LORRAINE HEWIT

CW01021752

The Broken Wall

The Broken Wall

A Study of
the Epistle to the Ephesians

MARKUS BARTH

REGENT COLLEGE PUBLISHING
VANCOUVER

THE BROKEN WALL
Copyright ©1959 The Judson Press

First published 1959 by Judson Press
PO Box 851, Valley Forge, PA 19482-0851
800-4-JUDSON, www.judsonpress.com

This edition published 2002 by Regent College Publishing
5800 University Boulevard, Vancouver, BC V6T 2E4 Canada
www.regentpublishing.com

All rights reserved. No part of this publication may be reproduced, stored in a retrieval
system, or transmitted, in any form or by any means, electronic, mechanical,
photocopying, recording of otherwise, without the prior written permission of the
author, except in the case of brief quotations embodied in critical articles and reviews.

Views expressed in works published by Regent College Publishing are those of the
author and do not necessarily represent the official position of Regent College.

In this book the author has employed his own translation of the Greek text of the
New Testament. In some cases, in order to bring out the meaning clearly, he has given
a free translation or paraphrase. A few of the quoted passages are identical with the
Revised Standard Version of the Bible, copyright 1946 and 1952. These are used by
permission of the Division of Christian Education of the National Council of .
Churches of Christ in the United States of America.

National Library of Canada Cataloguing in Publication Data

Barth, Markus
  The broken wall

  Includes bibliographical references and index.
  ISBN 1-55361-054-7 (Canada)
  ISBN 1-57383-229-4 (United States)

  1. Bible. N.T. Ephesians—Criticism, interpretation, etc. I. Title.
BS2695.2.B37 2002   227'.506   C2002-910662-1

CONTENTS

FOREWORD

THIS IS A STUDY BOOK FOR EVANGELISM. Laity are in mind, and not the clergy only. Though written at the request of one communion (the American Baptist Convention) for specific use in its own churches, a wider reading among other communions is hopefully anticipated. Schools of evangelism, in a six weeks' study preparation for active witness, will use this book as their basic text.

Questions immediately arise. Why a book on evangelism that deals little with techniques and methods and almost wholly with biblical theology? How can laymen "get into" a book like this? What does a theologian know about evangelism?

These questions betray the grave crisis in our churches. Obsessed with production and numerical results, evangelism has been so prostituted as to become a means of institutional growth; workable programs and efficient methods have claimed prior concern over the nature and meaning of the Gospel.

But the crucial questions in evangelism are theological and demand theological answers. "Wherein lie our authority and urgency?" "How do we resolve the dilemma of the evangelist: God using broken creatures like us to proclaim the Gospel of the new life, and while Christ is ultimately the Evangelist, calling us also to evangelize?" "What successful methods of evangelism must not be used, because incongruous with the nature of the Gospel?" These and other questions are tormenting the churches, as the Bossey consultation on

7

evangelism pointed up. A recall to a fresh awareness of the divine mandate rooted in the Gospel will drive us to the Scriptures and to a sensitive understanding of the world. Hence the need of a study like this.

But how can the laity . . .? The laity can and must! At every other level, laymen are expected to have responsible concern and insight. In fact, the distinction we have made between laity and clergy does violence to our common responsibility as a people of God. Actually, we all must grapple with the basic issues in evangelism or there will be little witness in the world. Our essential role is in the world. Our real field of service and witness is not in "churchly" ecclesiastical functions and activities, but in the "worldly" functions of secular society. Concerning this kind of real evangelism, the book speaks with eloquence and power.

Dr. Markus Barth is a biblical scholar, and to the perplexing theological questions which trouble us all he addresses himself with a disarming candor and sincerity. We may take real issue with some things he says. We may feel challenged or threatened in our most cherished prejudices or beliefs. But he dodges no issues which confront him in the course of this study. He speaks with utmost frankness and honesty.

Professor Barth is an evangelist at heart. He is an evangelist by virtue of his self-identification with the world. The salvation of the world concerns him more than his own salvation, but he is unsparing in his criticism of the churches as the greatest obstacle to evangelism!

—JITSUO MORIKAWA, *Secretary*
Department of Evangelism Planning
American Baptist Home Mission Societies
of the American Baptist Convention

November 1, 1958

PREFACE

THIS BOOK HAS BEEN WRITTEN with the intention of offering to Bible readers guidance in understanding some of the main themes of the Epistle to the Ephesians. May it encourage them to become faithful and brave ambassadors of Christ! Still, an exhaustive study of all the problems presented by Ephesians, or of all aspects of the Christians' high calling, should not be expected.

For guidance, advice, and warnings received before and during the preparation of this study, I am greatly indebted not only to scholarly Bible interpreters and pioneering evangelists, but equally to the actual life of congregations in this and in other countries. Whenever in the past and present times people were gathered around, or stooped into, the open Bible, there remained no basic difference between the men in the pew and those on the pulpit, or between scrutinous theologians in their libraries and venturous pioneers on the crossroads. I am grateful to all of them.

But for brevity's sake I have omitted all footnotes and almost all references to outstanding names, books, and documents. For the same reason no quotations are made from widely published or recently discovered Jewish, Hellenistic, and early Patristic texts. However, the collateral testimony of various parts of the New Testament could not be suppressed. In addition to the letters of Paul, the Gospel according to John and the Epistle to the Hebrews have proved to be the closest companions of Ephesians.

Most New Testament texts quoted in this book are presented in my own translation. The Revised Standard Version was used for the Old Testament and, on some occasions, for neotestamental references. Every translation (even King James') is a sort of exposition which necessarily neglects some overtones or varies the flavor of the text. Time and again the original language permits widely different interpretations. No preacher and teacher can avoid to make one-sided decisions and to take calculated risks. From day to day, and from generation to generation, there is need for deeper penetration into the original language, and for awareness of changing terms, idioms, and thought patterns.

The way of Bible study is steep and long, narrow and dangerous. But it is also scenic and rewarding, exciting and rich with discoveries. Our study of Ephesians is but a step made on that path. May it lead the readers to take more and wider steps! There is no reason to despair in the face of seemingly unsurmountable obstacles. Whatever their inclinations and prejudices, all pilgrims on that way are to keep together and to proceed with joyful boldness.

—MARKUS BARTH

Chicago, Ill.

PART ONE

PAUL'S PUZZLING EPISTLE

Paul's Puzzling Epistle

I. A Stranger at the Door

THE EPISTLE TO THE EPHESIANS comes to us as the voice of a stranger. If Paul be the author, then he humbles himself in this letter even more than elsewhere. Whereas in 1 Corinthians he calls himself "the least of the apostles," in Ephesians he uses an almost impossibly queer Greek formulation to denote himself as "less than the leastest" of all saints (cf. 1 Cor. 15:9; Eph. 3:8). The author submits himself to the judgment of the readers: may they perceive his understanding of the mystery of Christ (3:4)![1] Yet he speaks almost impersonally, as if from a great distance and in awe of "the holy apostles" (3:5). What appears like a bewildering contradiction may be important both for the author and for the ancient or modern reader of Ephesians. An evangelist does not impose himself upon anybody. He is free to submit himself and his message to others. Nevertheless he hopes by the grace of God to continue joyfully and boldly to open his mouth as a messenger of the Gospel (6:19). No imprisonment can silence him (3:1, 13; 4:1; 6:20). He has been made an ambassador of a mystery that cannot and must not be hidden (3:4 f., 9 f.).

Whether or not the readers of Ephesians like what he has to say to them, the author of this epistle cannot be stopped from calling and exhorting each of them to press forward with him. Not only in intercession (6:18) but also equipped

[1] In this work, when no Bible book is specifically named, it is to be understood that the Scripture reference, as here, is to the Epistle to the Ephesians.

with "shoes of the Gospel of peace" (6:15), they all are to be
evangelists. In order to carry out his evangelistic task and
to win co-operators in the service of God, the author does not
abase himself before his readers. He is sure that he has something important to say, and that heeding his words will be
worth while.

Really? The reception and understanding of Ephesians
offer great difficulties of a formal and material character.
Why not admit frankly that many features of this strange
epistle are, at first look, more difficult than delightful, more
puzzling than persuasive?

In *formal* regard, there exists considerable uncertainty as
to the identity of the author of this letter and as to the recipients of it. The title which our Bible translations give,
". . . of Paul to the Ephesians," has been challenged for many
reasons. The author of Ephesians addresses himself only
to Christians of Gentile origin (2:11 f., 19) — to "saints" of
whose faith and love he has but "heard" (1:15), to people
who know him only from hearsay (3:2) and who may have
learned of Christ from other teachers and preachers (4:20 f.),
to readers who still have to perceive by reading, rather than
by remembering, what understanding of the mystery the
author may have (3:4). But according to the Acts of the
Apostles (chaps. 18–20), Paul had been working in Ephesus
for several years, "teaching in public and from house to house
. . . both Jews and Gentiles" (Acts 20:20 f.). Why then does
the author of Ephesians behave like a stranger, if he was
the Paul of whom Acts speaks? Why, of all the Pauline epistles, should Ephesians fail to contain a list of greetings to
individuals in or near Ephesus? Finally, why do some of the
most ancient Greek manuscripts omit the name of Ephesus
in Eph. 1:1, if the church in Ephesus really was addressed?

These and other arguments are piled up against the
authenticity of Ephesians. They have, for some interpreters,
considerable evidential weight, and they have produced wild

chases and fanciful suggestions for alternative authors and addressees. Yet none of these suggestions convey any feeling of certainty. It is still possible to hold that Paul is the author of Ephesians; all theories created for showing a different author raise more problems than they solve. But Paul's authorship can only be affirmed with fear and trembling.

Not granted to the interpreter of Ephesians is that very substantial help which a reader or an exegete of an Old Testament prophetic book or of one of the Corinthian epistles may gain from some reliable information or plausible theory about the persons, places, times, and circumstances involved in the making and meaning of that book. In spite of the great name attached to it, this epistle retains strange elements that make it resemble a foundling. No attempt to unveil its secret will remove all of these strange features.

Though we may be unable u'timately to explain and demonstrate whence Ephesians comes and whither it goes, we nevertheless can listen to what the stranger has to say. Its words may prove able to raise and answer questions which are more important than those concerning authorship, destination, and exact time and place in or after Paul's life.

There is yet another formal difficulty. Can we listen to the message of Ephesians? The process of hearing, and understanding, and appropriating this letter seems to be more encumbered than is the case with other biblical books. For one thing, the language of this document has a character of its own. In the oldest available manuscripts it certainly is Hellenistic Greek, and in our translations it is more or less biblical English. But even within this Hellenistic and biblical environment, the language of Ephesians bears alien features. There are extremely long sentences (as 1:3-10 and 1:15-23) into which apparently is pressed in rather obscure, helpless, unaesthetical, or disorderly fashion, almost every topic between heaven and earth. The principle, "one [thought] at a time," is scarcely respected. There are innumerable relative clauses, coupled with consecutive dependent and final clauses. There are abstract nouns, cascading over one another, whereas in other Pauline letters verbs carry the main load of the argument. There are explanatory appositions and attributes, parallel phrases, and specifications (as in 4:12 f.) whose interrelation is anything but unequivocal. There are piles of synonyms connected by genitive constructions (as in 1:19: "greatness of power . . . according to the energy of the strength of his might").

There is an ample and sometimes awkward display of prepositions. Especially abundant is the use of the little word "in." It occurs most frequently either in connection with Christ ("in Christ," "in Him," "in the Lord") or with an abstract noun (as "in blessing," "in love," "in wisdom," "in insight," 1:3, 4, 8). The pleonastic, redundant, verbose diction used in Ephesians may have been entertaining and joyful play for its author. The words "the Holy Spirit of God" (4:30) do resound more musically than does a crisp reference to "the Spirit" (Mark 1:12; Rom. 8:16). But to the reader who abhors grammatic complications and loves brief statements, the style of Ephesians may seem anything but inviting to closer acquaintance. If not the author's breath, then certainly that of the modern reader, seems too short to last to the end of sentences in which the thoughts are coined in baroque, bombastic, or litanylike style.

So much, then, for these two *formal* difficulties raised by the stranger and his voice. Whether or not he stands in a wilderness, he certainly is bewildering! But considerable though these obstacles to understanding are, they seem but trifles when we face the *material* problems presented by the strange visitor. In the following paragraphs, we shall present five knotty points without as yet trying to resolve them. The reading or explaining of any part of the Bible always gains in depth and joy when the seriousness of the existing difficulties has been squarely faced.

1. Predestination: Ephesians proclaims (most outspokenly in 1:4 f.) that God has made a decision and election "before the foundation of the world." The reference to such election by God has given rise, and still seems to substantiate, a rigorous belief in determinism. By building upon the absolute "will of God" (1:1, 5, 9, 11) Paul seems to depict a despotlike god who made his blueprints before the creation, and who uses the world and man, as it were mechanically, to carry out his every whim. The plan of that god appears to be the determination of some for "salvation" (1:13), of others for "no inheritance in the Kingdom of Christ and God" (5:5). The love of God then appears like love only for those elected to be saved (2:4-10). Both the author and the recipients of Ephesians are boldly assumed to be on the safe side of God's ledger. "We . . . you are saved by grace . . . enthroned in heavenly places, in Christ" (2:5 f.). Correspondingly the others, the Gentiles, are readily denounced as "hopeless and atheists" (2:12); for they are "in the world" (2:12), and all kinds of nasty attributes are profusely spread upon their spiritual and moral life: "darkened mind, estranged . . . hardened heart, filth, and greed" (4:18 f.). They are called "children of wrath" (2:3; 5:6), while the saints feel safe as "beloved children" (5:1).

Now, if this is what the stranger has to tell us: that our dear Ego is saved, and that the others (the Greeks with all their glorious heroes and ideas, temples and statues, and also with their untiring search for truth and their suffering for freedom!) are lost, then the god of Ephesians is a god of conceit and of despair at one and the same time. Despite all the affirmations about the fatherhood (3:14; 4:6) and the love (1:5, 6; 2:4; etc.) of that god, that deity appears to back up the worst of Christian selfishness and of unchristian condemnation. Is God's church the country club of some privileged folks who have a good time while the world "goes to hell"? If Ephesians should really say and promote such things, what reason does anyone have to let the stranger enter his house and heart?

2. Intellectualism: Ephesians shares, along with documents of an ancient widely spread non-Christian religious movement (the so-called Gnosis or Gnosticism, cf. 1 Tim. 6:20), the strong emphasis which is put upon "revelation," "mystery," "knowledge," "wisdom," "understanding," and the like. Its author prays that God will give "the spirit of wisdom and revelation in knowledge of him, enlightened eyes of hearts, to know what is . . ." (1:17 f.). He is convinced that he, together with other apostles and prophets, was "made to know, by revelation, the mystery," and that he understands it (1:9; 3:3-5). And he is convinced that those elect not only have heard the "word of truth" (1:13) and can grow in understanding (1:17 f.; 3:19; 4:13), but also that they have something that can and must be made known to the universe (2:7; 3:10). Is this not a very narrow concept of Christian existence? How arrogant to claim that one knows "the mystery of God's will" (1:9) and "the word of truth" (1:13)! What nerve, boldly to ascribe such knowledge to "revelation" (3:3, 5). What conceit is displayed by Christians who presume that they can teach the powers that be, or (even worse!) that they must expose the evil of the world (3:10; 5:11-13)! What silly imagination to assume that the members of the church are saints and spotless (1:4; 5:27) merely because they know something extraordinary! Could the author of Ephesians have fallen victim to the assumption that mere knowledge of the good naturally implies the doing of the good, the being good, and the well-being of man? As if at all times and places Christians have not discredited, by their blindness, hardness, and ignorance, whatever they have pretended to "know"! And as if they have not had to suffer from persecution, slander, and malice whenever they have tried to be true to their calling! So the emphasis put by the Ephesian epistle upon knowledge looks hardly convincing.

Today, a man or a document that sells mankind no better
means of salvation than a kind of superenlightenment should
not expect to be welcomed as friend and helper in a world
whose very existence is at stake and in a church that pays
with the suffering of persecution when it is a true witness to
Christ. Few, if anybody, would want to be evangelists, "shod
with the gospel of peace" (6:15), if that ministry should
really produce or imply a haughty, magisterial attitude toward those who are strangers to, or are estranged from, the
church. For it simply is not true that Christians are brighter
or better than "worldly" people, or that they alone possess
all truth, and that all will be well, if only they are listened
to. In later sections of this book, the more detailed exegesis
of the role of "knowledge" in Ephesians will have to show
whether or not this epistle actually fosters intellectual pride
and vanity.

3. Superstition: That God acts in great love and grace
(2:4 f., 7 f.), and that Christ loves the church so much as to
give himself for her (5:2, 25) and to become an example of
how everybody shall be subject to his neighbor (5:21), and
of how the husband shall love his wife (5:22 ff.) — this any
reader may like to read. Also sentences like "Christ shall
live by faith in your hearts . . . by love . . ." (3:17) contain
and confer deep meaning that recalls the best of Reformation
theology. But in Ephesians the plausible appeals to look
up to the love of Christ and to embrace Christ with the
whole heart are found not too far from passages that describe
and promote what has been called belief in a "cosmic Christ."
Just when attention seems to have become focussed upon
the requirements and abilities of man's heart or inner life,
the author of Ephesians moves to strange-sounding intimations concerning "heavenly places" and their inhabitants
(1:19 ff.; 2:1 f.; 4:8; 6:11 f.). In Ephesians, great emphasis
lies upon the love of God and Christ and the way of Christ
into our hearts. But with equal emphasis a descent of Christ

to low places and an ascent to high places are mentioned (4:8-10); thus a forceful subjection of all powers to Christ was effected (1:20 f.). This journey down and up and this seizure of power has obviously much wider dimensions than the human heart or the life of man. If Christ's "filling all in all" with his power (1:23; 4:10) is not an alternative to God's "love," it yet qualifies all that Ephesians says about love, and does so in rather surprising and disquieting fashion.

In Ephesians, what is made subject to Christ bears the name of principalities and powers (1:21; 3:10; 6:12), of aeons and generations (2:7; 3:5), of prince of the air, devil, or evil (2:2; 4:27; 6:11, 16). The whole world (1:10), the air, even the heavenly places (2:2) seem to be filled with and dominated by such spirits (6:12). We may shortly call them angels and demons.

Now if the call of Ephesians to faith be truly enlightened and enlightening, then it should, so it seems, make a quick end to all superstition and wipe it from the scene as is fit for a nightmare or spook. Instead, the author of this epistle speaks of Christ's dominion over these principalities and powers (1:21 f.), of the church's function to manifest God's wisdom to them (3:10), and of every Christian's duty to reckon with them and to withstand them (6:11-13). Faith in Christ in this epistle means more than that Christ can or will or must fill the church (1:23) and our hearts (3:17, 19). Rather it is faith that Christ is head over the whole universe (1:10) and that he fills it (1:23; 4:10). A similar thing is said in Colossians (1:20). Christ does not make war *against* the universe, for "through him God reconciles the whole by making peace."

Does this mean that a modern reader must believe in a universe organized under spirits and powers ere he believes in Christ, and even after he has come to faith? It is tempting to argue that a Christ who descends and ascends, who rises above all, even from death, cannot be "sold" to modern man.

It is easy to throw angels and demons and the cosmic character and relevance of Christ's work upon the scrap heap of
ancient superstition and mythology, and to consider them
but a manner of speech that is utterly irrelevant for our space
age. But if we should feel entitled to throw out one part of
the witness of Ephesians to Christ, why not the rest of it
also; for instance, Christ's Lordship over the church and in
the heart? It is unfair and scarcely honest to consider the
Bible or parts of it as a cake from which we can pick out
merely the raisins we happen to like. Speaking the truth in
love and witnessing to the biblical Christ may imply the
necessity to speak also of some very strange things. Ephesians'
reference to principalities and powers does but accentuate a
difficulty which the reader of every Pauline epistle and indeed
of every Bible book confronts. A Christ created and shaped
according to our hearts and supposed needs would certainly
look different from the Christ preached in Ephesians and
in the Bible. But what good could ever be attained when
we do follow Ephesians and try to believe and to make others
believe that a "cosmic Christ" shall fill the church and dwell
in our hearts? Ephesians makes us aware of a dreadful
dilemma: If we stand for a modernized Christ, we seem to
betray the biblical Christ. Or if we evangelize with the Gospel which Christ preached (2:17) and which Paul was "given"
(3:8), we look like defenders of superstition. Ephesians seems
to make evangelism difficult, if not impossible.

4. Ecclesiasticism: Ephesians is in its very essence a church
letter. Many other New Testament epistles are addressed *to*
churches in one or another city of the Mediterranean world.
Ephesians shares such a destination. But, in addition, Ephesians is a letter *about* the Church, and it can scarcely be
avoided that the word Church be spelled with a capital C
when decisive passages of this document are interpreted. Not
a local congregation's specific problems, but the oneness (4:3),
the holiness (1:4; 5:27), the apostolicity (2:20; 3:1 ff.; 4:7, 11;

6:15-20), and the catholicity of the Church are among Ephesians' main subject matter (2:19; 4:13; 6:18; and 1:1, *if* the words "in Ephesus" are omitted). In the focus of this epistle is found, again and again, the universal Church: her relation to God the Father (3:14 f.), to Christ the head (1:22; 4:13; 5:23-32), to the Spirit from whom all gifts come (1:13 f.; 4:7 ff.), to the commonwealth of Israel (2:12, 19-22), to the pagan environment (4:17 ff.; 5:5-13; 6:11 ff.), to the apostle, and to all the saints (1:15; 3:18; 4:13; 6:18 f., 24). Some commentators feel inclined to see in 1:4 even the nucleus of a doctrine of the Church's pre-existence! Of greater appeal, certainly, is the emphasis which is put upon the basic unity of the body and upon the manifold ministry given to its members (4:3-12; 5:30), and the idea of organic growth and constructive building upon the root and ground of love (2:21 f.; 3:17; 4:15 f.). These elements of Ephesians' witness were used to create and justify concern in the "process" and "building of the kingdom," and in careful and effective administration of the mystery of spiritual and bodily unity.

Ephesians' concentration upon the topic "Church" has, within the New Testament, some parallels in the Gospel of Matthew, in 1 Corinthians, in the epistles addressed to Timothy and Titus, in 1 Peter, and in the seven letters of Revelation 2 and 3. The more the Church has grown, the more the interest of devoted thinkers has settled on the problem of the "Nature of the Church." Today both the Vatican and the Faith and Order Commission of the World Council of Churches are fascinated by this topic. Those who most vigorously promote the Church (with a capital C) feel inspired by Ephesians. It need not be held that they hunt for an abstract idea. But does Ephesians really tell them to build a world church, whether in a Catholic or Protestant form? Is it really Ephesians that inspires them to build or to promote, in theory or in practice, or in both, a High Church? Ephesians does indeed teach that the Church is Christ's body

(1:23; 4:4, 12; 5:30); the Church is called "the fullness of him who fills all in all" (1:23).

However, do such formulations imply that the Church is the "extended incarnation" of Christ, that it is a "redemptive society" and has a "divine nature" besides her earthly appearance? Readers who by nature, birth, or inclination are Roman Catholics, right-wing Anglicans, or otherwise Ecclesiasticists rejoice in the justification which Ephesians seems so readily to yield to their beliefs and practices. Jubilant or anxious about the real presence of Christ in the Church, they seem not bothered by the fact that their "Church" may claim for itself, and factually seize, a mediatory place and function between God and man, while actually it forms a hindrance against man's access to Christ. Two Gospels tell a story of a lame man who by only very extraordinary means could be brought to Christ. Those assembled around Christ almost prevented his access (Mark 2:1-4; Luke 5:18-19). Is the Church of Ephesians really a wall which makes it difficult for Christ to look upon the world? Or is it a wall by which some "insiders" attempt to protect Christ from the onrush of the world?

Whatever answer may be given, the emphasis which Ephesians puts upon the growth and building of the One, Holy Apostolic, Catholic Church appears very strange, dangerous, and unfriendly — perhaps not to the members of the Church, but certainly to the people at its margin and outside. Happy possessors of life and truth, of fellowship and light, seem to claim God for themselves, to invite outsiders to nothing else but to joining their "redemptive society," to work for nothing else than for the enlargement of their sphere of power, and to feel quite safe in the midst of the ocean of the world's terror, darkness, and lostness. In the Churchly view of the Church, the doctrine of predestination as sketched above seems to find its natural implement. Whoever evangelizes for a church, or for his church, may comfort himself with the assurance that he acts according to a predestined path. But whether or not he has stumbled over a scandalous misunderstanding inherent in a frequent misinterpretation of Ephesians is still the question.

5. **Moralism:** No serious seeker of truth and wisdom in the fields of personal and communal ethics will ever question the value of terms like growth and perfection, love and justice, and power and unity. How bright these concepts shine in Ephesians against the background of pagan impurity, deceit, and greed (4:13 f., 18 ff.; 5:3 ff., 8 ff.)! But things look different when Paul goes into details, especially in the so-called *Haus-Tafeln* (household rules) in which he gives exhortations respecting the common life of man and wife, parents and children, and masters and servants (5:21–6:9). Here a patriarchal, authoritarian, petty bourgeois, or otherwise old-fashioned and narrow-minded spirit seems to lead his pen. Scholarly interpreters of Ephesians have observed that in these admonitions there is an absence of all references to the second coming of Christ, to the consciousness of having a special call in a specific time, to the readiness to live the life of strangers and even to accept persecution; in short, the peculiar flavor of truly Pauline or early Christian life and ethics is said to be missing. Instead, the readers of Ephesians are advised by the author on how "to fare well and to live long" (6:2) and on how "to love oneself" (5:28). Furthermore, the author of Ephesians appears to be lacking in originality. Jewish, Greek, and Latin literature of this period, outside the early Christian literature, contains exhortations similar to those of the *Haus-Tafeln* (e.g., the works of Epictetus, Seneca, and Philo). Indeed, the call for mutual respect and for the observance of the rights and duties of man and wife, old and young, master and slave, is uttered even more eloquently. In addition, the master key offered by Ephesians for all cases of doubt is found in the words "submit" and "obey" (5:21 f., 33; 6:1, 5), which seems to mean nothing else

than that an old-fashioned authoritarianism rules the day, together with a conservatism that excludes all just and necessary revolutions.

This drab and dry ethical system is, if we follow the same informants, poorly dressed up and Christianized by the occasional insertion of the formula "in Christ" or "as [to] Christ" (5:21 ff.; 6:1, 5). The Christianization seems not to reach very deep and far. For who knows whether by giving and receiving such advice, writer and readers of this epistle do not attempt to snuggle comfortably into the orders of this world? They seem to prefer conformity with the enlightened world to the courage required by a full-hearted attempt boldly to live "in Christ" at whatever expense of discomfort, slander, and persecution. The narrowness of the ethics of Ephesians should, so it is suggested, cry to heaven. For only life in the "house" is taken and treated seriously, whether "house" be understood in the wider sense of the "house of God," the Church (2:19, 21), or in the more limited sense of larger family life (which included servants).

If it is Paul who writes this epistle, has he no eyes for the responsibility of Christians in politics, culture, economics, and society? Is he blind to their responsibility to bear into all realms of life a bold and joyful witness to Christ, the Redeemer? Ephesians, unlike Philippians, 2 Corinthians, 1 Peter, and Revelation, seems not to treat of the confessing and suffering Church. Has the author of this epistle forgotten that "we have here no lasting city" (Heb. 13:14), and that we are "strangers and sojourners on earth" (Heb. 11:13; 1 Pet. 2:11)? While other New Testament writers refer to the "dispersion" of the Christians in the world (James 1:1; 1 Pet. 1:1), the author of Ephesians teaches explicitly: "You are no more strangers and sojourners, but fellow citizens and members of God's household" (2:19). What a prison is that city or household! How shameful is such "fear" of the Lord and of the earthly lords as is asked for (5:21;

6:5)! How bare of inspiration and how legalistic looks a counsel that opens no way to the liberation of slaves, to the emancipation of veiled women, and to other "rights of man"!

But enough of pointing out the bewildering strangeness of Ephesians! A first look at the stranger at our door, and a summary of much that current scholarly depth-analysis of the intruder yields, result in a frightful picture. The stranger apparently justifies the worst which blasphemers of the Gospel (not without contribution and coresponsibility of many that call themselves Christians) might feel or hold against it.

We repeat, this strange fellow resembles a fatherless and motherless foundling. He uses a tiresome baroque language. He builds upon determinism, suffers from intellectualism, combines faith in Christ with superstitious demonology, promotes a stiff ecclesiasticism, and ends with trite, shallow moralism!

Every thoughtful reader of Ephesians will be aware of the fact that this picture is incomplete and that, in addition, it may be a caricature. Ephesians has indeed its beauty also, and it tells movingly of love and grace, salvation and peace, truth and unity. But in order to stir readers to diligent reading, to show how rich Ephesians is in surprising features, how poor we may be in appreciating them, and finally to expose what most likely are the most widespread misuses of Ephesians, the strangeness of Ephesians has been treated thus extensively and acknowledged in all earnestness.

From the possible shock and horror which a devoted student of Ephesians may have felt when he went through the above-mentioned seven formal and material difficulties, he may get a tiny impression of what a non-Christian may feel when he is approached in what usually is considered an "evangelistic" way. How often have Christians confronted the world with nothing better than a series of "isms" that have a more or less suspicious halo. If Ephesians should be a letter promoting evangelism *for the Church's sake,* if what "seemed" to be the case with Ephesians should in reality be that epistle's true character and essence, then we should not despise or condemn any non-Christian for turning down with horror, disgust, or shrugs whatever message we bring. We should not assume that, if it comes to choosing between the Gospel of Christ (as preached by Paul) and the world, we stand "of course" on Paul's side. Only he will ever be a witness to so-called outsiders who recognizes and takes up full solidarity with the estranged, ill-advised, shocked, and shocking outsiders. Only while being evangelized ourselves can we hope ever to become evangelists. We are not proud possessors, spenders, and defenders of the Gospel truth over against a nasty world. Whatever "spiritual gift we may wish to impart" to others will be conveyed only when "together with them we are comforted" by God himself (Rom. 1:11 f.).

The only method of "preparation for the evangel of peace" (Eph. 6:15) and for the corresponding evangelism is not a study of "methods of evangelism," but an acquaintance with the Gospel itself. As a contribution to serious Bible study, the preceding negative and, much more, the following positive and explanatory remarks on Ephesians have been compiled.

II. THE CHARM OF ACQUAINTANCE

1. More extensively and intensively than other New Testament epistles, the letter to the Ephesians has the character and form of *prayer.* Not only the entire first half of the epistle (1:3–3:21), but also the entreaty to worthy conduct contained in the second part (4:1 ff.), is basically one long prayer or a series of prayers, rather than proclamatory preaching (*kerygma*) or school-like teaching (*didache*). When someone argues with you or tries to persuade you of something, he may or may not exert power over you. But when he has prayed and is praying for you, his relationship to you and yours to him are different. To be sure, power, persuasion, and reason

would not be excluded by prayer. But it is power of a different sort and reasoning after a specific logic that make themselves felt in prayer of adoration and intercession. So it is with the stranger at the door. Ephesians has gained a right to enter because its readers have a place in the intercession of the author.

And the author begs nothing else but that the readers join in praising the same God in thought, word, and deed. Therefore, the epistle contains several explicit "calls to worship" (5:14, 19 f.; 6:18); it reminds us that we have "boldness and approach . . . to the Father" (3:12; 2:18). It is difficult not to be pleased and not to "get up" (5:14) when such a call to join a festival assembly is extended, and when it is firmly asserted that our time of estrangement is over (2:12 f., 19). When Christ himself preaches peace to those far and those near (2:17), who would still believe in ultimate enmity and salvation by war? The author of Ephesians puts his readers in the position of the "poor and maimed and blind and lame" who are (according to the parable of the Great Supper, in Luke 14:21-23) invited and compelled to fill the Lord's house. It is a pleasure to be addressed and driven in this manner. If rich friends and relatives could resist the invitation, a beggar and cripple certainly could not. And everyone who hears of such an invitation and feast will certainly be glad to attend.

The prayer and the call to prayer extended by Ephesians obviously are more than a nice and expedient idea or method of Paul. Both are based upon something great that has happened and to which Paul must refer again and again. His prayer is not the sending up of a trial balloon, for he knows to whom to pray, why to pray, and for what to pray. The event to which he relates all that he says is included in the name of Jesus Christ; and it will be described at some length later on. For the present it must suffice to say that it is not an event or miracle that happened over our heads, but an action of God in every phase of which we were and are included. Paul knows that something has happened to his readers, an event that they cannot deny or delay. His epistle has power over its readers because it reminds both God and them of the real ground upon which God's chosen people stand, of the change which took place within them, and of the hope which is theirs.

There is an old Latin saying, *"Lex orandi, lex credendi."* It may be transposed into modern ways of thinking: dogmatics makes sense only as an act of worship, or: true faith is a matter of sincere prayer, or: let us pray for faith. Ephesians could well be considered the source and proof of the axiom. All that the epistle has to say about faith and life (dogmatics and ethics) is wrapped up (and not in appearance only) in the form of prayer. It actually is said to God and to the Ephesians at the same time in solemn, dignified, devoted prayer. "Blessed be God the Father. . . . I do not cease to give thanks . . . I bow my knees before the Father. . . . His is the glory in the Church and in Christ Jesus. . . . Give thanks to God at all times for all. . . . Pray at all times in the Spirit with all prayer and supplication. . . . Peace . . . love . . . grace be with all . . . " (1:3, 16; 3:21; 5:20; 6:18, 23 f.). There is another such prayer that is directed to God and yet is made audible to men, a prayer that carries in itself the Church with all its weak faith and its life threatened by divisions. It is yet a joyful and thankful act. We mean the great prayer of Christ which is found in John 17. His "High Priestly Prayer" and Ephesians show plainly that what Christ has done, is done before God for the sake of man and ultimately can only be confessed before God and man.

The peculiar logic and power of Ephesians over its readers, and the joy which it can create in them, stem from its thanksgiving and intercessory character. Should we not be thankful for a man who has prayed for us? In turn, how can we become evangelists and convince or persuade anybody, unless we have first and continuously prayed for him? It is by no means strange, but rather highly appropriate and fitting and worthy of deepest respect that the "Gospel of peace" (6:15) is carried into the world by the Son of God who prays (John 17) and preaches (2:17), by the apostle who thankfully intercedes (1:16-18), and by many "imitators of God" (5:1) who are called and willing to pray with him (3:14-21; 6:18-20).

If Ephesians is basically a prayer, the characteristics of its language, diction, and sentences are no longer amazing. In all Pauline letters (e.g., in Rom. 8:31-39; 11:33-36; 16:25-27; and Phil. 2:6-11), those passages in which the apostle explicitly or factually turns to prayer of adoration and supplication display exactly the same pastoral pathos, liturgical plenitude, and involved combination of thoughts which are typical of the greater part of Ephesians. Therefore, linguistic reasons and observations prove rather than disprove the authorship of Paul for this epistle. Could it be that Ephesians has been and still looks strange to many, because Paul's prayers as well as any prayers to God for others have become a strange thing for us? If so, we certainly have good reason to let the stranger enter and to treat him in such a way that we, rather than he, are put to shame.

We are now ready to turn to another positive and enjoyable mark of Ephesians.

2. The letter to the Ephesians makes no excuses and *does not apologize* for its existence and character. Its tone is by no means "apologetic." For leading some discussions, it may be virtuous not to presuppose anything in the discussion's partner, or to assume none other but the most feeble ground of common understanding, or to polemize sentence by sentence against real or alleged objections which the partner may foster or against distortions to which he is subject. For presenting the Gospel, Ephesians chooses none of these ways.

With the exception of 4:14 — that short, sharp reference to the impossibility of living in childish, unstable attitudes to truth — there are no polemics contained in the epistle. It is true that devil and darkness, impurity and greed, are mentioned. They have ruled in the Ephesians, they reign around them, and they threaten to make backsliders of them (2:1 ff.; 4:17 ff., 25 ff.; 5:5 ff.). But they are inimical powers of the past; Christians can, "in the Lord and in the power of his might," stand against them (6:10-14). Not fearful polemic against powers that be, but the encouraging call to live a soldierly life (4:22-24; 6:10 ff.), to hold the assigned place (3:17), and so to proceed with all the saints to attain the perfect faith and knowledge of the Son of God (4:13) — this is the ground swell of the exhortation.

Christians do not live from what they negate, but from all that they can and must assert and confess. About God and about man, about the community and about single persons, and about the extension of Jesus Christ's realm over the powers of this aeon, they are given to know the news of salvation. The great message which Ephesians brings or calls to the mind of the readers will need to be sketched out later. But about the method of its author in making his points, some remarks are due here. He is building neither on rational arguments, nor on widespread commonplaces, nor on sentimental compassion for his readers. He knows only one basis: what God has done and said. The wisdom and the will, the plan and the love of God; the preaching, the death, the resurrection, and the dominion of Christ; the power of the Holy Spirit as displayed in the life of the Church and the commission of its members — these are mission and motivation enough for speaking of the Gospel. Other logical bases or argumentations may come and go, increase or decrease in value, change with the changing moods of human hearts. If God himself is ground and motive, no change need be feared. The Church is built on the foundation of the apostles and prophets, Christ Jesus being the chief cornerstone (2:20). This Church obviously is not built upon apologetics.

There are Pauline epistles, in which the apostle seems to be on the defensive, because the truth of the Gospel itself, the addressed church, or his person, is under serious attack. In Ephesians, however, a jubilant tone, an "address to one another in psalms and hymns and spiritual songs; singing and praising in the heart to the Lord" (5:19), determines the character of every thought and sentence. We are reminded of Heb. 13:17: either a servant of Christ does his work "with joy without groaning" or it is "useless." The joy of one who was privileged to know good news that concerns all men, Gentiles as well as Jews, makes Paul in Ephesians omit extended references to the Scriptures ("Scripture-proofs"), all logically involved arguments, all polemic outbursts against adversaries, and all excuses for intruding into the private lives and affairs of his readers. His abounding gratitude for God's work and his commission as a messenger of that word are causative for his praying, preaching, and writing. The love of which he knows "surpasses knowledge" (3:19). It is, for that reason, independent of the requirements of a scientific structure, of a logical wholeness, or of a popular appeal. The contents of the Gospel are not dependent on how well a man can defend them, or how well he can fit them into the pattern of his own or other people's thought and life. They do not involve information for the curious about what God did "before the foundation of the world," about the origin of evil, or about the builder and location of the wall that separated man from man and man from God. The Gospel rests on its own strength and truth. It stands on the ground laid by the living God. It cannot be Gospel without saying again and again: "This is what God did, and this is what God has said." Therefore, the Gospel can only be proclaimed — kerygmatically, not apologetically, to use the technical terms of present-day scholarly discussion.

We may ask whether such bold assertion of the Gospel's truth does not open a gulf between the evangelist and those

whom he wants to address. Is it possible to communicate anything to ancient or modern man without trying, in apologetic
terms, to explain why it might have some meaning and
relevance for the hearer? We answer: a stranger at the door
who announces that he has some urgent information for us,
a messenger who seems to be full from top to bottom of the
importance of what he has to say, is more welcome than an
uncertain staggerer who tries, with all kinds of instruments,
gimmicks, and tricks, to pry open the door. The opening of
the door of the mouth (6:19) or of the heart (Col. 4:3; Acts
14:27; 2 Cor. 2:12) can be prayed for and expected only when
nothing less than "the mystery of the Gospel" is being
preached "in joyful boldness" (Eph. 6:19 f.). The Gospel
cannot be stripped bare of its mystery character. It is and
remains God's mystery. Ephesians makes itself welcome and
is a charming document just because it dares to let shine
nothing else but God's love and election, Christ's death and
resurrection, and the Spirit's might and work among men.

There is no danger whatever that love for man or actual
communication shall be lacking, when an evangelist like
Paul trusts the Gospel to be self-supporting and self-authenti-
cating. The content of the Gospel he proclaims, includes
man in whatever situation he may be. What God makes
known through his ambassadors is that *we,* the sinners, the
former Gentiles, the tempted weaklings in faith, are reconciled.
So the Gospel is not only information *for us,* but equally as
much news *about* us. The messenger at the door does not
bring myths or fables about other beings, or else we would
gladly turn him away. Actually he brings the news, and calls
to our remembrance the fact of *our* former estrangement, of
our required citizenship among God's elect, of our share in a
rich inheritance. Why should we not make him most heartily
welcome?

3. A short *survey* of the contents of Ephesians will conclude
our introductory remarks. To the absence of apologetics upon

which we have just commented, corresponds the presence of
the following bold assertions:

Chapters 1-2: What God in his love has willed in eternity,
this has been and is being carried out with the Ephesians.
Because of Christ, such sinners as they were, are saved and
called to live a new life as members of the one people that
God has gathered from all mankind.

Chapters 3-4:24: What God has done, he also makes
known, first to the elect, then to the world also. He gives the
means to let his people grow in unity and truth, in faith and
hope internally and externally, from and to Jesus Christ, even
in the world in which they live. By the power of the Spirit,
God's work goes on. The New Man, Jesus Christ, will be
triumphant in the hearts of men, in the church, and in the
world.

Chapters 4-25-6: In all realms of life, the light of God's love
shall shine. Love and gratitude, submission and steadfastness,
testimony and prayer, are marks and means of the Church's
life in the world. The fear of God frees man from any fear
of cosmic powers. Nothing can stand against "peace and love
with faith from God and Jesus Christ" (6:23 f.).

While the first part of Ephesians deals with God's will and
deed, the second part describes God's ongoing work in his
self-manifestation to and through the Church. The third part
encompasses the realms and means of the Church's and every
Christian's mission. The message of all parts together is very
similar to John 3:16: God so loves the world that he gives
his Son and the Spirit; we are no more lost, but are gathered
to be one people that bears witness to all of grace and peace.
The movement which the epistle follows goes "from God"
(1:2), "through the Church" (3:10), to the bold and joyful
ambassadorship of the Christians in the world (6:15-20).

The straightforwardness of this movement gives the Epistle
to the Ephesians peculiar significance for all concerned with
the evangelistic tasks of the Church today. It cannot be pre-

sumed that a summary exposition of this letter can *make* its contents and traits actual. But an attempt can be made at showing how actual and incisive *are* both the message and the character of Ephesians for anyone who looks for help, strength, and companionship on the way upon which Jesus Christ has sent all Christians.

In three successive parts we shall now consider what Ephesians says about the groundlaying work of God, the gathering, the mission, and the equipping of God's people. Whether necessity and urgency of evangelism lie in the evangel itself, whether the commitment of the Christians to the evangelistic task is identical with the nature and destiny of the people God gathers, whether Jesus Christ, and he only, is Lord over man's heart and in every social texture — these are the propositions and problems to which special attention will be drawn.

THE PERFECT WORK OF GOD

PART TWO

The Perfect Work of God

PAUL HAS NEWS to bring to his readers. He reminds them of the ground upon which they stand. The information he brings does not deal with abstract ideas or principles, but with events that have taken place and call for attention. From passages like John 4:34; 17:4; 19:30; Heb. 2:10; 5:9; and 12:2, we derive the right and reason to call these events "the perfect work." In Ephesians, explicit reference is made to "God's workmanship" (2:10), to a "perfect man" (4:13), and to a "new man created after God's image" (4:24; the RSV translation "new nature" is misleading, cf. Col. 3:9 f.). The claim that there is someone who is perfect is too astonishing to gain a ready hearing. Maybe we did not ask for such information; yet we can listen, and having heard, we can see if the news which is announced deserves our faith or our skepticism.

The "good news" (gospel) which Paul is commissioned to bring to the Gentiles (3:8) deals basically with the death and the resurrection of Christ, and with the love and Spirit of God.

I. THE CROSS: THE ABOLISHED WALL AND OUR PEACE

One of the essential elements of the Epistle to the Ephesians is the tidings that the "wall of division" was "broken down" (or abolished) by Jesus Christ (2:13-18). Within the whole of this epistle, the account of Christ making peace by abolishing the wall holds the same central place which in some other New Testament epistles is occupied by strictly Christological arguments (see Col. 1:15-20; 2:14 f.; Phil. 2:6-11; Rom.

3:21-26; 2 Cor. 5:14-21; 1 Pet. 2:21-25; 3:18, 22; cf. Eph. 5:25 ff.).

What did Paul mean when he spoke of the "wall"? Four possibilities may be considered.

1. The wall mentioned in Eph. 2:14 may be an allusion to the wall between the outer and inner courts of the Temple in Jerusalem which kept the Gentile visitors away from Jewish worshipers. It stamped the pagans unmistakably as "those afar." Or it may allude to the wall around Jerusalem, or to the angel guard around the land of promise (Gen. 32:1-2), which kept off unwanted intruders. Then — at least implicitly — reference is made to the wall which according to the prophetic parable, God had built around his vineyard (Israel) for protection — and which was to be broken down (Isa. 5:5).

Some scholars, presupposing that the author of Ephesians is not Paul and that this epistle was written after A.D. 70, suggest that the destruction of the Jewish nation, of Jerusalem and the Temple by the Romans, may be reflected in Eph. 2:14. In this case, the great historical catastrophe of Jerusalem's fall is here adorned with Christological meaning. But nothing makes the acceptance of this hypothesis mandatory. For while 2:14-15 indicates that the wall was separating men from men (i.e., Gentiles from Jews), according to 2:16 the same wall means enmity between man (both Jew *and* Gentile) and God. The wall in the Temple, around Jerusalem, or around the Promised Land, therefore, cannot exhaust what the author had in mind.

2. The "wall" which divided men *from God*, and which was removed by Jesus Christ, may have reference to the curtain in the Temple of Jerusalem which separated the Holy from the Holy of Holies. In Mark 15:38 an incident is reported which took place at the very hour of Christ's death. This curtain was torn completely. That because of Christ's death we have access to God "through the curtain" is explicitly stated

in Heb. 10:19 f. (cf. Heb. 6:19 f.; 4:16). Eph. 2:18 and 3:12 probably deal with this same "access."

3. The wall and the enmity between men, and between man and God (Eph. 2:15 f.), might be identified with a function which the Law had assumed after it was "fenced in," as the rabbis used to say, by man-made statutes and ordinances (cf. Mark 7:7 f.; Col. 2:22 f.; Gal. 3:23 f.). Bounds (a fence?) set up at the foot of Mount Sinai were supposed to keep people from trespassing, impudent gazing, and consequent death in the presence of the Lord (Ex. 19:12, 21-24). So the statutes and ordinances of the scribes (of Ezra's kind) were meant to prevent any breaking of the Law that was given by God. But in Galatians and Romans, Paul has shown that peace with God, and the free life of a child of God, were not and are not achieved by doing statutory "works of the law." Only a slavish attitude could suggest the erroneous notion that merits were heaped up before God by performance of certain duties and rituals. In fact, according to Eph. 2:14-16, "the law of ordinances in statutes" (i.e., the Law fenced in by carefully elaborated and delivered Jewish interpretations and applications) divides Jews and Gentiles and hence serves as a divisive institution, keeping both in the state of "enmity" against God. In discussing "works," Paul in 2:5, 8-10 had already touched strings that sounded identical with the main chords of Galatians and Romans. Therefore, the teaching on the Law also may be identical in Ephesians, Galatians, and Romans. The broken-down wall may mean the abrogation of the divisive function of the Law.

The original dignity of the Law itself (cf. Rom. 7:12; 3:31) need not be questioned by this abrogation. In Gal. 3:19; Acts 7:38, 53; Heb. 2:2, there is taken up an honored tradition which said that the Law was "given through angels." But its misuse and malfunction are declared "abrogated" (Eph. 2:15). The destruction of the wall is, in this sense, the inroad through and past a host of alleged "mediators" to God himself. It is the one mediator, Christ, through whom a "new living way" has been made (Heb. 10:20). Now, "we have access to the Father" (Eph. 2:18) " . . . in him" (3:12). "We have peace with our God through our Lord Jesus Christ; through him we also have access . . . " (Rom. 5:1 f.).

4. Finally, by the wall may be meant a barrier between God and man, and between man and man, which consists of angels and other principalities and powers, such as are enumerated in Eph. 1:21. The author may have in mind a realm of invisible, uncontrollable powers, ideas, and rules which actually divide and separate the earth from the heavens from which God governs. What we call "hell" would then — if any topographical statement is worth making at all — be situated not under the earth, but between heaven and earth.

At any rate, the wall may be a metaphor for dominant powers of angelic or demonic character which make man's life miserable. These powers rule not only in relation to man but also on a cosmic scale. There are enough intimations of them, surely, in the conscious and subconscious, the scientifically examined and the unaccounted for chambers of the human psyche. The wall may also involve the rational and the irrational, the magical and the religious, the individual and the collective attempts to make sense of these "powers," to use them for one's own purposes, or to keep them out of one's life.

Later we shall have to discuss more fully the nature of these principalities and powers. That they are kinsmen of the Law (understood as a legalistic and meritorial stepladder) is indicated by Paul in Col. 2:8 and Gal. 4:3, 9. In these passages, "Law" and "cosmic elements" are practically identified. In Eph. 2:14, not only the wall of so-called "natural laws" and proven "facts," but also the wall of seemingly irresistible moral and immoral principles, and finally the wall of conscious or subconscious structures of mind and soul of man, may be declared dissolved, broken down, abolished and abrogated.

A selection of one of these four interpretations of "wall" can scarcely be made. Probably it must not be made. The great variety of meanings entitles and indeed compels the reader of Ephesians not to limit the meaning of the broken "wall" only to the realm of the religious. Political and cosmic, moral and righteous, intellectual and psychological, physical and metaphysical distinctions and divisions must also be thought of when Eph. 2:14 is read. To put it in more modern terms: this verse says that Jesus Christ has to do with whatever divisions exist between races and nations, between science and morals, natural and legislated laws, primitive and progressive peoples, outsiders and insiders. The witness of Ephesians to Christ is that Christ has broken down every division and frontier between men. And even more, Ephesians adds that Christ has reconciled men with God!

To confess Jesus Christ is to affirm the abolition and end of division and hostility, the end of separation and segregation, the end of enmity and contempt, and the end of every sort of ghetto! Jesus Christ does not bring victory to the man who is on either this or that side of the fence. Neither rich nor poor, Jew nor Greek, man nor woman, black nor white, can claim Christ solely for himself. All bear the stigma of "the old man that perishes in deceitful desires" (4:22; 2:2-3); whereas in Christ "the two are created one new man" (2:15). So Christ's victory is for both; it cannot be divided. We repeat with 4:24, there is now "a new man created after God." No longer can we boast of our human works. For here is "God's workmanship created in Jesus Christ for good works" (2:9 f.). It does no good to call Christ "Lord, Lord," unless we mean by "Christ" even this new man, the end of divisions, "one new thing made of both," "one new man," "one body" instead of two which formerly were antagonists of God (2:14-16).

To say "Christ" means to say "reconciliation" (2:16) or to say "peace" (2:14, 17). In negative terms, it means to say "abolition" and "abrogation" of every and all hostility (2:14 f.).

Abolition and peace — these great words will keep us from dreaming of, or scoffing at, a sexless, raceless, homeless, neuter superman, whom Christianity allegedly ought to promote or to produce. The words "neither Jew nor Greek, neither slave nor free man, neither male nor female; you are all one in Christ Jesus" (Gal. 3:28; Col. 3:11; 1 Cor. 12:13) by which Paul describes Christ's work, do by no means wipe out or deny distinctions between nations, sexes, classes, and occupations. Otherwise Paul would not have included in his letters special exhortations for Jews and Greeks (Rom. 2:17 ff.; 11:13 ff.), husbands and wives (Eph. 5:22 ff., Col. 3:18 ff.), slaves and masters (Eph. 6:5 ff.), etc. But, faith in Christ, even Christ himself, means that the two — whatever their distinctions are — can and do live together: those who were formerly opposed, mutually exclusive, separated by what seemed to be an insurmountable wall. To say "Christ" means to say community, co-existence, a new life, peace (2:14).

The implications of this equation are enormous. Excluded is the assumption that under any circumstance, Jew or Greek, man or wife, Westerner or Asiatic, bourgeois or proletarian, white or black, can claim to have Christ on his side or for himself only. Even if the claim were made by Christians, who with missionary zeal feel committed to bring Christ or Christianity to outsiders, non-Christians, and apostates, it would still be wrong, for Christians bear witness to Christ only when their words and deeds make it plain that Christ is as much the outsiders' and opponents' Christ as their own. He is the end of division and enmity. Christ is he who has made something new of the two: the near and the far, the insiders and the outsiders. "In Christ those afar have become such that are near" (2:13). Christ is that reconciliation which is greater and stronger than the hostility of either or of both. He is not what a Christian can give to others. He is the gift of God to both. If he "is peace" (2:14), then he is by nature a social, even a political event, which marks the overcoming and ending of barriers however deeply founded and highly constructed these appear to be.

In the light of Eph. 2:13-18, the continuing existence of "Christian" men's and women's clubs, of "Christian" managers' and laborers' associations, of suburbanite and colored churches, of American and indigenous congregations overseas, of communities for the educated and for those less sophisticated, are nothing less than a repudiation of Christ. When no tensions are confronted and overcome, because insiders or outsiders of a certain class or group meet happily among themselves, then the one new thing, peace, and the one new man created by Christ, are missing; then no faith, no church, no Christ is found or confessed. For if the attribute "Christian" can be given sense from Eph. 2, then it means reconciled and reconciling, triumphant over walls and removing the debris, showing solidarity with the "enemy" and promoting not one's own peace of mind, but *our* peace." If preaching the Gospel (evangelizing) is what its name suggests, then it is exactly the same as it was in Galilee, on Golgotha, and in the apostolic Church after Pentecost: "He came and proclaimed peace to those who are far and peace to those near" (2:17).

When this peace is deprived of its social, national, or economic dimensions, when it is distorted or emasculated so much that only "peace of mind" enjoyed by saintly individuals is left — then Jesus Christ is being flatly denied. To propose in the name of Christianity, neutrality or unconcern on questions of international, racial, or economic peace — this amounts to using Christ's name in vain. On the other hand, if true evangelism is carried out, it not only will involve *some* social action, but will be from beginning to end even that social, reconciling, uniting action with which Christ is identified when he is called "our peace."

We can now ask: *How* has Christ broken down the wall that separated man from man and God? If we did not ask this question, we might easily equate Christ and peace in such a way that Christ's own person and work would disappear and vanish behind the magic spell and possible dynamic of promoting or making a "peace" of our own. But to follow Ephesians means more than to say, "Christ is a political, social, unifying *event*." Ephesians bids us say with the same or even greater emphasis, "Only Jesus Christ is the one who brings about peace and reconciliation between God and man. Only he is the saving event."

How did he effect and proclaim "peace" according to Eph. 2? The answer is manifold. "In the blood," says 2:13; "in his flesh" (2:15, RSV); "in one body . . . through the cross" (2:16); "in himself" (2:15-16, Greek text; RSV drops [why?] the last repetition of "himself"); "in one spirit" (2:18). The words "blood" and "flesh," "one body," and "one spirit" circumscribe nothing else but Christ "himself." But we must specify what is meant when Paul says "Christ himself." It is not primarily the words of Christ, his example, his suffering, or his miracles. It means his whole humanity, and more specifically it means his death on the cross, his sacrifice. Therefore "the cross" is mentioned in 2:16 as the means of reconciliation. The sacrificial words "blood" and "flesh" set the tone of the argument (2:13-18). In 5:2 (cf. 5:25) Jesus Christ's "giving himself up . . . for an offering and sacrifice" is held before the reader's eyes as source and example of their new life. In a similar way in Col. 1:22; Heb. 2:14; and John 1:14 (6:53 ff.), the flesh and blood and death of Christ (i.e., the sacrifice of the man Jesus Christ) are declared to be the means by which grace and truth, reconciliation and life, are given to man. Paul can be very explicit: he declares in words which cannot be misunderstood that to preach means for him to "know" and "proclaim" nothing else but "Jesus Christ and him crucified" (1 Cor. 1:23; 2:2).

How can the cross break down the wall? To us, Christ's pain and shameful death appear to be unmistakable defeat and a deplorable end under human enmity and God's wrath, rather than reconciliation and peace. In Ephesians, the death of Christ on the cross results not in misery, but what in old English is called "at-one-ment." This epistle does not elaborate a doctrine of the incarnation or of the atonement. But since it calls Christ's death explicitly an "offering and sacrifice to God," and a self-delivering of Jesus Christ to God for our sake (5:2), enough hints are given.

In the Old Testament, mention is made of occasions where God "sought for a man among them [Israel] who should build up the wall and stand in the breach before me [God] for the land, that I should not destroy it; but I found none" (Ezek. 22:30). According to another passage God "said he would destroy them — had not Moses, his chosen one, stood in the breach before him" (Ps. 106:23; cf. Jer. 18:20). In Ex. 32:30-34 (also in Deut. 9:18 ff., 25 ff.) Moses' attempt to "make atonement" is described at some length: "If thou wilt forgive their sins . . . and if not, blot me, I pray thee, out of thy book." He offers to God his life. May God be "angry with him on account of the people" (Deut. 1:37; 3:26; 4:21) — if only God will spare the people that "have sinned a great sin" (Ex. 32:31).

The offering of Moses was not accepted; Moses did not die for Israel. If we follow Ex. 28:12, 15, 21, 29 f., 38, 41 and Lev. 10:17, it is not Moses' function, but the priest's, to bear before God the names, the judgment, and the guilt of the people. Various sin- and guilt-offerings and mainly the sacrifice of the Day of Atonement were instituted to attest the "peace" which God would "give" according to the Aaronitic benediction (Num. 6:24-26). But only of the Suffering Servant is it actually stated that he "makes himself an offering for sin. He shall bear their iniquities. . . . He poured out his soul to death. . . . He bore the sin of the many

and he made intercession for the transgressors" (Isa. 53:
10-12).

The sacrificial terms "blood" and "flesh," used in Eph. 2:
13-15, the allusion to Exodus and Ezekiel passages in Eph.
5:2, the frequency with which in the New Testament Jesus
Christ's death is explained by reference to Isa. 53 — such
facts make it probable that Old Testament texts such as
those just quoted, contain the most vivid answer to the question as to why Christ's death "made peace."

On the other hand, we should not be blind to the differences. While in the Old Testament a wall for Israel has to
be *built* and a breach in the wall has to be *filled* by a mediator, in Ephesians a different effect of the "offering" of the
mediator is described. Not for Israel ("those near") only,
and their protection from the wrath of God and the Gentile
onrush, but also for the Gentiles ("those far," Eph. 2:13, 17)
— salvation is now achieved.

But the elements common to both the Old and the New
Testaments prevail. In both Testaments, the chosen man of
God acts as an intercessor. He intercedes before God by
offering himself and his life totally, finally, for the good.
Aware of his election by God, he is not content to stand on
God's side against the sinners. Instead, he steps boldly to the
side of the offenders, the estranged, the outsiders, in order
to pray and plead for them to God. His prayer is his offering
of himself — his body, his soul, his life, his honor, his blessing,
his election, his love — to God "for the transgressors" (Isa.
53:12), "for us" (Eph. 5:2).

Why do the Ephesians have "peace" with God in Christ?
We can now answer: Because they have One who pleads and
intercedes for them. They do not stand alone. They are
prayed for by One who is righteous (1 John 2:1) and "beloved" (Eph. 1:6). What Ephesians does not say explicitly
about Christ's intercession is clearly taught in John 17:1-26;
1 John 2:1, and Heb. 5:7; 7:25, and is dramatically de-

scribed in the passion narratives of the Gospels where they point to Christ's cross between those of two criminals, and to the last words of the crucified. The intercession made by Jesus Christ is the sum total of his work and suffering.

In contrast to the Old Testament narratives and institutions, the peacemaker now is not a man whose well-meant offer of life was not accepted. Moses actually was "not able to carry all these people alone," for "the burden was too heavy" for him (Num. 11:14; cf. Ex. 18:18). Also the wish of Paul to be reprobate ("accursed") for his brethren's sake (Rom. 9:3) was not granted. And his prayer and intercession for the Ephesians, which give this epistle its particular flavor, did not remove the wall. Neither is it an institutional priest or sacrifice that has achieved actual atonement. Hebrews 7-10 describes extensively, in the light of Christ's death, why Levitical priests and sacrifices could not provide forgiveness and peace. But what was foreordained to be done "in Christ . . . the beloved [Son] of God" (Eph. 1:4-6) and what he actually did "in his blood . . . in his flesh . . . in his body . . . through the cross" (2:13 ff.) — this has abolished the barrier between man and God.

It has also removed the barrier between man and man. Whether proud insiders or self-sufficient outsiders, in both cases we are worshipers and slaves of a dividing wall. Christ's "proclaiming peace to those who are far and peace to those near" (2:17) speaks another language and exerts another power. It is his cross ("his blood") that "cries out" (Heb. 5:7; 12:24) louder than any blood spilled on soil can cry out for revenge and continued hostility. The depth, the truth, and the power of his confession of our sin and his plea for sinners make it impossible to dream of a redemption which is a private possession of the insiders, rather than a gift to all who are in need of it. If we do not believe that Christ prayed and died for the "strangers, the hopeless, the atheists in the world" (2:12), then we deny that he died "for us."

His death and his call, the peace and the reconciliation he brought, are for both and between both: the near and the far — or Christ is good for none, and his sacrifice is null and void. In Eph. 2:13-18, Paul asserts and we are called to believe that the death of Christ was *not* in vain — that whatever wall has separated man from God and from his fellow man was abolished.

The good news of the wall's destruction and the creation of one "new man" who shall live in peace is *unconditional.* Poison is injected into the Gospel of peace, if we limit its validity by any conditional restriction. To speak in the terms of Ephesians: We are elected in Jesus Christ (to have approach to God and to have peace one with another) — not *if* we are holy and blameless before God, but "*that* we should be holy and blameless before him" (1:4). Again, Christ did not give himself up for us because we are holy and pure, but "*in order* to sanctify the church by purification . . . to present her before him in glory, without spot or wrinkle or anything of that kind, but to be holy and blameless" (5:26-27). We observe in these sentences the absence of the conditional "if" and the presence of the final and consecutive conjunctions: "that" and "in order to." First comes the death of Christ; after this has taken place, it can only be announced and called to mind. Then comes its meaning for us and the change it effects in man's life. First is the good news: we have been prayed and pleaded for by him. Then comes the admonition to "walk worthily of the calling with which you were called" (4:1). First is God's eternal will and plan to redeem us "in the blood" of Christ, "in love" (1:4-7). Only upon this ground follows the second: that "we have redemption" (1:7) and "have access to the Father" (2:18; 3:12). First Jesus Christ descends to the lowest and ascends to the highest places in order to fill all (4:8-10; 1:20 ff.); then we can hope and pray to "be filled with all the fullness of God"

(3:19). First we are "saved by grace . . . not of our doing; it is God's gift" (2:5, 8); then follows our "walk in the good works, which God has prepared beforehand" (2:10; 4:1 ff.).

The newness of our life and the worthiness of our walk are the purpose and consequence of Christ's death (cf. Rom. 6:3 ff.). They are not its condition. Any attempt to promote an evangelism which would withhold the message of the cross until a certain readiness of the church and the world can be observed, would betray the evangel which puts the cross first. The preaching of Christ is the precondition and ground of the proclamation of our new life and of our walk "in the beforehand prepared good works" (cf. Eph. 2:10). "Christ crucified" is more than a certain qualification of the Christians' message to the world and of their life in the world. Indeed, the "crucifixion of the Lord of Glory" (1 Cor. 2:8), i.e., the utmost humiliation of the Son of God (Phil. 2:6 ff.), is the very start, center, and source of all and everything that Christians have to attest by word and deed.

And yet there is one event, as unique in kind as the crucifixion of Christ, which belongs to the heart of the Gospel and which has not yet been mentioned. To it, we must now give our attention.

II. THE RESURRECTION: ONE ABOVE ALL

The resurrection is the miracle of all miracles. We cannot argue for it; we cannot explain it; we cannot prove it. We can only ponder over it and study what a New Testament book such as Ephesians says about it.

It is noteworthy that Ephesians nowhere gives any indication of *how* Christ was raised. Like other New Testament reports and reflections on Christ's resurrection, in contrast to apocryphal documents of early sectarian groups, this epistle does not probe into the secret of an event that is without parallel in human history and experience. But while the mode of resurrection remains hidden, its meaning, power, and results demand interpretation and proclamation.

We ask first, how can one man's deed and death affect and change the course of centuries and the lives of millions of people? We might derive plausible answers from all kinds of analogies that are present in the life, work, and posthumous effects of illustrious men. But in so doing we would fail to follow the line of argument chosen in Ephesians and other New Testament books. If, together with John's Gospel and the Epistle to the Hebrews, we consider the sacrifice of Christ as an act of (intercessory) prayer to God, then the validity and effect of that act is dependent neither on a famous man's potential influence over others, nor on the readiness of later generations to let themselves be moved by it. The prayer of Christ is actual, real, present, and effective, regardless of whether *we* hear, respect, or accept it. A prayer offered to God depends on *God's* acceptance of it. In cultic terms, a sacrifice is only good when it is "accepted" by God, when it is a "pleasing odor" before him (Eph. 5:2; Gen. 8:21; Ex. 29:18; Ezek. 20:41). The resurrection of Christ by God's power is the solemn acceptance of Christ's sacrifice.

The way in which Christ's sacrifice is accepted corresponds to the totality and uniqueness of his death. Neither only the intention of the worshiper, nor only the blood, the choicest parts, the odor, or the smoke of an animal slaughtered upon an altar, but Jesus Christ himself is accepted by God. This is the meaning of resurrection in Ephesians; namely, that the same Jesus Christ who had descended to the lowest places (4:9 f.) was by an act of God's might raised to the highest place of honor (1:19-22; cf. Heb. 2:9). Not only Jesus' words and deeds and sufferings, but the whole, Jesus himself, is received by God and installed "at God's right hand" (1:20).

If the resurrection be viewed only from the angle of questions like these: How could a dead man come alive again?

How can we believe what cannot be proved by scientific tests? Or why should one miracle change the boring routine of ordinary people's lives? — no wholly satisfactory answer will ever be given. But where common experience falls short, the Bible still may open aspects and use arguments that speak for themselves.

The biblical utterances about Christ's resurrection have this in common, that they connect the resurrection inseparably with the crucifixion. The resurrection of Christ belongs to his crucifixion. The resurrection shows that the sacrifice made on the cross is a pleasing odor. The resurrection is the hearing and fulfillment of the high priestly prayer for the sinners. The resurrection is the glorious manifestation of the love that made Christ die on the cross; and it is the source of our love to God and fellow man. In Ephesians, three features are underlined with specific emphasis:

1. The resurrection of Christ by God is an act of such *might* and such *grace* as could be exhibited only by God. "The abounding greatness of God's power" (1:19) and the "abounding riches of his grace" (2:7) — not a healing, restoring, helping power analogous to human powers — are made known by the resurrection (1:18-20; 2:5-7). Resurrection means that such power and grace are in God as to reverse the normal order of life-death (under which we seem to be captive and hopelessly intimidated, cf. Heb. 2:15), and to make of it the sequence of death-life. "He who descended is the same who also ascended" (4:10). "You . . . we who are dead . . . he made alive . . . in order to show the riches of his grace in kindness to us in Christ Jesus" (2:1, 5, 7). "He says: 'Stand up, sleeper, and arise from the dead' " (5:14). To the author of Ephesians, to speak of God means to speak of the might and the grace of God; of that God who reveals himself by raising the dead. If we kept silent about the resurrection, we would not be speaking of God. Our "faith would be futile . . . we would be the most pitiable of all men" (1 Cor. 15:

17, 19). To say "God" in the valley of death and the tribu-
lations of life, means to believe in and to say, "Resurrection"!

2. The resurrection of Christ is an act of *cosmic* relevance.
Among all principalities and powers that influence or determine the course and life of nature and history, of society and
the psyche, none appears to be so omnipotent, final, and
devastating as death. Despite all embellishments and subterfuges, death is not unjustly called "the last enemy" of those
who live (1 Cor. 15:26). If nothing else, then death seems to
guarantee and to prove that wherever man is and however
he feels, decay and destruction are his final lot. To be in
the world — this certainly might mean nothing else but to
be sown for death, and therefore, to live "most pitiably."

But there is God who establishes something: even his crucified and risen Son, "above all rule and authority and power
and dominion, and above every name that is named not only
in this age but also in the age to come" (1:20 f.). To say
"resurrection" means that there is One who (though not
detached from, nor strange to, nor unconcerned with the
predicaments of man's life) is yet stronger than the laws of
nature to which we are subject. Resurrection triumphs over
death.

3. The resurrection of Christ is a *final*, confirming act.
From where he "sits" (1:20), Christ can and will "fill all in
all" (1:23; 4:10), even the most resistant place, the human
heart and understanding (3:17, 19). We cannot now discuss
at length why the second coming (the *Parousia*) of Christ is
not explicitly mentioned in Ephesians. The last judgment
certainly is not bypassed (5:6; 6:8 f.). And in Colossians (3:4)
a direct reference to the future appearance of Christ is distinctly made. In Ephesians, the finality of resurrection and
ascension floods with its light over all future events. What,
then, does it mean, that this One, Christ, is sitting at God's
right hand? What is made final and triumphant by his
enthronement? Because none other but the crucified, sacri-

ficed, interceding, wall-breaking Christ has been raised, we can answer: The intercession made by Christ is taken up to God's right hand! "He lives always in order to intercede" (Heb. 7:25). And he did not grasp this glory for himself with a robber's hand, or win it by courting public favor and applause. Not by human value-judgments or opinions, not by majority vote or by an accident of history, but from God himself Christ and his mediation have received that place. "God has highly exalted him and bestowed upon him the name which is above every name" (Phil. 2:9). By God himself the "one new man" for whose creation Christ died (2:15) is warranted as preferred to all, as honored above all creatures. Therefore, we need not vaguely wish or dream that there might be sometime, somewhere, somehow, hope, or at least some pleading for mankind before God. Rather, Ephesians asserts that there *is* hope and security and peace for men, and that these have been established by, before, and with God. For the mediator Jesus Christ, the crucified priest, the peace in person, the destroyer of the wall is enthroned "above all" (1:21), and eternally. "He says to the Son: Thy throne, O God, is for ever and ever. . . . Earth . . . and heaven . . . will perish; but thou remainest" (Heb. 1:8, 10 f.). So *He* is set above all; He, the "beloved" of God (Eph. 1:6), He who "loved us" (5:2), and in whom we are "beloved children" (5:1). We can conclude that in Christ's enthronement the "great love with which God has loved us" (2:4) was unshakably established in glory above all creatures.

The result of the resurrection is frequently described in political terms. If Christ is "enthroned" (1:20) on the securely established throne of God, then he is to be respected by all as king and monarch (Phil. 2:9-11). Whoever is in authority over a given realm will invariably affect the lives of its inhabitants. So Christ's monarchic rule "over all" makes not only all angelic and demonic powers (1:21 f.), but also all men — whether or not they know and like it — subject to the terms of his dominion. In the Gospels and Epistles alike, the "Gospel of Christ" is introduced and presented as a sort of political news or declaration. It announces that a change in government has taken place — as from a tyranny to a legal order, or from a revolutionary to a constitutional government.

This change was not due to "democratic procedure" and is by no means dependent on it. It has taken place, as it were, overnight (cf. Mark 4:27). It is God's work; it is complete. But it is also a work which from beginning to end involves men. In Ephesians, terms like "commonwealth" (2:12), "fellow citizens" (2:19), and "fellow heirs" (3:6) underline the political character of our belonging to the royal ruler, Jesus Christ. Col. 1:13 speaks of the "Son's Kingdom of love" (or Kingdom of the beloved Son) into which we have been "transferred" by "deliverance from the dominion of darkness." While Paul in 1 Cor. 15:23-28 seems to distinguish between the Kingship of Christ and the Kingship of God, Eph. 5:5 combines the two. The Kingdom of God is not ruled by two rulers who follow each other or compete with each other. Rather, the resurrection and enthronement of Christ reveal the eternal election, pleasure, and plan of God, to have Christ rule royally over mankind through sonship, grace, and redemption. God rules through Jesus Christ. The resurrection means that God solemnly identifies his own rule with that of the intercessor and breaker of the wall.

How does the resurrection of One involve the lives of the many on earth? The Epistle to the Colossians and the Epistle to the Ephesians speak with a boldness that is equalled only by that of the Fourth Gospel, of an astonishing, far-reaching, and joyful effect of Christ's resurrection: "We [you] have been raised with him!" (Col. 2:12; 3:1; Eph. 2:5). In the epistles to the Thessalonians, to the Corinthians, and to the Romans, our *future* resurrection with Christ is derived from Christ's resurrection. He is the first fruit or first-born (1 Cor. 15:20; cf. Col. 1:18; Acts 26:23) of many that *will* follow him on the last day. As we have died with Christ, we *shall* rise with him (1 Thess. 4:14; 5:10; 1 Cor. 6:14; 15:22; 2 Cor. 4:10-11, 14; Rom. 6:5-8; 7:4; 8:11, 17; Phil. 3:11, 21, etc.).

Colossians and Ephesians speak distinctly of a resurrection with Christ that has already taken place. "In Christ you have also been raised with him through faith, in the energy of God who raised him . . . he made you alive with him" (Col. 2:12 f.). "You have been raised with Christ" (Col. 3:1). He made us "who were dead through trespasses alive together with Christ . . . and he raised us with him and enthroned us with him" (Eph. 2:5 f.). We may compare John 11:26: "Whoever lives and believes in me, shall never die in eternity," with John 5:25: "The hour is coming *and now is,* when the dead will hear the voice of the Son of God, and those who hear will live." In Rom. 6:4, 11, 13; 14:8 f.; 2 Cor. 4:12; 5:17; Gal. 6:15; and Phil. 1:21, statements about newness of life or new creation are made that point in the same direction. Life from the dead is not only promised but already given by what God has done. The variety of situations in the churches caused Paul to place the accent sometimes on one aspect, sometimes on another. Libertine sinners are reminded of the future resurrection and judgment. Legalistic perfectionists are reminded of the completed work of God for man. Characteristic of Ephesians (and unlike Col. 2:20) is the omission of any explicit reference to our having "died with Christ"; instead, it is boldly preached: "With Christ we *have* been raised"!

What can this sentence mean? If it is more than a symbolic or rhetorical overstatement, it implies at least three things:

1. The resurrection of Christ cannot be spoken of or attested, unless we recognize that his resurrection is a miracle

which affects our being as radically and miraculously as it affected Him who was buried in the garden. Once (1 Cor. 15:12-19) Paul goes as far as to say: Only if we believe and confess that the many dead rise, can we say that Christ has risen. In 1 Cor. 15:16 it is declared, "If the dead are not raised, then Christ has not been raised"! When we confess that Christ has risen, our belief is not in a faraway, impotent "fact," but in a mighty event that reaches out and includes *us*. We confess, together with the resurrection of Christ and inseparably with it, that man, the man dead in sin (Eph. 2:1, 5), shall live! God does not will his death. The living God wills life and gives it! No aspect of death can prevent this. If spiritual death is even worse than death's physical work (we shall describe it later), then Eph. 2: 1, 5 shows that we inherit from Christ's resurrection precisely what we need here and now, that which alone can "save" us; namely, Spiritual resuscitation.

2. The resurrection of Christ means that with the supplication and intercession of Christ (Heb. 5:7 f.; 7:25) and with the person of Jesus Christ himself, all our human affairs, our very predicament and condition, have been accepted by God, taken up, given hope, installed in a place of glory. "Your life is hidden with Christ in God" (Col. 3:3). There is no reason to despair of man, of peace, or of life in the world. Though the "life of God" (in Eph. 4:18, this term is used for the true and real life which God grants as participation in his own life) is still "hidden" and confessed only in stammerings and stutterings of feeble faith, though we hardly perceive anything "glorious" in the life that we observe, there is yet a glory that only waits to be revealed (Col. 3:3 f.), and there is Christ giving himself "that the church might be presented before him in glory" (Eph. 5:27; cf. 1 Cor. 4:10). This means that because of Christ's resurrection human affairs are in a new state; they have a new look. The principalities and powers which seem so entrenched and invincible do not have

the last word. By our resurrection together with Christ, God displayed for all ages "the abounding riches of his grace" (2:7).

3. The resurrection of Christ is, as we observed before, the exaltation of the crucified man from death. When the resurrection is preached, it is not an abstraction or a lofty state of mind that is spoken of; resurrection concerns that man who could not and would not run away from death nor attempt to escape from the fear of it. It concerns that life which is our life — in fear and trembling (Eph. 6:5) in "*evil* days" (5:16), pressed by overstrong "powers" (6:12), distinguished by "chains," "sufferings," and the danger of "losing heart" (6:20; 3:13). The outstanding men of the Old Testament, that is to say, the servants of God, the prophets and kings, the priests and the psalmists, surprise and move us because of their blunt humanity. They have full share in what is human. In the same way, if indeed not in a more obvious way, the "perfect, the inner, the new, and the one man" (Eph. 2:15; 3:16; 4:13, 24) who is created by the resurrection, is real man and not a fiction or ghost. In consequence, we are not left with the notion that an ideal man "has been raised with Christ;" but concrete things are said about the new life which the new man is called to live in this present "world of darkness" (6:12). There will be occasion later to sketch what Ephesians has to say about it.

The message of Ephesians concerning the resurrection is more outspoken than that of many other New Testament books. Only the Gospel of John brings home the results of resurrection more emphatically. The resurrection is so strongly in the foreground of the Epistle to the Ephesians that explicit references to the sufferings of Christ and of the Church are almost completely omitted. The words "to suffer," "suffering," "temptation," and "tribulation," which are frequently used in other Pauline epistles, do not occur in Ephesians. Though the cross is preached with all vigor, there is nothing to be found of the sentimental, tragic, or pessimistic undertone characteristic of an abstract "Theology of the Cross." But the seemingly "scandalous" and "foolish" (1 Cor. 1:23) news of the sacrificial death of Christ cannot be separated from the good news of his resurrection.

The resurrection, as preached in Ephesians, leaves no room for any metaphysical or ethical dualism, as though the Gospel were only for the next world, while the hard realities of greed, cheating, and impurity are all that is left for the present world. The resurrection of the crucified Christ and the resurrection with him of those "dead in trespasses" mean that "*all*, the things in heaven and upon earth, are given *one* head," namely, Christ (or "are summed up in Christ," 1:10; the RSV translation of this verse is hardly adequate). By his descent and ascent Christ "fills all" (4:10; 1:23), so that there is no power that is not subject to him (1:21 f.). Upholders of a tragic dualism that would abandon to perdition the world, or the body of man, or the life of society, in order to strive for no more than the future salvation of a disembodied soul, certainly betray ignorance of the "Gospel of peace." They would dare to call the peace on earth which the Gospel announces a lie. Nowhere is it written that the politics of the great and small nations must follow a logic and ethic opposed to the Gospel. Even if they do, we still have no justification whatsoever for making out of the current tensions between East and West, or between hungry and overfed peoples, a neat dualistic system and world view equating evil with the East and justice with the West. In our day, Christian words, traditions, and institutions are often used to defend this tragic world view and to place a halo around some questionable politics. The message of Ephesians, the Gospel of peace, stands over against such abuse of Christ's name. The great work of God is too good to promote political or metaphysical tragedies.

In the following paragraphs, we must show that this work of God, its finality and perfection in the death and resurrection of Christ notwithstanding, is still going on.

III. THE SPIRIT: POWERFUL COMMUNICATION

The descent and ascent of Christ, the offer and the acceptance of his intercession for those dead in sins, and the faith and hope of all who live from him, might be nothing but symbols despite the firmness and incisiveness of Paul's thinking, preaching, and writing. In that case, it would not make much difference whether we considered those events and attitudes as part of a man-made myth or slowly growing legend, or as factual historical occurrences. The question remains whether all that was said about Christ and redemption and access to God is really more than a nice story, a dream house, or pie in the sky. After all, even "after Christ," Christians and non-Christians alike are living and dying in misery. There are those who hate and curse each other and God, and greedily steal and possess whatever they can lay their hands upon. Unless there be some communication from God to man concerning the validity of what was said about Jesus Christ and his work, mankind remains as divided, homeless, and hopeless as "before Christ." Despite all "preaching," the cynical shrugs, malicious grins, and shrewd arguments seem to triumph over the "good news." How are the love, the grace, the life, and the peace of which Paul speaks, actually communicated to the reader of Ephesians?

It is clear that the logic and rhetoric of Paul or of an interpreter of Paul's words cannot solve this problem. Neither can abstinence from careful thinking and self-abandonment to uncontrollable feelings provide an answer. The argument that the story of Christ is, after all, honored and commended by a long tradition and by respect-commanding teachers and churches is not used by Paul. The presence and actuality, the effect and validity, of God's work rest on a basis stronger than that which such things as rhetoric, feelings, and traditions can provide.

There appears to be a deep gulf between what is true "in the heavenly places" and what seems to be true on earth, between the clear-cut events and deeds that come from God's hands and our nebulous apprehension of what really matters, and, perhaps, even between Paul's faith and the faith of those who read Ephesians. Whatever the nature, depth, and breadth of the abyss, if it is to be overcome, it must be overcome by what we call "communication."

Now, for us, communication has become a sore and thorny problem. We tackle it by means of statistics, psychology, propaganda, and the like. But such instruments are scarcely adequate for dealing with the Gospel. Ephesians makes no use of them. According to this epistle, the facing and solving of the problem of communication is God's own affair, and it is handled by God himself.

The Holy Spirit is God's power that makes men realize, hear, feel, obey, and enjoy what God has done for them. "God blessed us with every Spiritual blessing" (1:3). "Hearing the word of truth, the Gospel of your salvation, and believing, you were sealed in him with the promised Holy Spirit who is the earnest of our inheritance" (1:13 f.). "In one Spirit we have access to the Father" (2:18). "You are being built for a dwelling place of God in [by] the Spirit" (2:22). "The mystery . . . is now revealed . . . by the Spirit" (3:5). "Be strengthened in [toward?] the inner man through might by his Spirit . . . that Christ may dwell in your hearts by faith" (3:16 f.). "Keep the oneness of the Spirit" (4:3 f.). "Do not grieve the Holy Spirit of God by whom you were sealed" (4:30). "Be filled with the Spirit, speaking to one another with psalms and hymns and spiritual songs, singing and praising" (5:18 f.). "Pray at all times in the Spirit" (6:18). The Spirit also is meant when Paul writes of the "gift of Christ" that is given to himself and to each member of the

Church (3:7; 4:7; cf. 1 Cor. 12:7). The riches and measure of
that gift are displayed in the different ministries entrusted to
the saints for the service they are called to render (4:11 f.), and
in the continuous building and growth of the "body of
Christ" (the Church) to its head and from its head (4:12-16;
2:20-22).

What do these references to the Spirit show us? While
describing the testimony of Ephesians to the resurrection, we
have already indicated that the crucified and risen Christ,
after his enthronement to God's right hand, has not retired
from working. Rather he has been "given all authority in
heaven and on earth" (Matt. 28:18) to rule over all principalities and powers (Eph. 1:20 ff.), until his enemies are
under his footstool (Heb. 1:13; 1 Cor. 15:25). John 14:16-17,
26; 15:26; 16:7 ff. (cf. 7:39); Acts 2:33 (cf. 5:32); and other
texts — among them Eph. 4:7 ff. — say distinctly that the glory
and rulership of Christ are demonstrated to us by the pouring
out of the Spirit.

For the author of Ephesians, the gift of the Spirit is the
evidence of Christ's resurrection. This gift proves Christ's
care for men, and his power to create praise to God in human
hearts, lives, communities, services, songs, and sermons. If
there were no Spirit we might be tempted to relegate the
crucifixion and resurrection of Christ to a place among other
tales and events. We might consider them to be the contents
of a religious story, legend, or myth. Or we might regard
them as spurious events of a bygone unscientific, miracle-
believing age. In either case, precisely their detachment from
ordinary, normal life would keep Christ at a distance from us
and us far from him. Yet the gift of the Spirit does not permit
cheap criticism which expresses itself in such terms as "unscientific," "mythical," or "antiquated." By giving the Spirit, God is
always able to seize man, whatever man's fashion of science or
his latest world view. In works of the Spirit, God is still
operating in the midst of history and experience, in the com-

munity of men, and in their psyche. The great events of crucifixion and resurrection may be decades or almost two thousand years removed, when the Ephesians, or we, read Paul's
epistle. But neither the godless nor the pious are left without
witness that God is ruling and that he rules through Christ.
The Spirit's operations on earth are proof to us that God's
work of salvation is still going on, and is not a past, completed
"fact" of history or mythology. It is by this very same continuing action and self-communication that the perfection of
God's work is revealed most clearly.

Four characteristics of this ongoing work deserve to be
pointed out, when the witness of Ephesians to the Spirit is to
be heard:

1. The Holy Spirit is the *power* of God — power demonstrated by the resurrection of Christ (1:19 f.) and from the
resurrected Christ (4:7 f.). It is needless to ask whether the
Spirit is God's or Christ's, as needless as to ask whether God
or Christ rules over all since Easter. In Ephesians the Holy
Ghost is called Spirit, Holy Spirit, Holy Spirit *of God* (3:5;
5:18; 1:13; 4:30, etc.); such nomenclature as Spirit of Christ
and Spirit of the Son (Rom. 8:9; Gal. 4:6) is not used. But as
the Gospels speak of the Coming One receiving and baptizing
with the Spirit (Mark 1:8-10), as Acts 2:33 treats of Christ's
receiving and pouring out the Spirit, and finally as Rom. 8:11
teaches that the same Spirit by which Christ is raised is also
dwelling in and operating in the saints, so Ephesians presupposes that Christ and the giving of the Spirit are inseparable. Christ's glory is declared by the gift of the Spirit to
Christ, and by Christ's gift of the Spirit to us. The Holy
Spirit is the resurrection-Spirit. His holiness may be identified with his peculiar power to give life even when and where
death seemed to triumph.

Now in Ephesians some of the same terms (*pneuma, ener-
geia, dynamis*) which are used for describing the name and

operation of God's "power," the Spirit, are also used for the devil and his satellites (2:2; 1:21). This means, on the one hand, that for the author of Ephesians "power" as such is not evil; for God himself acts in power. It means, on the other hand, that neither in heavenly places nor on earth can principalities and powers exert a dominion which does not find its match, and more than its match, in the powerful actions of God's continued self-manifestations. Evil demonic powers there may be; there is also the power of God, the Spirit! Communication by the Spirit is identified with a *power-demonstration* that meets and fights other "powers." May God's elect know that God is on their side! May they be "strong . . . in the strength of the Lord's might" (6:10)!

2. The Holy Spirit is the powerful *manifestation* of God. According to John's Gospel, the Spirit is the "Spirit of Truth." He makes known, teaches, reminds, witnesses, speaks, proclaims, and leads to the truth (John 14:17, 26; 15:26; 16:7). According to the Acts of the Apostles (Acts 2:33; cf. 2:14 ff.), he effects things that are "seen and heard." In 1 Corinthians the gift of God is called "manifestation of the Spirit" (1 Cor. 12:7). Ephesians calls the Holy Ghost "Spirit of wisdom and of revelation in knowledge" (cf. Isa. 11:2). Revelation of the "mystery" is effected by him (Eph. 3:5). The sealing by the Spirit (1:13; 4:30) is obviously an event of which the Ephesians were aware and conscious. Where there is communication by the Spirit, there is always and indispensably revelation, or manifestation, or to put it more plainly, information. "He will teach you . . . he will speak" (John 14:26; 16:13).

This emphasis of Ephesians on the informing capability of the Spirit results in a rather sober and disillusioning picture of the Spirit's work. Absent from Ephesians are all references to enthusiastic marks of the Spirit's presence, such as are described, for instance, in 1 Cor. 14 and Acts 2. No mention is made of healing or of speaking in tongues. Also, the prophets of 3:5; 4:11 (and 2:20?) need not have been an ecstatic band like those who met the freshly anointed King Saul (1 Sam. 10:10-13). A sharp warning is uttered against confusing "drunkenness with wine" with "fullness in the Spirit" (Eph. 5:18). We ask accordingly what sign of the Spirit takes the place of such extraordinary, ecstatic, and enthusiastic occurrences?

Not only in John 14–16 and Acts 2, but also in Ephesians, the essence of the Spirit as revealer is pointed out by reference to what we might call "action by words," i.e., to speaking, witnessing, and hearing. It is not just any word or talk whatsoever that is meant, but "the sword of the Spirit . . . is the word *of God*" (6:17). "Hearing the word *of truth,* believing," and "being sealed by the promised Holy Spirit" (1:13) cannot be separated as different manifestations of God's election. In contrast to Rom. 12:3 ff. and 1 Cor. 12:4 ff., Ephesians goes so far as to enumerate only *ministries of the word;* i.e., apostolate, prophecy, evangelism (mission), shepherding (pastorate, or counseling?) and teaching, when the "gift" of the risen Christ to the Church is mentioned (4:7,11). Also, the praying and singing done "in the Spirit" (5:18 f.; 6:18) show that Spirit and word are inseparable. The risen Christ does not rule by word and Spirit as though by two swords. But his rule is by the witnessing word which the Spirit makes men say to one another and to God.

We can now sum up tentatively what Ephesians says about the Spirit by saying that the truth, validity, and reality of Christ's death and resurrection are proved and experienced by the preaching, praying, and praising which takes place among the Christians. And we conclude from this statement, that if Christians begin to neglect, to doubt, or to despise preaching and prayer, or if they dare to put them on the same level with any church "activity," they would "grieve the Holy Spirit of God" (4:30) and could never be or become evangelists.

3. The Holy Spirit is the power of *unification* (at-one-ment). He assembles men by and under God's work. What the Spirit calls into being when he makes men preach and teach, pray and praise, do mission work and engage in brotherly exhortation, is (a) hearing "the Gospel of salvation" (1:13), (b) "hope in God's calling" (4:4), (c) knowledge of "the riches of the glory of the inheritance" (1:18), (d) "insight into the mystery of Christ" (3:4 f.). The Spirit attests mightily nothing else but what we have called the perfect work of Christ crucified and risen, and what we have described (on the basis of 2:13-18) as the making of peace and the creation of the one new man who has access to God. The love of God for his Son (1:6) and for us (1:4 f.; 2:4; 5:1), the love of Christ (3:19; 5:2, 25, 29) and the love among men (1:15; 4:2; 5:25, 33; 6:21, 23) — this love is not a matter of words and feelings only, but is effective and creative power. According to Rom. 5:5, "the love of God is poured out into our hearts by the Holy Spirit." This love draws together what was separated and apart; it creates at-one-ment, oneness; it is the "bond of peace" which we are to strive to hold fast (4:3).

To know, by the operation of the Spirit, what are the riches of God's glory, and to enjoy access to him by the same Spirit (1:18; 2:18) — this is the gift of God (4:7) that builds and causes growth of a community on earth; namely, the Church (2:22). The Church is the work of the Holy Spirit; and the Church is — as then, so now — the exhibited evidence for the resurrection of the crucified Christ.

We can now formulate a third meaning of the term "communication by the Spirit." It means not only action of overwhelming power and information of the truth which matters for life and death; it means also the gathering of a community — a community with God and with formerly estranged fellow men. The risen Christ manifests himself in the founding and the sustaining, in the building and the growth, of the Church. The Church is the people who live "in Christ" as "one new man" (2:15). She stands before him "glorious" (5:27); day by day her members throw off the fetters and shackles of the old hostile man (4:22). As God's chosen, holy and beloved, the members of this (Christ's) body put on compassion, kindness, lowliness, meekness, and patience (Col. 3:12); i.e., the "new man" (4:24), the "workmanship of God" (2:10), the "whole armor of God" (6:11).

The community of the Church, inspired and enlightened by the Holy Spirit, is a oneness that grows and is being built (2:21 f.; 4:12-16); it is not a historical society that has no other interest than to preserve a status quo. It is an assembly, not of cowardly compromisers, but of those "made strong in the might of the Lord's strength" to withstand principalities and powers (6:10 ff.). The Church is an evangelist that proclaims the removal of the wall between the insiders and the outsiders of the kingdom of God, rather than a capitalist who claims rights solely for his own benefit and enjoyment. The Church cannot justify her present and secure her future by erecting and observing demarcations and curtains between nations, denominations, congregations, or clerical and lay orders. Instead, it will bear witness to that Christ who entered into solidarity with the hungry, the naked, the captives, even with the criminals, who obviously seemed *not* to belong to his disciples or to the Church (Matt. 25:31-46; Luke 23:32-43). By the sealing with the Holy Spirit (1:13; 4:30), not only the community of saints, but the whole of mankind is sealed — even as circumcision (2:11) was sign and seal of the whole man's belonging to God. The Church that lives by the Spirit in the midst of the world is the stamp, footprint, and sign of God. It shows that all the world is God's property and that God does not give up, but upholds his claim upon all (1:22 f.).

4. The Holy Spirit is the *pledge* for future consummation. Eph. 1:13 and 4:30 point out in similar terms that the Spirit

already given is a sign of redemption still to come. The nouns "promise" (1:13; 2:12; 3:6; 6:2), "hope" (1:18; 2:12; 4:4) and (future!) "inheritance" (1:14, 18; 5:5) do not point in a common direction in vain. Ephesians is as full of "eschatology" (i.e., of a doctrine of completion, perfection, and fulfillment of God's work at the "end") as the average New Testament book. The question is not whether or not there will be a last judgment (6:8 f.), a victory of Christ over "all" (1:10; 4:10), a final unity of "all" before and by the one Son of God (4:13). Ephesians permits no wavering in that regard. But a serious problem is whether or not a self-centered understanding of the future day of "redemption" is valid. Should that day promise good only to the Christians? A Christian hope that yearns only for the Christians' own personal perfection, peace and happiness, looks deeply suspicious to all who crave for a hope in promises that are greater than those of egoistical and meritorial systems.

Paul's message in Ephesians is not one of individual perfection, wholeness, or happiness. It rather is Jesus Christ "filling all in all" (1:23; 4:10); it is the hope to attain to the stature of his fullness and perfection (4:13); it is the manifest triumph of God as Father "of all, over all, through all, and in all" (4:6). By the Spirit, a hope and a triumph are granted that go far beyond some egotist's private concern. If God is "all in all" (1 Cor. 15:28), there is no need to be anxious about individual post-existence. Ephesians does not promise heavenly pastures, but it promises the triumph of God's cause. The Holy Spirit given now is the seal that cannot be removed.

So much about the Spirit as the guarantor of God's perfect work and of the Spirit's impact upon us. More will have to be said about the Church and her members under the guidance and seal of the Spirit. For the present, it is sufficient to know that in Ephesians all that needs to be said about communication is said upon the ground of God's self-manifestation by his Holy Spirit. When churches arise from their sleep and become evangelists today, they can hardly improve upon Paul. Because the Holy Spirit is at work, no men "on earth" (1:10), "in Ephesus" (1:1), or "in the world" (2:12) can escape or deny the great work of salvation God has wrought in Jesus Christ. By the Holy Spirit, through the exalted Christ, the Father unceasingly continues to see to it that his perfect work shall be known, effective, and all-embracing.

Much could be said in support of the view of those who claim that the Holy Spirit has abandoned many of today's congregations and that few of them show convincing signs of true inspiration. And yet, grievance and complaint about the alleged absence of the Spirit could easily be a form of "grieving the Holy Spirit of God" (4:30). If the Holy Spirit were not at work, there could be no "word of truth," no "gospel of salvation," no Church, no witness, no service, no exhortation, no prayer in the name of Christ. On the basis of Ephesians, we can argue very directly that despite our "being tossed to and fro and carried about by every wind and doctrine, by the cunning of men, by their craftiness in deceitful wiles" (4:14), there is still a people gathered for preaching and prayer, and there are men living for obedience in faith and mission. Therefore, the Holy Spirit is at work. Whether in contempt or in despair, to deny the Spirit's activity would be blasphemy against the majesty of God.

IV. God's Majesty in His Work

The work which God did through Jesus Christ and by his Holy Spirit is by no means only a segment or an aspect of God. In Ephesians there is no appeal from God's operation and manifestation to God himself. We cannot speak of God except by speaking of that love, that plan, that mystery, and that word which has been and is revealed by the Son and the Spirit. And there is no way of rendering thanks to God ex-

cept by reference to what has been done in the past, is being
done in the present, and is anticipated in future blessings, in
the name of our Lord Jesus Christ (5:20).

In Eph. 1:3-12, the author explains that what God has done
and is now doing corresponds exactly to and expresses "the
counsel of his will" and "his good pleasure" (1:5, 9, 11). This
will was motivated by no factors outside of God. "Before
the foundation of the world" (1:4), "according to his good
pleasure" (1:5, 9), "according to the riches of his grace"
(1:7; 2:7), "in mercy, because of the great love with which
he loved us" (2:4), it pleased him by just one man and one
means, even "in Christ" (1:3-13), to elect and destine us to
be his holy and spotless children (1:4 f.),

We observe that not even human need or anxiety appears as
motivation of God's work. If either did, changing "needs"
might abrogate the goodness of God's work, might demand
other works — perhaps even another God and another revelation. Then God's mercy would be dependent on our misery.
Actually, what determines the course of God's action is
exclusively God's good pleasure to love us. To what end did
he elect us? "To the praise of the glory of his grace . . . that
we be [for] a praise of his glory . . . to the praise of his
glory" — so it is written three times (1:6, 12, 14), as though the
author would make sure that no praise or glory for the
church, or for men, or for human work would ever be substituted for what belongs to God alone (2:8 f.).

But what is the "glory of God"? His glory can be compared
with the bright splendor of the sky in the immediate sur-
roundings of the sun. For as the brightness of the sky discloses the light and heat of the sun, so the glory of God is
the radiance of God's own essence, power, and existence. The
value and the limitation of this comparison become evident
when we observe that in 1:19; 2:7, and 3:19, the greatness,
riches, and love of God are described as "going beyond, surpassing, abounding" ("immeasurable," in the RSV, expresses

only part of what is meant); and that in 1:8, the riches of God's grace is said to be without any restraint, "overflowing," or "lavished." God wills that his glory be seen (cf. John 1:14; 2:11; 12:28; 17:4 f., etc.). He wills not only that his love and riches and power be made known, but also be reflected in the special praise that among all creatures is expected from man alone. The specific plan of God is that "we [men] be [for] a praise of his glory" (1:12).

For referring to that "plan," the epistle uses several times (1:10; 3:2, 9) a word from which the English term "economy" is derived. The Greek word means management of a household, governmental principle, administration, strategy, or dispensation. Whatever sense we feel bound to prefer, it is made clear in Ephesians that Jesus Christ and the revelation of his work are not only a part, but are the very heart of God's eternal will and plan (1:3 ff., 15 ff.; 2:4 ff., 13 ff., etc.).

Whereas in Colossians (an epistle denouncing with much vigor a doctrine that apparently limited Christ's omnipotence) much stress is laid on the "fullness" of God "that dwells bodily in Christ" (Col. 1:19; 2:9), in Ephesians it is stated repeatedly that Christ is to "fill" all in all (1:23; 4:10). To become "filled with all the fullness of God" means for Paul nothing else but to let "Christ dwell in the heart by faith" (3:19, 17) and to let the church be what it is meant to be: "his fullness"; i.e., the people already now filled with him, with the Spirit (1:23; 5:18). It is not impossible — though convincing evidence is still missing — that the terms "fullness" and "fill" contain an allusion to some religious, pagan-syncretistic vocabulary and system. It is certain, however, that the majesty and totality of God present in the work of Christ (cf. 2 Cor. 5:19) are implied, and that the right and success of Christ over the whole world are proclaimed when his "fullness" is mentioned. It was and is God's will that there should be a tabernacle (2:21, a "holy temple") in which, and radiating from which, the glory of God should be seen. John speaks of the "glory" of the Son of God, "full" of grace and truth (John 1:14). Therefore, whoever perceives that glory of God which is revealed in the perfect work of Jesus Christ, is confronted by God's full might and grace, even by God himself.

Nobody could prevent Paul from building his prayer for the Ephesians upon the ground of that work for which he was ambassador and of which we had to speak. Preposterous is the thought that current religious needs or feelings of the twentieth century should be reason enough to criticize or correct what God has willed, planned, done, and what he is still doing according to the "good news." The grace and salvation of which Paul speaks are not a theory or a possibility. They are truth and reality, regardless of who may doubt them. Only as the "word of truth," authenticated by God himself, can the Gospel be borne forward — in our time, even as in Paul's.

Is the view which Ephesians presents of God's work too "objective," too concerned for "God's initiative," too miraculous or "mythical" in character, or too cosmic or wordly in its ramifications? A warning against such charges must be added. The special character of God's work is not its objectivity, but its subjective nature. The God who loves, plans, and does whatever is his will, performs all in his Son, the man Jesus Christ. So he acts very "personally" and he treats men as creatures made after his image. By enabling and calling us to be thankful with the praise we give him and the love we show for one another, he reveals that he desires us to be living, free, responsive persons, not objects. On the other hand, to talk of "divine initiative in the drama of redemption" is far too weak to convey an important meaning. Initiative is displayed when a car with a good engine pushes and starts a stalled car. God's work, however, is more than an initial push that enables man to continue under his own steam. God's work is the resurrection of people who were dead in sin. Those raised with Christ remain gladly dependent on God's Spirit in every move they make in the world as witnesses, in the Church as members, and in the closet in prayer. They know that nobody rises from spiritual death by pulling himself up by his bootstraps. Nothing less than the miracle of Christ's intercession and resurrection can terminate the hostility and fear that keep mankind in prison and bonds. No man has reason to abhor the "cosmic" relevance of Christ's person and work as they were described by Paul. The "cosmic" features of the message of Ephesians show that God loved "the world," so much so that in the perfect work of his love, hope even for "peace on earth" is well founded.

Before we can concentrate on how the Christians are to act in social, political, economic, and other "worldly" realms and regards, we must describe what are the proper marks of that people, commonly called "the Church."

THE GATHERING OF GOD'S PEOPLE

The Gathering of God's People

THE CHURCH, IN ITS ORIGIN, constitution, and life depends upon three elements: (1) God's self-revelation, which manifests his pleasure to save men from death and make sinners to be saints; (2) God's knowledge of the world, which determines what is needed by man for man's own good; and (3) God's grace, which actually creates of formerly hostile men an assembly which consciously and joyfully praises God and invites all men to do the same. On the following pages, we shall direct our attention to the revelation of the living God to dead men, to the judgment of God on the world, and to the gracious result of that revelation and judgment; namely, a people who live to the praise of God. We hope to show that dependence upon the living and loving God is what really constitutes the Church and determines her life. All talk about the Church's autonomy and democratic constitution, whether it be at the denominational or local level, will have to be gauged by this reality, or it will prove to be "unconstitutional." Where and when the Church is true to her constitution and determination she will grapple with the issues of her time. Firmly rooted in the love of the living God, she will be enabled daringly and realistically to see man as he is. From these facts it should be clearly seen that the Church's service will be expedient and efficient to the extent that it stems from the revelation and judgment of God.

I. REVELATION: OUR SALVATION FROM DEATH

In Christ, God has eternally planned and intended to love us. In Christ the perfect work of love was accomplished. In Christ also "the mystery of his will was made known to us" (Eph. 1:9). In him we were sealed by the "gospel of our salvation" (1:13). But an eternal election, a promise and an inheritance, a perfect work, would mean little if it were not made known that such love is real, active, and effective. Love that does not declare itself and fails to call for a free response of love is not love at all, or most certainly not God's love! Had God not revealed himself, he would not be glorified by men.

But it was "his good pleasure" that "the abounding riches of his grace" should be "shown in the coming ages in the kindness [exhibited] to us in Christ Jesus" (2:7), that "to him" there should be "glory in the Church and in Christ Jesus, for all generations for ever and ever" (3:21).

This "eternal purpose" (3:11) was realized in time chosen and measured by God. "When the fullness of time had come" (Gal. 4:4), the "plan for the fullness of time" (Eph. 1:10) was carried out. Christ was made head over all (1:10) ; the "mystery of Christ which was not made known in other generations to the sons of men, was now revealed" (3:5) and "was made known to us" (1:9). A Servant was appointed and equipped to "enlighten [the Gentiles] as to what is the plan of the mystery hidden from ages in God, the creator of all, in order that it be made known . . ." (3:9 f.). Little wonder that the apostle who was made recipient and instrument of this revelation (3:5, 7 ff.) prays and calls upon us to pray: "Glory to Him . . . for all generations for ever and ever" (3:21)! "Blessed be God . . . who has blessed us in Christ with every Spiritual blessing" (1:3)! That the "riches of God's grace" is shown "in kindness to us" (2:7) — this precisely is cause and reason for such jubilation.

In certain circles of theologians much is said and written on the need of man to understand himself in order that he participate in authentic being. The author of Ephesians, however, is little concerned with the self as subject matter of understanding. That "understanding" is an object of prayer and a quest of faith, he does not deny, for he asserts fervently: "The father of glory shall give you the Spirit of wisdom and revelation in the [full] knowledge of *him* . . . that you [may] know . . ." (1:17 f.), and "that you have power to comprehend with all the saints" (3:18 f.). From reading Paul's letter (or letters?) the Ephesians shall "perceive his insight into the mystery of *Christ*" (3:3 f.). Yet that which has to be understood is not "my own self," but the many dimensions of God's work (3:18), "the love of Christ that surpasses knowledge" (3:19), the mystery of Christ (3:4), the power that works in the resurrection (1:19), and the hope and inheritance given to the saints (1:18).

God's revelation is a challenge to, rather than a denial of reason. Ephesians does not ask from us a "sacrifice of intellect" to grasp or "comprehend what is the breadth and depth and height and length" of this revelation (3:18). Though the love of Christ does "surpass knowledge," this "surpassing love" shall be "known" (3:19). It is a "mystery" indeed (1:9; 3:3 f., 9; 6:19). It was "not made known to the sons of men in other generations" (3:5); it was "hidden from (or for?) ages" (3:9) and even angels longed to look (or to "peep") into it (1 Pet. 1:12). But to us it was made known through the Good News (1:9, 13); and where it is not yet known, it shall be made known by preaching (6:19; Rom. 15: 19-24; Acts 1:8, etc.). This is what we shall "understand" — even the mystery of Christ which by "preaching of the evangel" is to be made known to the Gentiles (3:4-10). God wants himself and his work to be known and understood.

Therefore God reveals in his work nothing less than the full mystery, i.e., his love, his might (or "his righteousness,"

Rom. 1:17; 3:21, 25, 26) — in short, "his fullness" (3:19). His whole work has the character and purpose of revelation. What he did "in Christ" was done "in order to manifest" (or "to show," 2:7; Rom. 3:25, 26). So both the doer of the work and the work (Rom. 3:26: "that he *is* righteous *and* that he *makes* righteous") can be known and must be made known. Generations and ages, regions and rulers, individuals and groups which do not yet recognize what is revealed, deserve to be told. God gave them the right to know. So they have a *right to know*. This is why Paul calls himself "a debtor [RSV, under obligation] to Greeks and barbarians, to wise and to foolish men" (Rom. 1:14).

In summary, how can we know God? Only by his work and revelation! As impotent and incompetent as we are to perform the great work which is "not from men, but God's gift" (2:8 f.), even so we are hopelessly unable to think for ourselves what God makes known through revelation.

The nature of God's revelation is described in clear terms. Neither propositions about attributes of God (saying, for instance, that God is immortal, invisible, inaccessible, cf. 1 Tim. 1:17; 6:16), nor a code for moral living, nor a "perfect law of freedom" (as in James 1:25), are put in the foreground. Rather, what is revealed can be summed up in the following statements: "God is rich in mercy, because of the great love with which he has loved us" (2:4). He is the Father, whose riches "overflow upon us" (1:8). He, the One Spirit, the One Lord, the One God and Father (4:3-6), is revealed in the creation of one new man (2:15), in our calling to be one body in one hope and one faith (4:4), and in the promise that we shall "all attain to the oneness of faith and knowledge of the Son of God" (4:13). Therefore, God accepts the sacrifice as a pleasing odor which is offered for peace and which proclaims peace (2:14-18; 5:2). Through Christ, he makes those far to be near, and to have access to himself as to the Father of all (2:13, 18; 4:6). He strengthens men with his power so energetically that they are enabled ("armed") to withstand the worst of onrushing powers (6:10 ff.). All of this and more is "revealed" after it had been "hidden for ages" (3:9).

We observe that it is always an *act* of the living God, and never information about an inactive "being" of God, to which Paul refers when he speaks of "revelation" and "knowledge." It is not in Ephesians only that this is stated. "What is known of God is evident . . . because God has revealed it. . . . Since the creation of the world, his invisible essence (his eternal power and deity) is being intelligently perceived in [his] works" (Rom. 1:19). To "know Christ" is "to know the power of his resurrection and [the] communion in his sufferings" (Phil. 3:10). God gave us the Spirit "to know what God has granted to us" (1 Cor. 2:12). In his work — in faithfulness to his eternal will, to the crucified Christ, and to the promises given to Israel — God reveals *who* he is: even "our Father" (1:2, etc.), and *what* he is: how rich, how gracious, how mighty!

In this self-revelation of God, man has the largest possible place. The thought that man is nothing because God is all in all is absurd. Actually, man alone is declared to be the beneficiary of God's great act of self-manifestation. Dead, impure, greedy, divided, hostile — however he may be described — man is the recipient of God's love and kindness (2:4, 7; 5:2). Sentence by sentence, what God makes known through revelation works out in salvation for man. "The Gospel . . . is the power of God for salvation" (Rom. 1:16). "The word of truth" is identified with "the Gospel of our salvation" (1:13). The glory proper to and due to God "in the Church and in Christ Jesus" is one and the same glory (3:21). What God does "in Christ," he does for men, as the existence of the Church on earth makes manifest.

We may say also that men by revelation became participants and beneficiaries in the life of the triune God. "No more" are they "alienated from the life of God through the ignorance which was in them" (4:17 f.). As children they partake in the Father's wisdom (1:17) and kindness (2:7; 4:32), so much so as to be called "imitators of God" (5:1)! Raised with Christ, they are "enthroned with him" (2:5 f.). As members of his body, they are one body; i.e., one flesh with him (5:30 f.; 2:16; 3:6; 4:4). Empowered by the Spirit, they can stand against principalities and powers (6:10 ff.). To use the daring formulation of 2 Pet. 1:4, they are "partakers of the divine nature." By uniting with himself such as were "dead" in their sins (2:1, 5); by acquiring as property those held captive before (1:14; 4:8); by making holy and spotless those who were walking "in the lusts of the flesh" (1:4; 2:3; 5:26 f.) — in this way God operates. He "showed it" for all future time (2:7). He wanted to "make it known" to the principalities and powers (3:10); namely, what sort of God he is and what is the extent of "his manifold wisdom" (3:10).

This revelation "through the Gospel" (3:5 f.) shows a solidarity of God with man, and it creates a participation of man in God's riches, which indeed "surpass knowledge" (3:19). No man can speak with such confidence concerning God's care for man and God's hope for humanity as the man who has received God's revelation. Paul is aware that other "saints," and also "the holy apostles and prophets of God," received this same revelation (3:5; Col. 1:26). But he cannot resist the consciousness that to him, the "less than least of all the saints," a special insight into the mystery of God and a particular charge were given (3:3, 8; 6:19).

God made himself known to men by the salvation of sinners in Christ. To explain the full significance of this summary, we need to add a few remarks about the meaning of the words "knowledge" and "know" in the biblical books. What today is called the "Greek concept of knowledge" corresponds to the rationalist and scientific understanding which triumphed in the Western world in the nineteenth century. "Knowledge" in this sense may be understood as the sum of objective, impersonal, controllable, and conveyable information about persons, events, or things. It is acquaintance with facts, truths, and principles, with laws, methods, and skills acquired by study, investigation, or exercise.

"Knowledge of God" obviously does not fit into this kind of definition. Why should something which appears like the expression of mystical feelings or the affirmations of blind faith, be considered an evidence of the "knowledge of God"? A dead body can be dissected and a knowledge of bones and muscles, of arteries and sinews, even of latent diseases and possible cause of death, can be gained, and may be utilized or forgotten again. The knowledge of an object or skill implies that man is free to gain or to display some mastery over it. But God is not a dead object, and if religion is no more than a skill, then it has lost the last of its possible credentials and values.

In the Bible, the right relationship between God and man (Matt. 11:27; John 6:69; 17:3, 25, etc.; Gal. 4:9; 1 Cor. 8:1-3; 13:12) is called "knowledge." God, or Christ, "knows" his own and they "know" him (John 10:14). The worst separation is confessed when one person says to another, "I don't know you" (Deut. 33:9; Matt. 25:12). In the Old Testament, the most intimate community between man and wife is described by the verb "to know" (Gen. 4:1, 17, 25, etc.). According to Hos. 2:16, 20; Jer. 31:31-34; and Ezek. 16, there is a close analogy between the knowledge that unites God and man, and the knowledge that unites man and wife. In both cases, knowledge is the togetherness and union of persons between whom call and response, giving and receiving, caring for and being cared for, complement each other. From the knowledge of God, man learns what it means to know a fellow man. But the knowledge between humans can also illustrate what knowledge of God means.

The union between him who knows and him who is known is called a "covenant" (Jer. 31:31; Ezek. 16:59-62). The making and keeping of the covenant does not wipe out, or disregard, the distinction of the partners. Rather, due regard for the difference between God and Israel, man and wife, the king and the people, is stipulated and "acknowledged" by the covenant. Knowledge is life of the two together: even of two unequal partners. In care and trust, in giving direction and answering with obedience, they lead a "life together." In the Bible knowledge is acknowledgment, submission to partnership, and enjoyment of it, but it is by no means superiority over, or skill in manipulating, an object.

The Old Testament treats oftener of this knowledge than the New Testament. It is full of commands and promises for the future that Israel shall know the Lord. But the expression, "We . . . ," "you . . . ," or "they know Him" (in the present!) cannot be found. Hosea observes bitterly, "There is no faithfulness or kindness and no knowledge of God in the land" (Hos. 4:1). And Isaiah states, "The ox knows its owner, and the ass the master's crib, but Israel does not know [God], my people does not understand" (Isa. 1:3).

According to Ephesians, the plan of God to reveal himself by "making men know the mystery of his will," "of Jesus Christ," and "of the Gospel" (1:9; 3:4; 6:19) is motivated by the love and grace of God (2:4, 7). The purpose of his self-manifestation is the "praise of his glory" (1:6, 12, 14) by a holy and spotless people (1:4; 5:27). Neither the mystery nor its revelation points to a manageable object. To his readers whom he addresses in Greek, Paul sometimes attempts to explain what he means by knowledge. He does so in a profound play on words: The saints are *knowing God,* or rather, are *known by God* (Gal. 4:9; 1 Cor. 8:2 f.; 1 Cor. 13:12; cf. John 10:14; 2 Tim. 2:19). Paul bursts out against a concept of knowledge that "puffs up" its possessor (1 Cor. 8:1; 13:2; cf. 4:6, 18 f.; 5:2). That he has in mind exactly the same concept of knowledge which we have just described by means of references to Old Testament texts is clearly shown in Ephesians. Many interpreters of this epistle have rightly pointed out that the argument of Ephesians (as of other Pauline epistles) is developed in two great steps: 1, God has made himself known in his great work (Eph. 1–3). 2, "Therefore I, a prisoner in the Lord, exhort you to walk worthily of the calling with which you were called, with all lowliness and meekness, with patience, forbearing one another in love, striving to hold fast the oneness of the Spirit in the bond of peace" (4:1-3). In this exhortation, as in the following admonitions and warnings of Eph. 4–6, Paul treats of the conduct and walk of those who receive knowledge. The verses of Eph. 5:8-14, by using the metaphor of "light," refer to the "enlightenment (1:18, i.e., to the knowledge) received from God which makes us "walk as children of the light" (5:8). Paul does not speak of a sum of propositions, axioms, objective insights, or rules which the Ephesians now possess, or might forget. Knowledge of God, rather, is a way of life. It is new existence — "new creation" (2 Cor. 5:16-17) — no more in "alienation," but "near" the covenants of Israel (2:12 f.). As in Hosea, Jeremiah, Ezekiel, so also in Eph. 5:21-32, the relationship between man and wife is treated as an analogy to the relation between the Lord and his chosen people.

We conclude that in Ephesians the verbs "to know" and "to make known" — except when an allusion to Hellenistic "knowledge" (gnōsis) is made (3:19) — denote that existential relationship between God and man which was promised in the Old Testament. Jeremiah wrote: "They shall all know me, from the least of them to the greatest" (Jer. 31:34). Isaiah promised: "The earth shall be full of the knowledge of the Lord" (Isa. 11:9; cf. Hab. 2:14); and "By his knowledge shall the righteous one, my servant, make many to be accounted righteous" (Isa. 53:11). Zechariah, John the Baptist's father, pointed (according to Luke 1:77 f.) in the same direction when he foresaw that his son would "give knowledge of salvation to the Lord's people in the forgiveness of their sins, through the tender mercy of our God." Ephesians speaks of this same "knowledge of salvation in forgiveness."

The intellectualist misunderstanding of the "knowledge of God" is as fatal as an antirational definition of revelation. If we cannot define God and the revealed mystery by our reason, even less can we pretend to praise and serve him only by swallowing propositions. God is to be loved "with all your heart, with all your soul, with all your might" (Deut. 6:4), "and with all your mind" (Luke 10:27). The totality of man is chosen by God to love him. Knowledge of God is never a handed-down possession to be treated like some second-hand acquisition. It is always new. Neither does it concern a part of man only, such as his brain or feelings. Rather, knowledge of God is that "holding fast the bond of peace . . . with all lowliness and meekness, with patience, forbearing one another in love," to which Eph. 4:2 f. exhorts. The "salvation" which God works for and in us will be "worked out with fear and trembling" (Phil. 2:12 f.). God's revelation, the Gospel of salvation, calls and enables man to "awake . . . and stand up from the dead" (Eph. 5:14). It does not negate man.

Therefore, precisely where God's revelation is graciously "made known" and gratefully "known," a people of God arises, stands, and walks in a way "worthy of the calling with which it is called" (4:1).

Before we turn to further characteristics of that people, we have to consider from whence it is gathered.

II. Judgment: The Truth About the World

When a man announces to his fellow man, "I shall tell you the truth about a certain person," it rarely happens that "all that becomes [makes?] manifest is light" (Eph. 5:12 f.). Secret things are dragged into the light which all too often are "a shame even to speak of." The man-made observations, analyses, and condemnations can scarcely be identified with the "word of truth, the gospel of our salvation," of which Paul speaks in Eph. 1:13. But the warning of the Sermon on the Mount not to judge or to condemn one another (Matt. 7:1 ff.), and the insistence of Romans (2:1-16; 3:4-19) that God alone is the true and righteous judge, seem to be contradicted by Ephesians: "Expose (or convince, correct) . . . the works of darkness" (5:11)!

Is the world left to the mercy of man's analysis? To be sure, keen observations are made about "hidden persuaders" which manipulate human wills, about "organization man" with his tyranny and boredom, and about "the lonely crowd" to which we belong. Not only anthropologists, sociologists, and psychologists, but also painters, actors, and writers of drama, novels, and modern music give their varied analyses of the human predicament. An increasing number of theological documents begin with a diagnosis of the anxieties and needs of man, of the mobile and multistructural society, and of the world at large. Indeed, it seems quite fashionable to build a whole "systematic theology" and to decide upon counsel and cure for modern man on the ground of such analysis. Why should not a statistical basis of psychological and sociological observations form the only reliable ground upon which to determine advice and consolation for mankind?

But where this is the chosen method, the great work and self-revelation of God are rejected and cease to serve as the criteria of truth. Man's analysis of his fellow men and of the self becomes too "objective." In our modern and popular Christian and non-Christian analyses of the world, a vague reference, at best, to the "religious needs of man" replaces knowledge of God, the creator, redeemer, and judge (who addresses man personally and provides for him to be a free member of the covenant). But the personal God whose name is "I AM WHO I AM" (Ex. 3:14; Isa. 43:11, 25; John 14:6, etc.) and man who, in God's love, is deigned to be a partner of God and to stand before God as a responsible person, are usually left out of the picture.

It is different with the prophets and apostles when they speak of the world. From them we hear what we may call God's own diagnosis or analysis. Not only a value judgment, but *God's* judgment then takes the place of human self-analysis. Then all is measured by God's act, by his love, by his revelation. The difference between good modern novels and drama and average sociological and psychological diagnoses of modern man, and between inspiring historiography and a haphazard compilation of facts lies in the presence of a prophetic element. Great literary and artistic works always show a concern for solidarity in the face of estrangement, hope in the midst of despair, and peace despite all wars and rumors of wars. Ephesians is literature that definitely has this concern. It contains radical judgment on the world, but (to state this in the words of James 2:13) "mercy triumphs over judgment." For it is God's judgment (Eph. 6:8 f.; cf. Rom. 1:17) and mercy, God's wrath and grace (Eph. 2:3; 5:6; 1:4 ff.; 2:4 ff., etc.) which is proclaimed. It is possible, then, that the real man of all time (and therefore also modern man), is addressed and reached at least as effectively and realistically through what Ephesians has to say about the world, as through all contemporary philosophical, psychological, sociological, and artistic analyses.

What is the world of man in God's sight, according to the Epistle to the Ephesians? The words "all," "the all," and "each," are used so frequently in Ephesians, and they are found so often in direct relationship to God (4:6) and to Christ (1:10, 22 f.; 4:10, etc.), that we can expect at least some light on the nature of (the) "all," as it appears before God. Three features can be distinguished.

1. The most surprising is the frequent reference to "rules," authorities, powers, dominions" (1:21) which are not of blood

and flesh (6:12). They occupy "heavenly places" (3:10; 6:12).
The "prince of the air" (2:2), the devil or evil one (4:27; 6:11,
16), is the "spirit" that rules according to the "age of this
world" (2:2). Demons (RSV, "spiritual hosts") of wickedness
are "world rulers of the present darkness" (6:12). They deserve nothing but "resistance" (cf. 6:13). Twice reference
is made to the "methods" (RSV, "wiles") of the devil to
whom the saints are exposed (4:14; 6:11). The word "method"
occurs in Ephesians only in an evil sense, and it is used nowhere else in the New Testament. Together with principalities
and powers, "every name that is named not only in this age,
but also in the coming one" is mentioned (1:21). It is
not said that all "rules, authorities, powers, dominions" or
that all "names" are evil or serve the evil one. But all of
them obviously are exerting an influence over the world, an
influence that is matched and overcome only by the power
of God which was "working in" Christ's resurrection and
which even to the present time is empowering the Christians
(1:19 f.; 3:16; 6:10).

Whatever may be meant by "names" and "principalities,"
they are invisible powers. Their rule is felt as coming from
somewhere above us, and they are given "names" which express our respect for them. They seem to form a whole empire, and defy easy control; else there would have been no
need of the resurrection of Christ to put them under his feet.
We may learn from what is said about them, that for the
author of Ephesians *not* all that is beyond rational or scientific grasp, not all that is invisible (cf. Col. 1:16) and that
occupies "heavenly places" (6:12), is to be identified with
God or considered worthy of religious reverence. An invisible,
spiritual counterrealm to the Kingdom of God seems to be
presupposed.

But what can Paul mean by "principalities" and "powers"?
It is no answer glibly to explain away these words as mythical
encumbrances or "Paul's belief in a world of ghosts." For if

the faith of which Paul speaks was not make-believe, but faith in Jesus Christ, the cavalier attitude of the modern demythologizer is as ineffectual in the interpretation of Paul as the barking of a dog at the moon. Actually, the Pauline epistles and the Jewish and Hellenistic background from which Paul arose, offer enough indications — if not to identify or define these principalities and powers, at least to describe them by reference to four features of Paul's thinking and terminology.

(a) In Rom. 13:1 ff. the political government, the state, is called "authority," "authorities," and "rulers." Not only the Roman officials, but also the political, judicial, and ecclesiastical authorities of the Jews may be meant by "rulers" of this world, as mentioned in 1 Cor. 2:8. Non-Christian judges in court are spoken of as "angels" in 1 Cor. 6:1-3. (b) In Rom. 8:38 f. "angels and rulers and . . . powers" appear closely related to expressions familiar to us, such as "death and life," "the present and the future." Also, in 1 Cor. 15:24-27, death appears under the hostile "rules, authorities, powers" which become subject to Christ. (c) In Gal. 3:23 and 4:3, 8 f. (cf. Col. 2:8 ff.) moral and ritual law, even religious principles and statutes, are meant by the world "elements." Elements, in turn, are in the same passages equivalent to angels, principalities, powers, even "gods" (Gal. 4:8 f.). (d) The economic and social position of the slaveowner is described by the word *kyrios* which is also the root of the term which is translated "dominion" (*kyriotēs,* Eph. 6:5-9; 1:21). Therefore, it is probable that the structure of economics and society is involved where "dominion" is mentioned.

We conclude that by principalities and powers, Paul means the world of axioms and principles of politics and religion, of economics and society, of morals and biology, of history and culture. He also refers to "names" that are "named in this world and the next" (1:21). Whether Paul thought only of titles and dignitaries in general (such as emperor, legislator, philosopher), or of some specific names (such as Moses and Nero), we are free to think of representative names, heart-warming or heartbreaking, such as John Bull, Uncle Sam, Lincoln, Stalin, Socrates, Sartre, Einstein, Freud, Augustine, Savonarola, Don Juan, and Brigitte Bardot. We are not reading Ephesians with open eyes and ears, unless we apply it to the burning questions of Western and Eastern ideologies, of the London slums and South African statutes, of the schools and the stage. To acknowledge that Christ is greater than these problems — this is to confess that Jesus Christ is "above" every rule and power and name (1:21) and "head over all" (1:22). The fact that Paul mentions these "powers," does not make his Gospel old-fashioned, superstitious, or speculative. Rather, it shows that it is of the essence of the Gospel to include utterances concerning political, social, economic, cultural, and psychological situations, dogmas, and problems.

We are unprepared, or perhaps we dislike, to see constituents and axioms of all these "worldly" realms treated as angels and demons. The contemporary world of Paul, with the exception of some Jewish groups and some later mixers of religions, did not like it either. Paul was *not* expressing the religious or scientific world view of his time when he spoke of principalities and powers. And the references of the first three Gospels and of Acts to "demons" or unclean spirits were not expressive of a common belief. But, according to Mark 1:21-28, such powers did make their appearance with, and were hostile to, the Son of God. When God reveals himself, unseen powers and factors of the world become revealed also. The "enlightenment" provided by God (Eph. 1:18; 3:9; 5:8) opens man's eyes for a quick, sharp look at the principalities and powers and their work behind and in the world of man.

So much for the surprising references to rules, authorities, principalities, and powers.

2. Most disturbing of the statements in Ephesians about the world are the utterances about man "apart from Christ" (2:12). Men who walk in trespasses and sins are declared "dead in trespasses and sins" (2:1 f., 5). Man without Christ is the "old man." Of him, but one thing is to be said: he "perishes in deceitful desires" (4:22). Of course, it can be said, even by Paul, that the sinners "live in them"; i.e., in "immorality, impurity, passion, evil desire, and greed, which is idolatry" (Col. 3:5-7). But such life is, as we would say, "No life at all!" The prophet Ezekiel has an even better name for life in separation, enmity, and sin. He calls it "a valley full of bones, . . . lo, they were very dry" (Ezek. 37:1 ff.). He who believes that life in sin has any promise or hope, promotes "deception with empty words" (Eph. 5:5 f.). Actually, he is "alienated from the life of God" (4:18), "clean cut off" (Ezek. 37:11). To "live in sins" is equal to being dead (Col. 3:7; 2:13; Eph. 2:1, 5). In Luke 15:24, 32, the father of the prodigal son makes a similar statement: the son "was dead." To the angel of Sardis it is said, "You have the name of being alive, and you are dead" (Rev. 3:1). A voluptuous widow is called "dead even while she lives" (1 Tim. 5:6).

There are many Psalms in which disease, sin, captivity, pressure by enemies of all kinds, or lostness in the wilderness or on the sea, is seen as a characteristic of the "realm of death" or "sheol" (cf. Ps. 88:3; 143:3; 31:12). Perhaps the most moving descriptions of that dark realm from which only God can save one are found in Hezekiah's prayer (Isa. 38:10-20) and in Psalm 22.

We observe that in both Testaments, in the Psalms and in the epistles to the Ephesians and the Colossians (cf. 1 John 3:14; John 5:24 f.), the deadness of the sinners is not an impersonal, detached, objective value judgment or a post-mortem diagnosis. Instead, only those whose life was "brought up from the pit" by God (Ps. 30:3; Jonah 2:6), whose soul was "delivered from death" (Ps. 33:19; Job 5:20, etc.), sing in psalms of the miserable sinners' death. Not a post-mortem, but a "post-resurrection" is made in each case. The same applies to Ezekiel 37, to Colossians and Ephesians, to Luke's Gospel, and to the Book of Revelation. Nobody is called dead unless he has been or is to be resurrected. "Us who were dead . . . God made alive with Christ" (Eph. 2:5; Col. 2:13). "He was dead and he is alive again" (Luke 15:24, 32). "You are dead. Awake, and strengthen all others that are on the point of death" (Rev. 3:1 ff.)! "Arise from the dead" (Eph. 5:14)!

In contrast to most of the Old Testament Psalms to which we have been referring, in Ephesians only one cause, means, and sign of death is named. "Trespasses and sins" are the cause of the verdict, "You, we, were dead," (2:1, 5). While disease is not referred to at all, enmity (2:14, 16), estrangement, homelessness, hopelessness (2:12), captivity (4:8), being tossed and carried about by winds (4:14) are mentioned. Yet all these features are but enlarged descriptions of what is meant by "trespasses and sins." Always spiritual death is meant, from which nothing and nobody but God can save.

Now it is possible to declare "deadness in sins" only a figure of speech — as we may speak of "hell upon earth." But the Old Testament precedents and the indissoluble connection of utterances about our deadness with statements about deliverance or resurrection from the dead by God, call for a more thorough interpretation. What God has made known by revelation and what Paul as the servant of the Gospel proclaims, includes the fact that those who are "saved by grace" (2:5, 8) are saved from death (2:1, 5). So miserable and dreadful was their captivity, error, enmity, and sin, that only "death" is adequate terminology for their status and predicament. Had they been only morally or intellectually "asleep" (cf. 5:14), sick, stained, or weak, other means than revelation, redemption, or resurrection would have helped them to stand again upon their feet. The whole great work of

God would have shot far beyond its mark. Some enlightened philosophy, some religious discipline, some holy tradition, some moral principles, or some measure of good will on man's part might have brought salvation. In Col. 2:8 ff., Paul warns of a heretical (religious) system that used Christ, apparently, merely as one among many divine or redeeming factors. The emphasis throughout the whole of Ephesians lies on the positive assertion that only in Jesus Christ are the plan, mystery, and power of salvation to be found. Only the love of Christ is capable of saving men from their real predicament — from death "in trespasses and sins" (2:1).

Symptoms and signs of "trespasses and sins" are described with a wide array of terms. The typically Pauline (and Johannine) terms "flesh" and "darkness" are used for them (2:3; 5:8). "Flesh" means the totality of man's spiritual, psychic, and physical perversion and bondage to evil. Whether men are circumcised or not (i.e., whether Jew or Gentile by origin), they all are "in the flesh" (2:11). "By nature" (2:3) men are "sons of disobedience" (2:2; 5:6) and therefore "children of wrath" (2:3). They are aliens and strangers from the promises, the covenants, and the community of Israel. They are hopeless and godless in the world" (2:12). Not knowing of the mystery of Christ (3:9), they live in the vanity of their minds. Because of a hardened heart, their status is alienation from the life of God. They are callous, and they deliver themselves to licentiousness, impurity, and greediness (4:17-19). They are "darkened in their disposition" (4:18). "Darkness" refers to the "ignorance" (4:18) that rules in men who are "without Christ." As with "knowledge" in its biblical sense, this term describes not merely or even specifically intellectual deficiency, but a whole way of life (see Ps. 14; 53; 1 Sam. 25). According to Eph. 5:5, a man who lives as a fornicator or as an impure (homosexual?) or greedy man, is an idolator. Sin is not directed against man only. The man dead in sins serves false gods. By giving opportunity to the devil, man is a "thief" (4:27 f.). And of what his heart is full, his mouth overflows: lies, foul words, bitterness, anger, wrath, clamor, and slander proceed from it (4:25, 29, 31). Ephesians is eloquent and incisive in its catalogue of vices. Neither thought, nor words, nor deeds, nor omissions are overlooked. There certainly is no lack of realism in these descriptions of the sinner's life "without Christ" (cf. 2:12).

The sum total of what is said about man is contained in the words death, enmity, alienation, and darkness (2:1, 5, 12, 14, 16; 4:18; 5:8). All these terms describe a separation and presuppose the existence of an insurmountable wall. We have shown above that the abolition of this wall was the work of Jesus Christ.

3. What is the purpose of this prophetic analysis with which Ephesians is spiced so thoroughly? The answer can be brief: Paul wants to show not what man is and remains before God, but what man *was*. The writer emphasizes the radical antithesis between what "we were" and what God has done ("But God . . . ," 2:2, 4). It marks the separation between "once . . . at that time . . ." and "but now . . ." (2:11-13; 5:8); between an earlier state and a "no more" (RSV, "no longer"; 2:19; 4:14, 17, 28). Not for their own sake, but rather *pro memoria* (2:11, "remember!") and as a warning (4:17), the respective descriptions of the past sins (death in sins) were given, and the still present and felt "energy" of the evil spirit is mentioned (2:2). The references to what man without Christ was and what the devil still works, show that God's call does not go out to an ideal or nonexistent man, but to man who seems to be tied up in death and sin, to man who makes life miserable for himself and for his neighbor, and who prefers idols to the knowledge of God. That God loved with so great a love as to love this man (2:4 f.), that in Christ so great a power was exerted as to

raise and keep upright these our dead bodies (2:5 f., 6:10 ff.; Rom. 8:11), that the Spirit of revelation enlightens such darkened and hardened hearts (1:17 f.; 4:18) — this is shown by the many references to the sins of men.

What an abyss or wall sin has produced can actually be seen and described only in the light of grace. Paul has good reason to start out (in 1:3 ff.) by blessing God for his love, grace, and mercy. Sin is not the foundation of grace. Neither is speaking of sin the logical foundation for speaking of grace. But where the fullness of God's grace is praised, there man will not be ashamed to confess how miserable a sinner he is. The Gospel of peace cannot be preached by first analyzing and denouncing the people, and then by demanding that the people recognize their sin and need. It would not be the "good news" that would be announced by that method. But when an evangelist knows of God's riches and deeds and power, then he will, like John the Baptist, not withhold from his fellow men the message that all that God is and does, is bestowed precisely upon those outside the sacred ground, far from God, hopeless, captive, and dead in sins.

We can say the same in entirely different words. A minister of a Protestant church in the crime-ridden and misery-filled East Harlem section of Manhattan put it this way: One cannot persuade or convince another of sin. Sin cannot be proclaimed or treated as a topic of teaching. Sin can only be confessed in prayer. When sin really is spoken of, man does not speak against fellow man; he must not do so, even if he should be the "holiest Joe" dealing with the most insulting backslider. We can only speak of sin in solidarity with fellow sinners, and before God. In the prayer in which we praise God for the crucifixion and resurrection of Jesus Christ, and in which we cry "Father!" through the Holy Spirit, we can and will also confess, "Forgive us our sins."

The rabbis had a name of their own for "confession of

sins." They called it "to give God the glory" (cf. John 9:24). It is probable that it is only "to the praise of God's glory" (1:6, 12, 14), and not for the promotion of a gloomy, pessimistic, stoic, or existentialist world view, that God's judgment over the world is described by Paul with such clarity. We note that sin certainly is unmasked and dethroned by God's works of power and grace, of resurrection and revelation. But sin is never "revealed" or "made known." "All that is exposed is revealed by the light. For all that is revealed is light" (5:13 f.). This means that God's judgment is not an alternative to his grace, but that it is full of grace. Even in God's judgment, light for the man in darkness, life for the dead, the Father's home for the prodigal, are manifested. We are under judgment, indeed — but under judgment of grace.

III. GRACE: A NATION FOR GOD'S GLORY

God's judgment and grace are not in vain. His self-revelation is not an offer only. His word does not return to him empty, but it accomplishes his purpose and prospers in the thing for which it was sent (cf. Isa. 55:11). On earth a carrier or singer of the "praise of his glory" (Eph. 1:12, 14) is called into being. This singer of God's praise (5:19) is called in Eph. 1:22 "the Church" (see also 3:10, 21; 5:23-32). It was the will of God that "we be [made] for the praise of his glory" (1:12). Salvation by grace is identical with "workmanship": with an artfully planned, executed, and completed work. "Saved by grace . . . we are God's workmanship" (2:5, 8, 10). It is by no means astonishing, neither is it merely a metaphorical overstatement, when at least three times in Ephesians the saving work of God is called a work of creation. "We are created in Christ Jesus upon the ground of good works, which God has prepared before" (2:10). Christ destroyed the wall "in order to create in himself the two into one new man" (2:15). "The new man is created after [the image of] God in true righteousness and holiness' (4:24;

Col. 3:10). Only in 3:9, where God is called "creator of all things," is it possible that the creation of heaven and earth are in the author's mind. But even in that passage, Paul may be thinking also, and quite distinctly, of all that was created by revelation and salvation; namely, the Church. To take seriously "creation" and "God's creature" means for the reader of Ephesians to ponder seriously on the Church, rather than on nature and history in general.

Paul affirms that the Church is created out of God's grace and might. The Church is not a man-made, human institution. She cannot be sufficiently described by the observation of the laws of history, sociology, or psychology. She cannot explain her origin, maintain her life, or achieve her purpose by merely following scientific rules, democratic processes, or effective methods. Her past, present, and future are from God. Her head, and chief cornerstone, is Christ (1:22; 4:15 f.; 5:23; 2:20). Her very life is life from the dead (2:1, 5). Her guarantee is the Spirit (1:13; 4:30). In particular, there are three elements that need be pointed out, for they will help to explain what will be said later about the constitution of the Church.

1. It has often been observed that the two topics "Knowledge" and "Church" are more to the fore in Ephesians than in any other book of the New Testament. These topics belong inseparably together. The Church is the first-fruit of God's revelation. She knows already what is to be known and acknowledged universally. Until all in all is filled with the fullness of God, only the Church is called "the fullness of Christ" (i.e., that which is already filled by Christ). So far, only the Church has striven to attain the "fullness of Christ . . . of God" (1:22; 3:19; 4:10, 13). Only the Church has "heard and believed the work of truth, the Gospel of salvation" (1:13). "For to us God made known the mystery of his will" (1:9).

But the Church did not receive this knowledge solely for her private benefit. Rather "the manifold wisdom of God should be made known, now . . . through the Church" (3:10). For the salvation of those who already are resuscitated from death was granted by God "in order that he might show in the coming ages the overflowing riches of his grace" (2:7). Therefore the Church is made to go along — shod with the Gospel of peace and faithful in prayer, supplication, and intercession — with Paul the ambassador, who knows that he has to "make known the mystery of the Gospel" (6:15, 17-20). To receive and to convey knowledge of God's mystery, this is essential to the Church. God's self-revelation creates, sustains, and commits the Church. She is not only the privileged recipient, but also the chosen instrument of the manifestation of God's will, grace, and might.

The relationship between the Church and the knowledge of the mystery of God can also be summed up with words taken from Matthew's Gospel: "No one knows the Son except the Father; and no one knows the Father except the Son and anyone to whom the Son chooses to reveal him. . . . To you it has been given to know the mysteries of the kingdom of heaven, but to them it has not been given. For to him who has, [more] will be given and he will have abundance. . . . Blessed are your eyes because they see and your ears because they hear. . . . Many prophets and righteous men longed to see what you see, and did not see it, and to hear what you hear and did not hear it. . . . Do not be afraid. . . . Nothing is covered that will not be revealed, and nothing is hidden that will not be known. What I tell you in the dark, say it in the light. What you hear [whispered] in the ear, this proclaim upon the housetops" (Matt. 11:27; 13:11-12, 16-17; 10:26-27). In Ephesians, the same privilege of the Christians to receive and to carry knowledge is described under the metaphor of light: "Once you were darkness; now you are light in the Lord. Walk as children of light" (5:8).

The proudest and the most committing title of the Church which the New Testament contains is found in 1 Tim. 3:15. It has reference to the Church's trusteeship in regard to knowledge of the truth. In that passage, the "house of God, the Church of the living God" is declared to be "the pillar and bulwark of the truth."

Such titles look not a little pretentious. They may smack of the claims of infallibility issued by the Vatican. They may call to mind the distortion of the Christian Gospel by Gnostic sects since the first century. They may seem to have found validation in the snobbish intellectualism of 19th-century Protestant "biblical criticism." They lead ill-advised churches and committees to fill the world with an abundance of analyses, counsels, and reprimands that arrogantly presume to show a sense of superior wisdom. Is this really what Paul wanted to say, when he described the Church as those who already know what the whole world eventually is to know?

Far be it! "Knowledge that puffs up" is discredited most explicitly! "If any one imagines he knows something, then he does not yet know as he ought to know. But if one loves God, this is known by him" (1 Cor. 8:1-3). According to Ephesians, knowledge of God is not a system of thought or information to be received, possessed, and conveyed. It is much more. Knowledge or "enlightenment of the eyes of the heart" is and remains a gift of God, which can only be prayed for. "I do not cease praying thankfully . . . that God . . . may give you the Spirit of wisdom . . . in knowledge" (1:16 f.). Since knowledge is a way of life, total existence as partner of God and recipient of his grace, it cannot be seized from God and secured in definitions and institutions. Neither can it be stored in man or in the Church. Nor can it simply be given by one man to another. Christians are not made tombs, depositories, masters, or sources of knowledge. They are but "children of the light" (5:8). This means that their first need is to grow in knowledge, so that they be "no more babes" (4:14). The Church is not already the "oneness of faith and knowledge, the perfect man, the measure of the age (or stature) of Christ's fullness." But she is on the way "to attain to oneness, manhood, and fullness," which belong only to the Son of God (4:13); so she is on the way to knowledge. And her wisest members will confess that she "knows only in part," whereas perfect knowledge of God remains a matter of promise and hope (1 Cor. 13:12). The word of truth and the knowledge of God are not static. They are living as they "grow and bring fruit" from the first day of their appearance until today and into the future (Col. 1:5-6, 9-10). A proud church, denomination, or seminary which rests on institutional form, creedal definition and other laurels of the past, or imposes itself upon the minds and lives of other people, betrays the revelation and knowledge from which she actually lives. Only one who is continually receiving knowledge is able to impart insight.

On the other hand, the Church need not despair over differences and contradictions between varying insights into God's work. The Church is not left alone in her struggle for knowledge. The "promised Spirit" with which she was "sealed" (1:13) does not leave her alone or go to sleep. He bears testimony to the one Christ, and uses, despite all divisions, now this, now that, congregation or man as his instrument. A church that gives up hope of finding "oneness of faith and knowledge" and of "understanding the breadth and length and depth and height [of the mystery of God's fullness] together with all the saints" (4:13; 3:18-19) would not be the Church of which Paul speaks in Ephesians. It would not be the Church that lives by the Gospel and for the Gospel. It would not be "shod with the preparation for the Gospel of peace" (cf. 6:15).

The word of truth and the knowledge of Christ's mystery are never possessions of the Church. The Church is, however, called to seek and to respect truth and knowledge with the meekness, lowliness, and patience equal to, if not greater than, the humility of a serious research scientist or philosopher. The Church is a learner, along with the world, in the school of God. Knowledge exists only where there is growth in knowledge. The Christians are "light" (5:8) only as they continue to be "enlightened" by the Spirit (1:17 f.) and by Christ (5:14). The Church is on the way to attain to the fullness of God (3:19; 4:13).

It is obvious that many American churches and church members care little for the vital relationship between the Church and knowledge, of which Ephesians makes us aware. In theological seminaries and in church schools, knowledge of the Bible, theology, or church history, has been superseded by a cult of education, methodology, fellowship, and organization. To be sure, "knowledge" in the biblical sense *is* common life and mutual responsibility. It creates forms and functions and ministries. But common life, beautiful programs of action, and organizational forms cannot replace the learning and acknowledging of the mighty acts of God.

2. The Church is "not of the world . . . but *in the world*." So we read in the High Priestly prayer of Christ (John 17:14, 16, 11; cf. 15:19). Christ does not ask that his disciples be "taken out of the world" (John 17:6, 14, 15). Similarly in Ephesians, the Church is a community that lives on earth. Ephesians treats of the "catholic" Church; i.e., of the one, universal, world-wide community to which all regional and local assemblies, congregations, and members belong.

But we ask, where on earth *is* this one Church really present? Is it in the Christians' brains and feelings, in ecstasies and dreams? Sometimes statements are made concerning the Church (with a capital C!) that seem to treat of an unearthly, other-worldly, abstract oneness, perfection, and holiness. Such utterances have little to do with the life of congregations and denominations, with the Sunday wor-

ship and weekday activities, with the great ecumenical assemblies, and the intimate "bull-sessions" of small groups, as
they wrestle for truth.

The question is whether Ephesians, since it does not treat
of the local church, promotes a kind of Platonic idea of the
Church. Who or what (except Jesus Christ; but cf. Mark
10:18) could be "holy and blameless" (1:4; Col. 1:22), "having no spot or wrinkle or any such thing" (5:27), and yet
live on this earth when "the days are evil" (5:16; 6:13)?
Interpretations of the statements made in Ephesians on the
holiness of the Church vary. According to some, the Church
is destined to be like a spotless sacrificial animal; then little
or nothing of moral character is implied in her "holiness."
Others see in these utterances a challenge to gather and
build a morally ideal church. Still others feel entitled to the
conclusion that the Church, washed and clothed by Christ,
cannot and does not sin, for as Paul says elsewhere, "there
is no condemnation for those that are in Christ Jesus" (Rom.
8:1). A pessimist would hold that only as victims of the
world, sacrificed to the inscrutable God, can we be perfect.
An ethical idealist would call for ruthless striving to attain
higher levels. An ecclesiastical perfectionist would maintain
that the worshiping Church is already a perfect servant of
God. And a friend of compromises would dodge the issue
by speaking of the two natures of the Church: of the earthly
nature, which is conditioned and mastered by the imbecility
of the flesh and the powers that be, and of the heavenly
nature, truly given, fully ruled, and amply nourished by the
Spirit of God and the Gospel of Jesus Christ. The fatal distinction between the "visible" and the "invisible" Church
accounts for the growth of this compromise.

We observe that these interpretations presuppose and teach
either that the Church actually serves two masters and is
conditioned by two factors, Christ and the world, or that she
is so completely identified with one that the other does not

really affect her. The dualism which results from one of these schools of thought may be expressed in terms of time. Then the "two natures" of the Church are said to reflect the tension between what the Church is "already now," and what she is "not yet." Or the tension between appearance and essence, between fact and ideal, or between history and eschatology is put into the foreground. The perfectionism of the other school of thought relies on what the almighty God can "create" (2:15; 3:9; etc.), and on what faith asserts despite all evidence to the contrary. What does Ephesians contribute to such views and discussions?

In many Greek manuscripts of this epistle, the issue is taken up in the first verse of the first chapter: the saints are both "in Ephesus" and "in Christ Jesus." (See KJV and RSV footnote.) Something besides topography or geography finds expression in these statements. Ephesus and Christ are more than mere localities. Spheres of power, means of enforcement, and a resulting status are described by the little word "in," and by the name which follows it. If "Christ" stands for God's perfect work, "Ephesus" stands for the world and its influence. Those addressed in the epistle are both "Ephesians" (according to the title) and "saints who are faithful" in Christ Jesus. A mixture of both designations is not made. For Paul there are no "Ephesian Christians"; neither does he know a "Roman Church," a "German Christianity," or an "American Christendom." But a relation is stated: the saints live "in Ephesus" and are faithful "in Christ Jesus." Paul does not know, or address any of his epistles to, Christians in the abstract, or to Christians who are suspended in mid-air. It is typical of his thinking that he speaks only of churches and of the Church on earth.

This Church, wherever on earth it meets in the form of a house-church, of a local congregation, or of a regional assembly, is the bride of Christ (2 Cor. 11:2; Eph. 5:26 f.). This Church is washed (like a bride before her marriage? Eph.

5:26). This Church is elected to be "holy and spotless" and is so to stand before him (1:4; 5:27; 2 Cor. 11:2). The "praise of his glory," which is the purpose of God's will and work (1:6, 12, 14), is to be sung now on the "evil days," at all times in Ephesus (5:16-20). Ephesians differs from the Book of Revelation in that in Ephesians only the praise of the saints on earth is described, whereas in Revelation much emphasis is put on the eternal praise of angels and of a heavenly assembly of raised martyrs. A corresponding fact is that in Ephesians, instead of discourses about what is "already now" and what is "not yet," there is a major emphasis on what is "now" and what is "no more." "Now" (already) resurrection, enthronement, gathering into God's house and Kingdom, revelation of God's mystery, and testimony to a new way of life have taken place; therefore the rule of death, of sin and estrangement, and of ignorance is valid "no more" 2:1 ff., 11 ff., 19; 3:1 ff.; 4:17 ff., 28). A future consummation of God's work, a handing out of the inheritance which is now guaranteed (1:13) on the "day of redemption" (4:30) is not ignored by Paul. We mentioned already that Ephesians contains an "eschatology," a doctrine of the last things. The Church lives, but in "hope" (4:4).

But the Church is not described primarily in future terms. The eschatology of Ephesians concerns much more the present Church that lives in the world. True doctrine of "last things," biblical eschatology, deals not of the future only, but also of all works by which the eternal God manifests himself fully in time. "Last things," and the "last days," actually are present when the Spirit of God is abundantly poured out upon the Church (Acts 2:17 ff.); when the Good News of the fulfillment of God's promises is preached (Luke 4:18-21); when the hour comes "and now is" in which dead men hear the voice of God, believe, and live (John 5:25). These things: the presence of the Spirit, the presence of the Gospel, and the presence of resurrection on earth, among the Ephesians and others that were "far," are announced in Ephesians. The Church lives from this presence and fulfillment of promises given for the last time. Scholars have labeled this fulfillment of God's promises "realized eschatology." Living from the outpoured Spirit and sealed by it, the Church is indeed an "eschatological" sign erected *in* the world. However, the awareness of the blessings received already, the "now," does not blind it to what lies ahead. The church knows that God's revelation is not over, but continues "now . . . through the Church" (3:10) for the benefit of "the coming ages" (2:7), and is to have its consummation on the "day of redemption" (4:30). Therefore the Church is also a sign *for* the world. By its very existence, it is a living sign showing that nothing less than holiness and spotlessness are the contents of God's plan and will for *all* those dead in sins.

The holiness and spotlessness of the Church (1:4; 5:27) are a gift and commission which God already has given, and is giving, to the assembled saints upon earth now. The Christians cannot make or call themselves holy. They would be ridiculous pretenders if they did. But they are called to acknowledge what "the word" does and says to them. By the word they are "purified." Paul says explicitly that the Church is "purified in the water bath *of the word*" (5:26). And in John's Gospel it is said: "You are clean because of the word which I spoke to you" (John 15:3). The Reformers called this purity the "imputed righteousness" and in so doing followed what Paul had said in Romans (4:3 ff., etc.). Should holiness and spotlessness then be only a verbalism, only a matter of words? The spirit proves that more than "only" a declaration of righteousness is uttered. For he calls, gathers, builds, and empowers those justified in such a way that they realize that the work of God stands behind "the word." They are made something by this word, even God's chosen "holy and spotless" ones. "Hearing the word of truth and believing, you are sealed" (Eph. 1:13). Despite all the counsel which the Ephesians needed concerning their worship, conduct, and testimony, they were actually God's elect. They were commissioned and committed to be holy and spotless. They were entitled to believe and proclaim that God, despite all the sin and weakness of man, creates people called saints!

We now can draw two conclusions which contain the alternative to what we called dualism and perfectionism. The Church's Lord is not God *and* the world, but God reveals his Lordship by creating and maintaining the Church in the world. And the Church is One, Holy, and Catholic, not by capacities she acquires, possesses, or exerts, but because of the work which the Spirit does in her and through her by the word of God and in faith. She is not a perfect assembly, but an ongoing fellowship for growing and gathering. She lives always "in the process of formation."

In other words, only what lives on earth as a result of the enlightening, calling, gathering, building operation of the Holy Spirit of God, is called the Church. Without faith, there is no Church.

Now, this Church lives on earth. She lives in Ephesus, but not in Ephesus only. Should the dispersion of the congregations over the world imply an inevitable overpowering of the Christians by diverse local, national, cultural, economic conditions? The difference between the Pauline epistles indeed shows differences between the lives of individuals and the problems of congregations, as real as those between different denominations, between city and country churches, and between theological schools today. Should there be a different holiness and spotlessness available for Christians in different countries and towns?

If the holiness of the Church is God's gift, then it is indivisible. Then the oneness of the Church is incorruptible, wherever and however its members meet. The catholicity (world-wideness) is real in spite of all regional problems. This is what Paul attests when he refers at least seven times to "all [the saints]" in Eph. 1:15; 2:3; 3:8, 18; 4:13; 6:18, 24; (and 5:20 if we interpret: "give thanks for all [saints, or people]"). In other epistles he speaks also of "all the churches" (Rom. 16:16; 1 Cor. 7:17; 14:33; 2 Cor. 8:18, etc.). Whether he treats of regional, local, or house assemblies, he always makes clear that they are of the same flesh and bone as the one church he addresses in the respective letters. The one Spirit, Lord, and Father, and the one hope, faith, and baptism (4:3-6), the one perfect man and the fullness of Christ which they all are to attain (4:13) — this is what keeps them together. Obviously, the oneness of the churches spread over the world is (if we follow Ephesians) not a question of better organization, administration, and boards, or of mixing creeds, or of planning programs and making demonstrations. Such things come and go. The unity of the Church would rest on weak legs, if they, as things, were its support, standard, and means of achievement. According to Ephesians, the unity of all Christians is guaranteed by the one truth preached to them and believed by them. It is effected and upheld only by what Paul calls the "bond of peace" (4:3). We may consciously or unconsciously "grieve the Holy Spirit of God" (4:30); we may deserve scolding as a sleeping and dead church (5:14), but we cannot prevent the Spirit from giving testimony to the one Lord, the one people of God, and the one hope for all men. Rather than grieve the Spirit, we are called to "keep the bond of peace" (4:3); i.e., to acknowledge that we cannot let go of one another, since God keeps us together. To know of the pre-given, guaranteed, and indestructible oneness of all churches and Christians is a great source of hope and the greatest possible impulse to work for unity.

The holiness and the oneness of the Church belong together. Even the scandalous sins of congregations, denominations, groups, and individuals cannot abrogate God's gift, promise, and commission. May the Church show knowledge of the rich and mighty God's gift and commission! May those who were made light, walk as children of the light (5:8)! May there be visible signs on earth which indicate what the Church is and is called to be!

Of the living Church's existence on earth, there are many signs. All that Ephesians says about the difference between the Gentiles' and the saints' conduct (4:17 ff.) could be mentioned here. Even more, a sign is what happens in preaching and hearing, praying and praising, when the saints are assembled. But the forms of the Church's service and obedience will be discussed later. At this point, only a few general remarks are needed.

Where the Church is, there growth and building take place. It is characteristic of the Church, not only to be "rooted and grounded" in love (3:17) or "built upon the foundation of apostles and prophets, Christ Jesus himself being the chief cornerstone" (2:20), but also to grow visibly. Roots and foundations might remain invisible. But it is a visible evidence of the Church's presence and life in the world that it is a structure "growing by being joined together" (2:21), and a body being built and building itself up (4:12, 16). It is a sign of the Church that it resembles in part a living plant, in part a growing human body, in part a house in the process of being built. The metaphors "rooted" and "growing" refer to the mystery of growth and of life that sustains the Church. The metaphors "body," "joints," "babies," "measure of maturity" (4:13-16 f.) point to the one new man who shall no more bear the signs of infancy (4:14; cf. 1 Cor. 13:11). Finally, the metaphors "building, temple" make clear that elements from outside are fitted to be added to the growing construction.

These and other metaphors which Paul combines into a (seemingly incomprehensible) unit, are illuminating precisely because they mutually complement and correct each other. The inward and outward, the invisible and the visible, life of the Church, the power given by God, and the activity displayed by its members cannot be separated. This is the Church: God's plantation in the world, the new man created by God of former enemies, the construction lot of God on earth. Wrong is the alternative: either the Church is a place for quiet contemplation of God's work, or she is the ground for tumultuous or organized human activities; for quiet growth *and* busy building are indispensably present, vital, and apparent where the Church lives. God gives that growth, in Corinth (1 Cor. 3:6 f.) as well as in Ephesus (2:20-22; 4:16; cf. Col. 2:19). He gives it on earth, to a gathering of men of flesh and bone. Always the Churcn of which Paul speaks, is the Church that manifests God's work nowhere else but on *earth*.

We can now proceed to a last general feature of the Church.

3. It is not without public, *political relevance*, that the Church lives on earth from the knowledge of God. Much more, the people of God that "grows" in knowledge and in building activities, is given a head and an order, a form and a history; indeed, all that is necessary to convey to it a political character and to make it a nation or "a people," rather than a loose and irrelevant gathering of some people with individual concerns. The concept "nation" may best sum up what is meant when God's people are called a "commonwealth" into which the Gentiles are admitted, or when the Ephesians are called "fellow citizens of the saints and members of God's household" (2:12, 19). Not as if Paul wanted to establish the foundation of a special Church-State, State-Church, or world-wide Vatican; but when he speaks of our "citizenship" (or commonwealth) which is in heaven (Phil. 3:20; cf. the "civic walk" worthy of the Gospel of Christ mentioned in Phil. 1:27); when he reminds the Ephesians of their

inheritance in the Kingdom of Christ and God"; also when in Hebrews (12:22; 13:14; cf. Rev. 3:12; 20:9) the church is called a "city" (*polis*) or a "camp"; then a terminology is used that comes close to identifying the Church with a colony of heaven on earth, comparable to the colonies of the Greek states in Asia Minor. Then it is stated that the saints (their racial, historical, and social ties to Ephesus, country, or town, notwithstanding) are full citizens and subjects of a special "kingdom," the kingdom of Christ and God (5:5).

There are not only privileges and duties of worldly commitments; there is also God, and Christ at God's right hand, and the Spirit proceeding from Father and Son. The Church and those in the Church are God's house and belong to the commonwealth ruled by God in the same political sense that is characteristic of Israel's belonging to God (2:12, 19). This is one of the reasons why Paul calls Jerusalem "our mother" (Gal. 4:26), and the Church "the Israel of God" (Gal. 6:16; cf. Rom. 2:29).

The Greek word for "Church" (*ekklēsia*) which is frequently used for denoting God's people in the New Testament, described both before and in Paul's time a political assembly, and it is used in that sense in Acts (19:32, 39, 41). If the political connotation of the term "Church" and of the Church's character be overlooked, the Church can all too easily understand herself to be an irresponsible and unconcerned club for the promotion of ideals and culture. She could keep her hands clean, while statesmen and citizens get involved in the vital issues of the nation and the world. Since, however, the Church is the continuously growing gathering of those who "know" the mystery of Christ, the abolition of the wall and the making of peace between God and men, she cannot remain within a safe circle. Christ stepped "into the deepest places of the earth" (4:9). He dared to meet the mockery and wrath of the "rulers of this world" (1 Cor. 2:8). The Christians are "coheirs, members of the same body, partakers of the same promise" (3:6) with Israel and with Christ only when they grow "from Christ" and "into him" (4:15 f.) as a visible, responsible, active community. To "keep oneself unstained from the world" in order to maintain "religion pure and undefiled" (cf. James 1:27) does not mean to keep hands clean and idle when social, economic, and political needs or scandals cry to high heaven. The saints are called to be holy and spotless (1:4), not by walking like Gentiles with a hardened heart (4:17, 19), but by "speaking the truth in love" (RSV, 4:15). So the Church is God's people which has, where it fulfills its commission and lives up to its high calling, a deeper concern for questions of peace, truth, and justice than the "Gentiles." "The fruit of light consists of all that is good, righteous, and true . . . walk as children of the light" (5:8 f.; cf. Phil 2:15; 4:8)l

It is clear that the Church's existence on earth as a nation may call (and has called) for conflicts with governments, nations, and national interests as conceived by thinkers or activists who do not recognize what the "knowledge of God" is and means. Paul is not blind to the consequences of his teaching. The nation, the state, the culture, and the purpose of a given society belong to the principalities and powers which the Church may have to "resist on the evil day" (6:12 f.). Let us remember that Ephesus was one of the well-known cities of the Hellenistic world and of the Roman Empire, and that the Mother and Love cult of devoted priests and masses (cf. Acts 19:23-40) gave the city outstanding importance and safe income. We observe, however, that Paul presupposes that conflicts and attacks will start from the principalities rather than from the Church. Paul exhorts the Ephesians carefully to "watch out how they walk." May they do it "not as unwise, but as wise men, making the best of the time; for the days are evil" (5:15 f.). Search for God's wisdom (1:17; 3:10), rather than some "wise guy's" pat answers or clever subterfuges, is here recommended. Paul obviously does not have in mind a possible withdrawal from the world and its "greedy men, robbers, and idolators" (1 Cor. 5:10). Neither is it fear or insecurity to which he gives expression. Rather, he encourages the Ephesians to be strong (6:10). They are wise and able to stand against all that rushes against them, when they take up the "whole armor of God" provided for them (6:10-17). The church appears finally, therefore, not only as the assembly of citizens (2:19) which is a shining light in and to the world (5:8 f.; cf. Phil. 1:27; 2:15), but also as the militant army of God, equipped with the right spirit and the right armor to ward off the disturbing fire ("flaming darts" 6:16) of ill-advised potentates.

A citizenry ready to wage war when it is imposed upon them: this is a third definition of the Church peculiar to Ephesians. This definition supplements the two which have been elaborated. It has been shown that the Church is the community of those who know God's work, and that the Church is a community living on earth and manifesting God's will and God's success in making sinners holy. This Church is not afraid or ashamed of being "in the world," "in Ephesus." It is so constituted that it will not flee into lofty places, devote itself to harmless activities, or surrender to unconscious slumber. It shall live according to its constitution.

IV. The Constitution of God's People

In the preceding section, we have seen that the Church can only be spoken of where certain events take place; namely, the acknowledgment of God's work by a new way of life, the assembling and commissioning of his people on this earth, and the submission of all forms and needs of this world to the judgment of God's wisdom. The Church is where these things happen. They may not be plain or convincing to every man in the Church or outside the Church. These events have the nature and aspect of sowing, waiting, and enduring defeat and anguish, rather than the quality of untroubled joy and gathering of much fruit. They may look ambiguous because men associate the Church now with one, now with another secular system of thought, method of operation, or organization, popular or unpopular. Yet, by its ongoing formation and information, and by its incessant change and growth, it will be revealed that the Church is not just another man-made club, a historical phenomenon, or natural product, but a people that hears and follows the call issued by God in the Gospel of peace.

The Church is always an event of public manifestation. One can be a veteran without joining a Veteran's Association, or an heir without caring for his inheritance. One can belong to a nation without acting as a responsible citizen. But it is impossible to be a Christian, unless day by day acts of testimony and obedience take place. The Church is a living and dynamic body. Its every breath and step come from the energy and power of God, who gathers, builds, enlightens, and commissions her, or it is not the Church. The signs of the Church are evident; if not, there is no Church.

But the question arises whether the Church has not also an inflexible, unchanging, institutional structure which protects her from lapses into wild spiritualism or occasionalism. Ephesians does refer to the eternal will of God (1:4 ff.; 3:11), to the word of truth (1:13), to the foundation upon an immutable ground (2:20), to the divine gift of the ministry (4:7-12), and to the "incorruptibility" of the Christian's love (6:24). These statements are indicative of a certain unchanging, inflexible character of the Church. With these references we have now to deal.

The unchangeable constitution (some call it the Divine Law) by which the Church is the house and citizenry of God and according to which she lives and exists, is not a letter or a document written on paper. Neither is it a perfection which the Church possesses or attains by her own power. It is not a glorious past or a future prospect which can easily be documented and proved. Instead, it is a threefold relationship. In Ephesians the personal relation of the Church (1) to Christ, (2) to Israel, and (3) to man is set so clearly in the foreground and underlined so heavily that it deserves our special attention. Only when and where this threefold relationship is in order and lived up to will the Church be right and true. In the Bible "rightness" or "righteousness" are never considered to be individual virtues, but are always life lived according to the spirit of a covenanted relationship.

1. In Ephesians, the relationship between *Christ* and *the Church* is summed up in the title "head" which is given to Christ, in the metaphor "body of Christ" used for the Church, and in the term "members of his body" which is employed for describing the saints (1:22 f.; 4:4, 12, 15 f., 25; 5:23, 30; cf. 2:15; 3:6). Paul uses parallel terminology in other epistles (Col. 1:18, 24; 2:19; 1 Cor. 11:3; 12:12 ff.; Rom. 12:4 f.). In Ephesians and Colossians, when these terms are used, the focus (primarily, not exclusively) is on the interrelationship between Christ and the Church, in Romans and First Corinthians it is on the mutual bond between the Christians.

The description of the perfect work of God (given in Part Two) should make it sufficiently clear why Christ is called the head of the Church and why in him "all things in heaven and upon earth," even the principalities and powers that be, have received a head and superior (Eph. 1:10, 20-23). But the special reasons why only the Church (and not the world too) is designated the body of Christ, call for some comments.

Head, body, and members, according to Greek and modern views (cf. 1 Cor. 12:27; Eph. 4:16 in many Greek manuscripts) are primarily *parts* of man. But wherever Old Testament or primitive psychology prevails, the total man rather than anatomic subdivisions is meant by references to soul and body, head and members, hands and eyes. In the Bible (except in

1 Cor. 12:12) man does not *have* a soul, a head, an eye, a body. But he *is* soul and body, and he *is* what his eyes and hands do (Matt. 5:24-30; 6:22-23; Luke 19:22).

That Paul in general and Ephesians in particular have to be understood on Old Testament premises was observed before. When, therefore, in Ephesians Christ is called the head of the Church, he is not considered to be merely the noblest part of the Church. Rather he is identified as the indispensable ruler who dominates, as the life that quickens, as the lord who protects, as the will that directs, or as the leader that nourishes the body. And when the Church is called his body, she is not designated as an appendix to, or as an extension of, the head. But she is the manifestation of his government and life, a manifestation made upon earth, before the ears and eyes of man, within human society and history, but also in defiance against powers and principalities that include death. God "raised us with Christ . . . in Christ, in order to show the coming ages the abounding riches of his grace, in the kindness [exhibited] to us in Christ Jesus" (2:7), . . . "that the manifest wisdom of God be made known now to rulers and authorities in heavenly places through the Church" (3:10).

This, then, is the basic meaning of the equation, "The Church is the body of Christ." *The Church is the manifestation of the risen Christ upon earth.* When she is persecuted, he is persecuted (Acts 9:4). "When Christ who is our life will appear [in glory], then you also will appear with him in glory" (Col. 3:4). "We [the apostle] are always carrying in the body the death of Jesus, in order that even the life of Jesus may be manifested in your body . . . in your mortal flesh. Therefore death is at work in us, but life in you" (2 Cor. 4:10-12).

Now it is never said that Christ extends himself into the Church, or that *he* grows (himself) by creating, sustaining, or perfecting the "one new man." Christ is not a plant that grows by consuming sun and rain from above and earthly elements from below. Neither is he ever compared to a statue that "grows" under the sculptor's hand, by the insertion of hands and feet. Therefore all the talk of "incorporation into the body of Christ" is inadequate. It is not Christ who grows; but saints and the body grow according to biblical teaching. "We are to grow up in every way into him, from whom the whole body . . . makes bodily growth" (4:15-16). "In him the whole structure is joined together and grows" (2:21). What grows is Christ's "body," the "whole structure" that was planned in him, and remains dependent on him.

In Colossians (1:6, 10; is 2:19 an exception?) the growth of which Paul speaks is qualitative rather than quantitative, in knowledge rather than in members. But the Acts of the Apostles speaks of the quantitative growth of God's people (Acts 7:17) and mentions happily the increasing numbers that "were added" (by God) to the church (Acts 1:13; 2:41, 47; 4:4; 5:14; 21:20). Whatever the kind of growth that is meant, "it is God who gives growth" (1 Cor. 3:6 f.; Col. 2:19). In Ephesians, the "growth of the body of Christ," and the building of the "whole structure" implies probably both this deepening in "knowledge," love and obedience, *and* this growth in numbers. The metaphor of "building" would not have been used together with that of bodily growth, unless the author intended to point out at least one important fact; namely, the Church cannot and does not live for herself alone, by fostering within her walls her "knowledge." Much as she needs knowledge, she needs for her very essence and existence building materials that from the outside are added to and inserted into her. In 1 Pet. 2:4 f., consequently, we find the (Gentile-born) saints spoken of as "living stones" that have approached and are built upon The Living Stone, Jesus Christ. The "joints" and "parts" mentioned in Eph. 4:16 may belong to both: the body and the building metaphor. If they do, they denote not only knees and elbows, feet and legs and arms, but also the joints and parts used as material in constructing a building. What goes into the construction is as important as what makes the structure grow.

We conclude that while Jesus Christ is the "perfect man" (Eph. 4:13), the *body* of Christ is *not* yet finished, not yet perfect. When the Church is called the "body of Christ" she is so designated because she is viewed as including many that at present do not yet belong to her. Many High Churches boast in our day through some of their theologians that they either are or represent (*bene* or *plene,* "well enough" or "fully," as some like to quibble) the "body of Christ in the sense of Ephesians," but they do not appear like a "growing body." They seek salvation in maintaining each its own traditional and past historical structure, rather than in openness and readiness for changes and new elements added to the "whole structure." Yet Ephesians is read with less than care when only the concept of the "body of Christ" is derived from it, and when the vital concept of the *"growth* of the body" (4:15-16) is ignored. The Church is not a dead, unapproachable, mighty or rich body, but is Christ's living and growing body. The Church includes, by this definition, virtually all who are still unbelievers.

At this place we must ask: Is Christ, then, the head of the godless as much as he is the head of the Church? And is, as indeed some Gnostic syncretists believed, the whole world, or at least all mankind, the body (or mantle) of the "Redeemer"? Ephesians and Colossians leave little doubt or obscurity: Jesus Christ is not only "head of the Church." He is as much, and by the same right by which he is head of the Church, head also of every man, whether that man believes in Christ or not. Therefore, Christ is called "seated above all," "head over all," and "fullness filling all in all" (Eph. 1:10, 19 f., 23; 4:10; Col. 2:10). Even the factual reconciliation of "all" is ascribed to him (Col. 1:20). "It pleased God . . . to reconcile all with himself, through him" (i.e., Christ).

But "all" (people) do not yet know (i.e., acknowledge) who and what Jesus Christ is, or what they are in and through him. Many walk still in the path of "ignorance which is in them because of their heart's hardness" (Eph. 4:17-18). Consequently, the all, the world and the powers that be, are never called Christ's body, though he is the head and reconciler. "Body" means, as we have shown, the manifestation of the life of the whole person. A body that does not express life, energy, and direction, would be a corpse and would look as though beheaded. Therefore, the world, the unbelievers, the powers that be — all that show no distinct marks of a specific "life of God" (4:18) in them — are not called the body of Christ. Until the many know the mystery of Christ, until they hear the call: "Stand up, O sleeper, arise from the dead! Christ will give you light!" (5:14), and until they are raised in faith to be living witnesses of the power of the resurrection, they cannot be considered and called the body and members of Christ.

In the terms of other Pauline epistles, Christ "has died for all; therefore all have died" (2 Cor. 5:14). The intention, love, and power of the crucified has no limits. We are not entitled to exclude anyone from having this redeemer. But not all have risen yet with Christ. For only the saints who "do not ignore," but who "know . . . believe . . . consider" (Rom. 6:3, 6, 8, 11) what has happened to them in the death and resurrection of Christ, live and walk in "newness of life" (Rom. 6:1-23). Even more dramatic is the way in which in Revelation 20 the same relationship and difference between the saints and "the rest of the dead" (Rev. 20:5) are described. The thousand-year empire (the millennium) is probably a symbol for the time of the Church between the Resurrection and the Second Coming of Christ. In this time "the dragon, the old serpent" [i.e., the Devil, Satan] is safely bound. The Gentiles need not be impressed or led astray by his behavior in chains and his later short release. But this does not mean that the Gentiles have already risen, or that there is no more death. In that period, only the witnesses (martyrs) of Jesus have already been made alive and enthroned with Christ (Rev. 20:1-6). Another passage (Rev. 6:9-11) shows that the number of witnesses to Christ is not yet full. Those alive *in* the Church know that the life which they have received will be given to many that are still dead and outside.

On the other hand, unless those who are now called body of Christ and members "remember" (2:11) that they them-selves were "dead in sins" and "saved by grace" alone (2:1-8), they betray their own salvation and the public manifestation of grace for which they were saved (2:7). To belong to the Church and to enjoy the intimate and glorious title "body of Christ" means remembering and confessing that it is by God's grace that dead men live, in acknowledgment and to the praise of the "head."

The Church is a living demonstration of the power of, and of faith in, the resurrection, or it is not the Church of God. In this "doctrine on the Church" is unlimited hope for neigh-bors, be they friends or enemies, for individuals and whole countries which today still refuse the Gospel. And here is hope even for sleeping churches. To know that the Church is the *growing* body of Christ, means to hope and to live upon sure ground and with a definite purpose. It means to accept inspiration, power, and direction only from Christ and his quickening Spirit, without any seeking for success or riches. The living Church always grows intensively and extensively. Her members have the same faith and hope for "those far and those near" (2:13, 17, 19). They cannot help but commu-nicate to them the Gospel of peace.

So the constitutional tie between Christ and the Church which is illustrated by the metaphors head and body, growth and building, makes the Church consider herself a prelimi-nary form and assembly of God's people. We speak of a "preliminary" form, because the building of the structure is not yet completed while it still grows (2:21 f.; 4:15 f.). The fullness of Christ's stature is not yet attained (4:13). The mission is still unfinished (6:15, 19 f.). But there is God who *gives* growth, and his eyes watch day and night over his creation and property. Therefore the structure of the body of Christ, the manifestation on earth of the power of resurrection, has to grow and is actually growing. *Growth "into Christ"* (4:15) in knowledge, and *growth "from Christ"* (4:15) in love and mission to those who are still far — this is the meaning of the glorious, but sadly misused title, "body of Christ." A dynamic, not a static, relationship between the Church and Christ is thereby described.

In Roman, Greek Orthodox, and Anglican literature, and in recent years in some Presbyterian and Lutheran utterances also, the term "body of Christ" is often explained in an entirely different way. We are told that this term calls for a mystical, and personal identification; as it is said, for example, that the Church is Christ, the Church is the mystical body or the extension of Christ, or the Church is a quasi Second Christ. Ephesians is used to support this sacrilegious nonsense. In Eph. 1:23 the Church is called the "body of Christ, the fullness of him who fills all in all." This and similar statements do not invite to self-glory and self-promotion of the Church. Rather, we find in them the *preliminary and missionary* character of the community, which is being filled now "with [literally, for] all the fullness of God" (3:19).

Special reason for refraining from speaking of an extension of Christ is offered by Eph. 5:22-33. In this passage Paul shows why and how the relationship between Christ and the Church is an example for the love and mutual submission between man and wife (5:21). The ethical counsel and the Christological discourse points immediately to the meaning of the head-body simile. When the unity between man and wife resembles the unity between Christ and the Church, then love and care and submission and respect become its mark.

We ask, are the terms "one flesh" (5:31, cf. 5:29, his flesh), "one body" (1 Cor. 6:16; cf. Eph. 5:30, his body), and "body of Christ" (1:23, etc.), indicative of a oneness greater than love and submission? Should there be an ontological, biological, or mystical relationship between God and Israel, Christ and the Church, or man and wife, which is more than the covenants of God promised to Israel (cf. 2:12)? We doubt it.

Attempts have been made to go beyond the relational and covenantal bond of love and submission, of word and faith. They result in such fabricated concepts as extension of Christ, mystical body of Christ, organic unity with Christ, divine nature of the Church, redemptive community or society, and Second Christ. If these terms really make sense, they should be applicable to the man-wife relationship also. The wife then would become the extended personality of the man, his mystical body, even a second man! Paul does not teach this in regard to the Church or the married woman.

As if he knew that the head-body simile alone was not sufficient to describe the nature of the Church's relation to Christ, Paul has used with it the foundation-building metaphor and the covenantal marital relationship for further illustration. Each form of speech has to be respected in its own right and place. Upon no one of them alone can the teaching on the Church be based. Eph. 5:22-33 adds to earlier passages about the Church one decisive element. The Church is not an impersonal outflow or process starting from Christ and expanding into the world, but she is his chosen bride who responds to his love in voluntary, glad submission. The Church is the one new man Christ created as personal partner who responds with hymns of praise. An impersonal extension of Christ, or a Second Christ could hardly give that free answer of praise, for which the Church was created (1:12, 14).

There are Protestant schools of thought and denominations which, since the Reformation, have insisted upon a recovery

of the covenant character of the Church. They have pro-
moted the formation of Free Churches and disapproved institutional and State Churches. To the "cage of gold" which
princes, parliaments, and High Church theologians furnished,
they have preferred the risks, poverty, and weakness of experi-
mental congregationalism, questionable order, and erratic
theology. The apostle Paul promotes in Ephesians neither a
wild spiritualism nor a comfortable establishment. The
Church of which he speaks has a constitution and respects
decency and order (cf. 1 Cor. 14:40).

We proceed now to the second article of the Church's constitution, which though less discussed and known, is equally
as important as the first.

2. The *Church* lives in a special relationship with *Israel*.
This special bond may best be called solidarity, or, as we hope
to show, conversation. By "Israel" we understand not only
ancient Israel which was promised and given God's Messiah.
Neither do today's Jews in their dispersion over the world
(or in the young state of Israel) exhaust what is meant. Nor
can the Israel according to the Spirit, the "true worshipers
in Spirit and in truth" of all ages, to which John and Paul
refer at times (Rom. 2:29; Gal. 6:16; John 1:47; 4:22) serve
as an exclusive definition. What we need to bear in mind is
that the total of *all* possible descriptions of Israel may be
involved when some passages of Ephesians are before us.

"In Christ we have been destined before and appointed . . .
to be for a praise of his glory — we who had hoped in Christ
as the first. In him you also . . . were sealed by the promised
Holy Spirit . . . to the praise of his glory" (1:11-14). The
explicit differentiation made between what God did to "us"
and to "you" might refer only to the "difference in equality"
that exists between the apostle and those who became Christians after him. But the weight of the following passages
presses us to another interpretation, which identifies the

word "we" with (Paul and) the believers of Jewish extraction, and the word "you" with the Gentile-born Christians. In 2:11 ff. it is stated: "Remember that you were once Gentiles in the flesh, called the uncircumcision by the so-called circumcision. [Remember] that at that time you were without Christ, alienated from the commonwealth of Israel and strangers to the covenants of promise, bare of hope and godless in the world. But now in Christ Jesus you who once were far have become near. . . ." In 2:14 ff. we read: "He . . . made the two [things? parties? groups? men? peoples?] one. . . . He abrogated the law of ordinances in statutes in order to create in him the two [men or peoples, to be] one new man by making peace, and in order to reconcile them both in one body to God by killing in him the enmity. He came and preached peace to you who are far, and peace to those near. For through him we both have access to the Father in one Spirit. Therefore you are no more strangers and sojourners, but you are fellow citizens of the saints and members of God's household, built upon the foundation of the apostles and prophets, Christ Jesus himself being the chief cornerstone."

To be noted also is 3:5 f.: "In other generations the mystery of Christ was not made known to the sons of man as it has now been revealed . . . that the Gentiles are fellow heirs, members of the same body, fellow-partakers of the promise [of God]." According to this last passage, the mystery of Christ is the brotherhood and fellow-citizenship of the Gentiles with Israel!

Such statements are too ponderous to be overlooked. The whole work of Christ, his "making peace" and his being "our peace" by "killing the enmity" (2:14-16) is not only related to, but also consists of the breaking down of the dividing wall between Jews and Gentiles. We observe that it is *not* related, primarily, to the partition between races and classes, nations and neighbors, ages and cultures.

It well may seem to us that political and social, racial and moral, sexual and spiritual, educational and psychological, tensions and contrasts deserve more attention than — of all things! — the relationship between the Church and Israel. Passages like Gal. 3:28; Col. 3:11; 1 Cor. 12:13 do indeed treat of the oneness of Jews and Greeks, slaves and free men, barbarians and Scythians, males and females. There the Jews and Gentiles are counted as but one among *many* of the inimical pairs that have been reconciled (at-one-d) in Christ. Now, in a preceding section, these passages led us to speak of the abolition of every wall and of the peace which Christ made for man and woman, master and slave, etc. We need not retract what was said about the social, political, and psychological dimensions of the perfect work of God. But we have to realize at this point that in the letter to the Ephesians, Paul does not from the outset generalize what he says about the "one new man."

In this epistle the "workmanship of God" (2:10), the "one new man" (2:15; cf. 4:24), is said to be created only of (RSV, "in place of") these two: Jew and Gentile (2:11-22). That both Jews and Gentiles are divided also into male and female, young and old, owners and slaves, is not forgotten by Paul. But social peace, between the sexes, between young and old, and between different classes, is no substitute for that unique peace which ended the hostility between the insiders and the outsiders of God's house. According to Ephesians, social peace in any realm and in any form is a consequence of the peace which was made between Jews and Gentiles. God's great deed ("workmanship," 2:10), and the preaching of Christ's blood (2:13-17) procure peace between those estranged from Israel's commonwealth and the Israelites. To walk "worthily" of this call and the bond of this peace (4:1 ff.) means to let thanksgiving and submission rule among all Christians (5:20-21), love and respect among married people (5:21-25, 33), responsibility and obedience among old and young, master and slave (6:1-9). But only the peace between Jews and Gentiles, which makes both together have peace with God and free approach to God (2:16-18), is the source from which peaceful coexistence at all levels of life is to be drawn.

This same peace also is the standard by which to test all efforts to peace, whether they be honest or escapes from the basic issues. Whether it be Hitler's attempt to establish a pure Germanic race, or Russia's purge of party ranks, or the concern in certain American circles for the conservation of the white race, or the flaming patriotism of some Arab nations, the test for the sincerity and good intentions of the movement is always to be found in the way it treats the Jews, politically, socially, and culturally.

Why are the Jews so peculiar? In the Bible they are declared to be both God's and mankind's "apple of the eye." Why of all the peoples of the world are they so dear to God as to be "kept as the apple of his eye" (Deut. 32:10; cf. Ps. 17:8)? Why is a man who "touches" and "plunders" them a fool who "touches the apple of his [own] eye" (Zech. 2:8)? Why cannot those who believe in Christ have peace with God and with each other without having peace with Israel and without approaching God together with Israel (Eph. 2: 16-22)? Ephesians answers: It is not because Israel doesn't need resurrection and reconciliation, gathering and building up "into the holy temple in the Lord." On the contrary, says Paul, not only *you* (the born Gentiles) "were dead in trespasses and sins . . . according to the age (RSV, course) of this world" (2:1 f.); but "among these [sons of disobedience] also all of *us* [Jews] once walked in the desires of our flesh . . . and we [the Jews] were by nature children of wrath, like the rest of them [RSV, of mankind]. But God . . . made *us* who were dead in trespasses alive together with Christ . . . in Christ" (2:3-6). "The two [Jew and Gentile] Christ made one" and "the two he created [to be] one new man" (2: 14-16). "He came and preached peace to those who were far *and peace to those who were near"* (2:17). Not in a different, but only "in *one* Spirit we both have access to the Father" (2:18) and we both are "built together for a dwelling place of God" (2:22). What is proclaimed by Paul in Ephesians is not the superior value of Jewish character or racial history, neither is it fraternization with the Jews at any price. The words "in Christ" and "in one Spirit" are far too prominent to permit a purely humanitarian approach to the problems of Israel's history to this present day. What, then, is Paul's argument for an indissoluble solidarity of the Church with the Jews?

Keywords like "election" (1:4), "grace" (2:5), "workmanship of God" (2:10), "promise," "covenants" (2:12; 3:6), "household," and "temple" (2:19, 21) of God point to the answer. The fact that the Ephesians were made alive together with Christ (2:1, 5 f.) cannot be considered apart from their election and gathering by a promise and word, into a house and temple that already existed before there was a church in Ephesus. God had a household and a people for the revelation of his grace and glory, even Israel, before the Gospel came to Ephesus. The people of God did not come into existence only when Gentiles, such as the Ephesians, were gathered into it (Luke 14:15-21; 22:14-20; Acts 2; etc.). Though "the house" was not "filled" (Luke 14:22-23), there was a people of God at all times. Israel heard God's word from the prophets, hoped in the Spirit, and was called to enjoy citizenship in God's kingdom and filial rights in God's house, long before the Gentile members of the present church did. The rights of a child and of a citizen in God's kingdom are granted by "love" and by "grace" (2:4-5), first to Israel, and only then also and equally to the Gentiles (2:19).

This is important for their knowledge of God. God did not become loving and gracious only when he inserted Gentiles into his house and his kingdom. Neither did he cease to love and to govern by grace those whom he had adopted and privileged before. If his love were a novelty or a thing that could cease to be, how could the Christians in Ephesus be sure that God would not change again? Instead, by reference to Israel, the Ephesians are reminded that nothing less than the eternal will and plan of God is revealed to them through the apostle. The God of Abraham, Isaac, Jacob, and not some other god, is their Father. To be sure, the love, grace, and peace which they enjoy was revealed to them only "now" (1:9 f.; 3:5, 10). But it is the same love, grace, and peace which was God's "purpose of ages" (RSV, eternal purpose; 3:11; cf. 1:3-14).

So they "have" nothing — whether redemption, forgiveness, peace, access to God, or hope (1:7, 18; 2:14, 18, etc.) — which they do not have together with Israel. Alienated from Israel they were "bare of hope and without God" (2:12). Joined to Israel they partake in "the life of God" (cf. 4:18; 2:14; 3:6). Therefore they cannot pray, "My Father." They can only speak to "Our Father" (1:2). It is of sheer grace that such prayer is possible. And this grace joins them to those who received grace before, and who are receiving grace with them, namely Israel.

In order that they do not forget to praise the grace of God, they are admonished to "remember" that they are newly, graciously, and miraculously admitted to the house and commonwealth of God, and are saved from estrangement and hopelessness (2:12; 4:18). Not long ago, their own life was nothing but erring, cursing, swaying, and swaggering around in vanity, ignorance, hardness of heart, and darkness (4:14, 18-19, 31; 5:6; cf. Ps. 107). It was a hopeless and godless affair (2:12). Their life was death (2:1, 5) and "captivity" (4:8), not "life of God" (4:18). All the while, others, even Israel, were at home and were always members of God's household. Now the Gentile-born Ephesians are privileged to know that they, too, shall "inherit the kingdom of Christ and God" (5:5), that they are sons of the same household (2:19), members of the same body, heirs of the same riches (3:6), and stones in the same structure as Israel (2:20-22). Now they are "no-more-strangers" and "no-more-sojourners" (2:19). It is Israel who reminds them of the miracle of their adoption — be it Paul with the other Hebrew-born apostles, the prophets of the Old Testament (2:20), or the Jews whose actions are described in such passages as Acts 19:8-10, 13-20. Whether these Jews live by magic and tricks, whether they slander and persecute Paul or receive the Gospel with open hearts, they are always the instrument of God to show two things with unique clarity: the estrangement from God and the grace of God, the death of the prodigal and the life of the accepted child of God.

To belong to the household of God means to live in brotherhood and fellow-citizenship with these Jews who unwittingly bear testimony to the true nature of God and man. Only "in Christ" do we come to see and appreciate why we live in such close solidarity with the Jews. And only "in Christ" do we discover that our solidarity with the Jew is proof of any serious concept of brotherhood. The privilege and the tension of solidarity with Israel test the depth of our brotherly emotions, words, and deeds. No Christian ethics can bypass this solidarity with Israel.

But what about the many rather sharp remarks against the Jews which Paul makes in most of his other epistles? Especially in 1 Thess. 2:14-16; Rom. 2:9-11, 16 ff.; and in Galatians, Colossians, and Philippians there are found outbursts against those who prefer the righteousness of the law by works, to grace and peace given in Jesus Christ (cf. the apostolic speeches which are summarized in Acts; also Matt. 23; John 8:31-59; Rev. 2:9; 3:9, etc.). They ignore the "righteousness of God" — this is bluntly said of the Jews (Rom. 10:3). Their father is the devil, we read in John 8:44. And Paul warns the Christians of Gentile origin against falling into the steps of his own past; i.e., against living like Jews ("to Judaize . . . in Judaism," Gal. 1:13-14; 2:14).

In Ephesians there is but one slight touch upon this side of the problem. After recalling that we "are saved by grace . . . not by works, lest anyone boast" (2:5-9), Paul speaks, not without irony, of the "so-called uncircumcision" that is given its name "by the so-called circumcision in the flesh which is a work of hands" (2:11). This hint is clear enough for a warning. Paul does not intend to lead the Ephesians back to a place where "the Law of ordinances in statutes" had erected a "wall" between The People and the peoples, and between God and man (2:14 ff.).

But Paul's main stream of thought is not polemic. When he refers to "Israel" (2:11 ff.) he points out that on earth, in the world of alienation, error, darkness, and death, there was and is always a people of God. It not only lives in God's mind, but it also has form and name, a history and a ministry. Whatever this people did with its election, with the prophecies and the Law — whether it gave and "gives the glory to God" (this is the meaning of the Hebrew word "Judah"), whether it boasted of man's own works and framed the Law in man-made statutes, or whether it murdered its prophets — nothing can wipe out the privilege and function of Israel. Even the faithlessness of Israel cannot nullify God's faithfulness (Rom. 3:3-4). The Israel of which Paul speaks in Ephesians is therefore Israel in whatever attitude and attire it meets our eye or confronts our ways. It is the Old Testament people and the Jew today, the true worshipers and those who, with the help of a disciple of Christ, and of a Gentile judge and his soldiers, crucified the "king of the Jews." By God's election to be his child and servant, Israel has *a character indelible.*

As brothers of the Jews the Christians are given an unchanging constitution and order. They are received into a God-given order of living in God's house. They are depend-

ent upon a word given and a Spirit promised by God to
others first. They are served by, and they are called to serve
in, a ministry that has preceded their own commission. It is
Israel who by right of God's choice always comes first in
questions of truth and righteousness, preaching and faith, fellowship and service. "The Jews first and to the Greeks . . ."
(Rom. 1:16; 2:9 f.; 3:9, 29; 1 Cor. 9:20; Acts 13:5, 24, 32 f., 38,
46; 20:21; etc.). "The Jews' King" was the crucified "Savior
of the world" (John 19:19; 4:42)! John's Gospel contains the
most radical and the most important sentence that was ever
coined in regard to this topic: "Salvation is from the Jews"
(4:22). In terms of Ephesians, this means that salvation, ministry, worship, and common life are not to be organized and
adapted by the Christians *ad libitum* — according to whatever need looks most urgent and whatever method looks most
efficient. But the "saints and faithful in Christ" (1:1) are
those who are being "built up . . . together" (2:20, 22) with
those who were the chosen people before them and who still
are chosen. The growth of the church takes place only where
the structure (the body of Christ) is "joined and united together" (2:21 f.; 4:16). The word "together" appears nowhere so frequently or in such daring combinations as in the
Greek text of Ephesians. It describes always (also when explicitly resurrection and enthronement "together with Christ"
are mentioned, as in 2:6 f.), community of the church with
Israel.

Now Paul shows in all his letters with great emphasis that
the Church is a community — not a casual collection of some
individuals with more or less common religious convictions.
He teaches distinctly that the Church lives as one body by
the mutual service which God's Spirit makes the members
render to one another. Both the diversity and the unity of
these manifold services are discussed most fully in 1 Cor. 12
and Rom. 12. However, Ephesians adds, as we have shown
before, an important specification.

It is not fellowship with fellow men in general that we need primarily and absolutely for our knowledge of salvation and for receiving and rendering service inspired by God. Essential for the growth and building of the Church are the Jews who lived before us and the Jews who live with, among, and around us now. And indispensable is our being joined and knitted and built together with them. We repeat: the criterion whether we are honest, thorough, uncompromising when we acknowledge that we need fellow man in order to stand before God lies in our relationship to the Jews. The "King of the Jews" is theirs before he is ours. He is theirs, before he is theirs *and* ours. After being "made one" (2:14), "both of us have access to the Father in one Spirit" (2:18). No access is open, no Holy Spirit is available and operative, that would admit either one of the two without the other to the throne of grace. Access to "our Father" is given to both the prodigal who enters the Father's house and the older brother who has never left it. The Father shows one and the same love for both (Luke 15:11-32). To "the Hebrews" it was written, but by Gentiles, too, it is still to be read, that "since we have a great high priest, let us approach the throne of grace" (Heb. 4:14, 16; cf. Rom. 5:1 f.; Eph. 3:12).

Not only Christ, the chief cornerstone, but also the foundation walls of the Church bear witness to the community with Israel. The church is "built upon the foundation of apostles *and prophets* (2:20). Because of the secondary role which New Testament prophets played in the theology of Paul and in that of the early church (cf. Eph. 3:5; 4:11; 1 Cor. 12:28 f.; Acts 11:27; 13:1; 21:10; etc.), and because of the honored place Old Testament prophets and prophecies held in earliest Christian preaching, we are well advised to consider the prophets mentioned in Eph. 2:20 as Old Testament prophets. Moses and David (as author of the Psalms) were counted among them (Deut. 18:15, 18; Acts 3:22; 7:37; Heb. 4:7); the whole Old Testament was spoken "by the prophets" (Heb.

1:1). The Church is built upon the Old Testament witness and the New Testament witness to God. She does not stand only upon that of the disciples of Christ, but on the search, foretelling, and witness of the old prophets as well (cf. 1 Pet. 1:10-11). This is said in Eph. 2:20. The church, built upon the apostles and prophets, can neither stand "in love" on its root and ground (3:17), nor grow internally or externally (2:21 f.; 4:13-16) unless it listens and learns continuously from the Old Testament people of God, and from the testimony given to and by them.

What about maintaining a sharp dividing line between the "value" attributed to the Old Testament and that attributed to the New Testament? The wall of division which was abolished by Christ includes the walls erected by our value judgments. The many Old Testament quotations and allusions which give flavor to every page of the New Testament show that the early Christians did not see any reason to erect a wall between the Testaments, or around the New Testament in order to eliminate the Old. It was left to sectarian groups to call the Creator God a devil, and to denounce his acts of justice as diabolic. The Ephesians are told to be built up in obedience and trust to the apostles and prophets, and to worship and glorify God together with the Jews. Whether all Jews will become Christians is not stated in Ephesians. It makes no difference for the saints' solidarity with them.

A recently completed constitution of a church in the Netherlands speaks of "the conversation with Israel," and makes clear that this conversation belongs as essentially to the life of the Church as the mission (apostolate) to the Gentiles. This excellent formulation deserves to be understood in its fullest and deepest sense. "Conversation" means complete turning to a partner, walking (and staying) with him in serious and friendly dialogue. It denotes, further, familiarity with his woes and joys, and sharing with him in patience, suffering, and hope. When the Church is awake and alive, it not only talks, but it lives and walks with the Jews, wherever and however they are.

Nowhere in all of his epistles has Paul put the conversation in word and walk with Israel so much in the foreground as in Ephesians. Only after what appear to have been immeasurable sufferings and disappointments at the hands of his Jewish "brethren" (1 Thess. 2:14 f.; Gal. 2:13 f.; 2 Cor. 11: 24 ff.; Phil. 3:2 ff.; Rom. 2:17 ff.; 9:1 ff.) did he come, not to a final condemnation of the Jews, but to the insight and preaching of the oneness of the "olive tree" (i.e., the people of God, Rom. 11:17 ff.), the "fullness" (RSV, full inclusion, Rom. 11:12) of Israel, the salvation of "all Israel" (Rom. 11: 26; cf. Heb. 11:40), the "one body" (Eph. 3:6; 4:4) and "one new man" created of those who "without Christ" were "two" and lived in enmity (Eph. 2:14-18; cf. Gal. 3:28; Col. 3:11; 1 Cor. 12:13).

But even before his teaching on the constitutional oneness of the Church with Israel became as explicit as it is in Rom. 11 and in Ephesians, Paul never denied being a Jew. He always referred to the history of Israel and to the testimony of its chosen fathers, kings, and writers. He built his explication of Christ's death and resurrection upon the Old Testament (1 Cor. 15:3 f., etc.). If we give up conversation with Jewish-born prophets and apostles of Christ, if we repudiate Hebrew thought and diction, if we attempt to form anti-Semitic churches, to keep Jews out of our communities, or to suppress all concern for whatever the Jews (including the state of Israel) do and suffer today, then we are not living as members of the one body, the Church, which is described in Ephesians.

In the daily life and conduct of today's churches and organization of denominations, congregations, conventions, and church boards, this vital element of Ephesians' message and call is little, or not at all, known and honored. During the

Nazi period of recent history, there were some declarations uttered and some timid or bold steps undertaken by a few congregations and individuals, to live, act, and suffer according to the implications of Paul's teaching on the Church. In the years since World War II, especially in Holland, deep and penetrating thinking is being devoted to the relationship between Israel and the Church. But the World Council of Churches at its Evanston Assembly defeated a motion that aimed at least at a clear-cut oral declaration about the hope of Israel and for Israel. Yet denominations and congregations, synods and boards, world councils and individuals can be ambassadors of the Gospel, evangelists carrying an urgent message, and missionaries equipped with good credentials only when they realize what thankful and responsible conversation with Israel means. Israel is the original and logical missionary of God. The mission of the Church is carried out only in fulfillment of Israel's calling and privilege.

In a simple or long-term program, it is impossible to outline the sum of decisions and actions that would have to be made by a church which acknowledges its solidarity with Israel. By no means will solidarity with Israel be exhausted by a minimum of resistance against secret or open, sophisticated or clumsy, anti-Semitism, and by some "mission" stations created in modern ghettos or in the young state of Israel. Not only serious study and concern of some theological thinkers, not only the ardent work of some minority groups and individuals, but an awakening in all echelons of the ecumenical movement, of denominations, of congregations, of all church members, is necessary. It will have to be an awakening to the confession of scandalous omissions and commissions of which the Christian churches were and are guilty, in past and present times. It will mean the acceptance of much suffering and loneliness, which we are not to avoid, but to bear as brothers. It will result in an exchange of help and advice which will show the world that the

Church's solidarity and fellow citizenship with Israel does not end in mutual disappointments and grievances, is not conditional or opportunistic, but essential and vital to the life and witness of the Church.

3. We turn now to a third and final article of the Church's constitution. The Church lives in a specific relationship to *every man*. As the Church's growth to the full stature of Christ, and the Church's brotherhood with the people of Israel are constitutive and indispensable, so also a very specific attitude and action of the Church is essential in regard to all men.

Not in vain has Jesus Christ become man and taken the side of both the outsiders and the insiders of God's house. Of him, who reconciled those far and near, the members of God's household cannot think or speak unless they accept his work, which is the abolition of the wall. Instead of the wall, they now know and acknowledge a "bond of peace" (4:3). The resurrection does not permit further walking among men after the (hostile) fashion of the "old man" (cf. 4:22)!

Further, not in vain has Israel as God's first-born a privileged place and an indispensable function in God's "economy." The factual position of the Jews before God and man may appear to be as ambiguous as that of the prodigal's older brother in the parable (Luke 15:25-32). The Jews do yet belong to the house of God! The prodigal straggler, after being received at home by the Father's open arms, has no right to despise or to belittle the labor and work of the first-born. He who is saved by sheer grace after a long life in darkness and in the realm of death, has every reason to honor other men who have been toiling in God's vineyard while he was lazy. Therefore all of Israel, whether they are kind or harsh to the saved Gentile sinners, need and have a right to receive respect, patience, and a testimony of gratitude.

Israel opens the eyes and minds of the Church and the Christians not to consider themselves the only children of God. The Jews, not only the belittled, despised, and persecuted Jews, but also the murmuring, rebellious, and self-righteous Jews make us realize of what sort and kind the many children of God are. By confessing that God is "Father of all and over all" (4:6; cf. 3:14 f.), we confess that we are surrounded only by children of God and that we do not know any man who is not our brother.

Now, the "brotherhood of all men" is an ideal that often was based on anything but Jesus Christ's work and Israel's special vocation. Reason and experience, the human or absolute spirit, and utilitarian arguments were supposed to vouch for it. The Bible does not speak of such an ideal. Furthermore, the Gentiles are not called children of God in Ephesians any more than "all men" are called the body of Christ. And yet, those who *were* "sons of disobedience" (2:2) and those who still *are* (5:6), are not left without hope. The saints in Ephesus have already received and are still to receive "knowledge . . . of God's calling" (1:17 f.), and those still disobedient shall receive "light" through these very saints (5:6-8). The number of God's children is not yet full (Rev. 6:11). "Still there is room" (Luke 14:22 f.). Not only Israel's salvation, but also her own salvation make the Church realize that by resurrection (Rom. 11:15) even he who appears to be stone dead today, can be manifested as a "child of God" and a brother of the saints tomorrow. "God is able from these stones to raise up children to Abraham" (Matt. 3:9).

What the Christians owe to Israel, what they learn from Israel, and what they hope for Israel, this they also apply to their conversation with every man — even with the "enemy" (Rom. 12:19-21). After treating in three long chapters (Rom. 9—11) of the Church's relation to Israel, Paul proceeds immediately (in Rom. 12—15) to describe the Christian's conversation with every man; i.e., with brother and enemy, with saints and pagans, with weak and strong characters. He does the same in Ephesians. After portraying Christ's work as the making of reconciliation and peace between Jew and Gentile, and between these two and God (Eph. 2:11-22), and after showing how this work is made known to, in, and by the Church (3:1–4:16), he concludes his argument with exhortations concerning the Church's life and the Christian's way of walking among and in relation to all men (4:17–6:20).

"Let all men know your fairness [your equity, forbearance, goodness]. . . . Bear one another's burden. . . . Since we have the opportunity, let us do what is good to all men, foremost to those who belong to the household of faith. . . . If possible, as far as depends on you, have peace with all men. . . . Love does no wrong to the neighbor. Therefore love is the fulfillment of the law." With these and other commandments and counsels, Paul reminds the Philippians (4:5), the Galatians (6:2, 10), and the Romans (12:18; 13:10) of their basic relationship to their fellow man. To these utterances correspond in the Epistle to the Ephesians the much quoted words: "Be kind to one another, compassionate, forgiving" (4:32). With Gal. 6:2 we may call this another formulation of "the law of Christ."

The reason for this "law," the criterion for its fulfillment, and the source of power to fulfill it are identical. "Be kind . . . compassionate, forgiving, as God in Christ has forgiven you" (Eph. 4:32). God showed "the riches of his grace in the kindness to us [exhibited] in Christ Jesus" (2:7). Therefore "walk in love, like as also Christ loved us" (5:2, 25). The call to be kind, compassionate, forgiving is nothing less than the call to "become [or, to be] imitators of God, as [his] beloved children" (5:1). God's own love and action of love (2:4) is both source and standard for "testing (RSV, trying to learn) what is pleasing to the Lord" (5:10), for "understanding what is his will" (5:17), for "doing God's will from the heart" (6:6), for doing what "is right" and "fitting among the saints" (6:1; 5:3), and for escaping from attitudes, actions, words that are "not fitting" (5:4). That which is "not fitting" and contrary to "walking worthily of the calling with which you have been called" (4:1) is three times described as "licentiousness, fornication, impurity, greed" (4:19; 5:3, 5). It is described also as lying and silly talk (4:25; 5:4), as bitterness, as wrath and blasphemy (4:31), as theft, and as eye-service (4:28; 6:6).

There are no individual virtues as distinguished from social virtues. The life of the new man is a life of true, pure, unselfish, witnessing relationship to his fellow man. The "neighbor" who receives the Christian's witness by words, actions, and attitude is sometimes denoted as the (fellow-) member of the Church (4:2, 25, 32; 5:21, 30); but Paul does not mean that the Church is a "light" only for the Church herself, or that Christians have to obey the "law of Christ" only in their conversation with fellow Christians. The special features of the Christians' life "in the world" and the equipment of the Christians for knowing and using the countless opportunities for witness, and for enduring and resisting in the actual or possible tensions, will be discussed later. Now we are concerned only with the ground swell of their behavior and attitude toward fellow man.

To the constitution of the Church belongs one great denominator which is common to all that Christians manifest, represent, do, and bear. This constitutional denominator cannot be described in terms of traits of individual perfection like courage, fear of punishment, hope for reward, or complete devotion. Though similar traits are not completely missing in Paul's admonition (cf. Eph. 3:16; 6:10 ff.; 5:5, 21; 6:8), they do not have the character and value of virtues or ultimate goals. The underlying common motive of Paul's ethical admonitions would be called, by a reader of Romans 13 and 1 Corinthians 13, "love." A student of Ephesians may refer to Eph. 4:32 and call it "kindness." Kindness to fellow

man — this is, simple though it sounds, one of the most startling and revolutionary key words of Pauline ethics.

Philosophers, lawyers, priests, humanists, poets, and ana-
lysts of all times have seriously worried, worked, and suffered
for the elaboration and propagation of one fundamental or
supreme virtue that could or should dominate all relationships. Ideals of freedom or righteousness, of democratic or
aristocratic order, of individualism and collectivism, etc., have
been sought, formulated, tested, illustrated, improved, and
questioned again and again. Christian denominations, congregations, and individuals have identified themselves under
different conditions with one or another of these. It may seem
as if the last, highest, and deepest idea which individual or
popular thought in the Western hemisphere can contribute
to this ongoing quest is a pessimistic world view, and a
fatalistic (be it heroically stoic or bitterly cynical) opinion
and explanation of the relation between man and man, or
between man and society. Whether the seat and core of what
is moral and what is immoral are sought and found in individual man or in society, always a gloomy view prevails. At
best, compromises, adjustments, delays between man and man
are expected, but not the doing of what is good. *"Lupus est
homo homini* (man is a wolf to man), so the Romans used to
say. And this axiom appears to be valid still, both in and
outside the churches of the world which was supposedly
Christianized after the fall of the Roman Empire.

But not in Ephesians! For we find in this document, as in
other Pauline epistles, no reason whatever for either primitive or sophisticated pessimism in regard to man's relationship
to his fellow man and to society. Paul holds and makes plain
that the Church and her members know and shall live out of
the acknowledgment that man is cared for and protected
by God. Whether he already is raised from death in sin, or
whether he is still to be awakened and raised (2:5 f.; 5:14);
whether he already is called or is still to be called and fitted

into God's household and growing temple (2:19-21; 6:18-20); whether he makes his bed in hell or heaven (4:14; Ps. 139:1-12), the glory of God shall be sung by him, the fullness of God will not leave him empty. Ephesians gives reason and courage to the conviction that something good can be done between man and man: "Whatsoever good somebody does, this he will receive from the Lord" (6:8). The members of the Church are equipped to do this by letting all men know the great work of God. By God's perfect work they are not incapacitated, killed, or annihilated, but they are resurrected and empowered to live and to act in gratitude and response "for a praise of God's glory" (1:12). "We are God's workmanship created in Christ for good works which God has purposed before, that we should walk in them" (2:10). What is the sum of these good works?

"Be kind to one another!" (4:32). These words and all the urgent and concrete appeals, counsels, and warnings that go with them, should certainly not be understood as an invitation, with smiles and smoothness, with handshaking and shoulder-patting, with tea parties and rummage sales, to cover up, to override, or to disclaim hypocritically what there is of enmity and misery, of pride and prejudice, of hardness and foolishness, between, in, and around those of different races, sexes, classes, and ages. But "kindness to man" (2:7) is the steel and iron with which God treated the wall of hostility between man and man, and between God and man, when Christ died "for all" (2 Cor. 5:14) and was raised "above all" (Eph. 1:20 f.). Kindness exists only where the Holy Spirit makes men walk "with lowliness and meekness, with patience . . . forbearing one another in love" (4:2). He is kind to man who acknowledges and manifests by his attitudes and actions that his fellow man, be he far or near, is cared for, and is reconciled and protected by God himself. God is his Father. Christ died for him. The Spirit is promised to him. We cannot keep at a distance the subject of God's love and might.

We cannot despair of our fellow man. Kindness is not dependent upon response. But it calls for response, since God's "kindness to us" (2:7) proves effective in the raising (2:5 f.) of "beloved children of God" (5:1) and in the "creation" (2:10, 15; 4:24) of "imitators of God" (5:1).

Kindness stands diametrically opposed to any attitude, whether displayed in thoughts, words, or deeds, that shrugs off a fellow man as a hopeless case, and that manifests toward him nothing else but contempt, disgust, despair, hatred, or unconcern. Without kindness, man stands against man. The church cannot join those who have given up hope for peace on earth. Kindness means protection of the threatened life — of one life as much as of the life of millions. Kindness means risk and resolution, a clear stand and wise action. Kindness is a sharp steel against gloom, boredom, and unconcern. It is a granite block against which commissions, statistics, experiences, and shrewd calculations will shatter. The little petting and indulgence which is commonly confused with kindness today, has little or nothing to do with what Paul says in Ephesians 4:32.

Kindness, if shown by the church today, would include a bold stand in the discussion about Israel and atomic arms and experiments, brave action in the burning issues and crying scandals of segregation and city slums, uncompromising and unconditional solidarity with and help for the victims of Western civilization and colonialism. We may agree with many non-Christians that it is of ultimate concern whether one man or some hundred thousand die or are born crippled because of hunger, war, or radiation. But we must still ask what difference it makes whether or not a handful of Christians speak the truth, give something to those in need, purge out all bitterness from their hearts, and forgive offenders (cf. Eph. 4:24-32). How should or could the Church be a hospital for all the sick of the world, a corncrib for all the hungry, a meeting ground for all inimical world powers and individuals, or a beacon and lighthouse for all in darkness? And after all, what "good" can we do that can stand before God's judgment (cf. 6:8)?

It is clear that such questions are nothing other than a cover up and masquerade by which we hope to extricate ourselves from the political, social, and this worldly relevance of the "bond of peace" and of the "gospel of peace" (2:17; 4:3; 6:16). But we cannot appeal or abrogate the constitution which God has given to the Church. It may well be that true kindness is as much the criterion of our belonging to the one Church as is the confession that Christ is our Lord and that the Jews are our brethren. It cannot be said that Paul treats the "ethical" questions with any less devotion, energy, and directness than the "dogmatic" issues.

"You are light in the Lord. Walk as children of the light" (5:8). This is the final aspect of Paul's teaching on the Church. By the will and work of God, the Church is so constituted that she bears "fruits of the light" given to her. The light bears the fruit of "goodness, righteousness, and truth" (5:9; cf. Phil. 4:8). Individuals and groups, academies and nations, world views and whole philosophical systems may end up in ultimate despair regarding man. The Church cannot follow them in this course, because of God's work and because she is God's work (2:10, 15). Despite her evident inability (and sometimes unwillingness) to teach and to feed, to heal and to reconcile, all her own members (not to speak of all the world!), the Church is the community of those called *not* to despair in view of both the ocean of death and misery and the frailty of her own theoretical and practical contributions to alleviate hostility and need.

We conclude: *The Church is for man,* or she is not the Church. She is full of hope and trust for every man, because God, the Father, the Son, and the Spirit is for man. Through the "word of truth" which she hears, believes, and carries into the world, the Church "knows" how well man is cared for and

144 THE BROKEN WALL: A STUDY OF EPHESIANS

provided for by God. Man "in the world" (2:12) cannot be more "dead" and "hopeless" and "godless" than the Church's members themselves have been (2:1, 5, 12). If they were saved and raised and made brothers, then God can do things that are beyond human power. Nobody else but the Church is called "to be strong in the Lord and in the strength of his might" (6:10). "Through the Church, God's manifold wisdom shall be made known" (3:10).

In slum districts of American, European, African, and Asiatic cities, in discussions of concerned groups gathered from all social and intellectual classes, in known and unknown actions and in evangelistic speeches, some attempts are being made in our time to show that the Church is for the whole man and for all men. Whether these attempts are bold or shy, successful or collapsing, convincing or queer, they are not an appendix to or a luxury in the Church's life. They belong to the very essence, nature, and manifestation of God's people. Either the Church manifests by word and deed that God is for man and that she knows that man's cause is not lost but is to be won in public, or she is unchurched, not-the-Church, a hypocritical, complacent, sleeping, and dead institution. Neither doctrines nor traditions, neither bishops nor presbyters, neither conventions nor expanding numbers of congregations can save the Church when she belies and denies the constitution which God has given her and the covenant which God keeps faithfully and upon which she stands. The constitution of God's covenant is unshakable ground. It is the "divine law," by which the Church lives in the world.

What it means for the Church to stand in the world as the house of God and as the growing body of Christ is treated in detail in Part Four of this book.

PART FOUR

THE CHURCH IN THE WORLD

PART FOUR

The Church in the World

IN THIS CONCLUDING PART of our study of Ephesians, we need
to consider how the community of those who "hear and
believe . . . the Gospel" (1:13) is to stand and walk in the
world. The second half of the Epistle to the Ephesians is
full of intimations showing that the actual, visible conduct
of the Christians in Ephesus was not too different from that
of their non-Christian Gentile neighbors. Yet in those same
chapters (Eph. 4—6) there are found many statements and
exhortations that show what difference it makes that God
has done the perfect work and has set forth his "workmanship"; namely, a people for himself that is gathered, built,
and growing, even his "holy and spotless" Church. All those
assembled and included in God's people are admonished
thus: "Walk worthily of the calling with which you have
been called" (Eph. 4:1). As "one new man" the Church was
created through the work of Christ (2:15). She is constantly
"renewed" from inside out and from outside in (4:23-24).
She "puts on" and "takes up" (4:24; 6:11, 13) what God has
created and prepared for her. For God is inspiring every
breath she breathes and every movement she makes. He gives
her direction and power (1:17 f.; 3:16 f.; 6:10). Therefore
the Christians shall "walk no more like the Gentiles" (4:17).
The relation of God's gift to their life and of their life to
the world is described in one long and aboundingly rich
sentence in Rom. 12:1-2: "Because of the mercies of God,
present your bodies as a living, holy, acceptable sacrifice to
God; this is your Spiritual worship; do not conform your-

147

selves [or, be not conformed] to this world, but be trans-
formed by renewal completely so as to test [or, to prove; or,
to try to learn; cf. Eph. 5:10, 17] what is the will of God"; i.e.,
good, pleasing, and perfect.

God's mercy and workmanship do not inactivate man, but
work as power of renewal in him. It was the "pleasure of
God's will" (1:5 f.) to give grace and life to those who had
been more than inactivated — even dead in sin (2:1, 5). This
same "will" is now also to be done "from the soul" (6:6) by
those that are no more "alienated from the life of God"
(2:12; 4:18). As the Lord's Prayer distinguishes between, and
yet compares, the doing of God's will in heaven and upon
earth, so Paul insists that "in Ephesus" God's will be learned,
tested, and done (5:10, 17; 6:6). He is far from offering or im-
posing casuistic prescriptions for all eventualities of life — as
if he or any other man could take the will of God in his own
hands, define it infallibly in words, and push it down the
throats of friends or fiends. He only gives admonitions, direc-
tions, encouraging or warning hints. In Ephesians the Christians are addressed not as Paul's children, but as God's children
(5:1). Brotherly advice for the present day rather than a
timeless code is given to the readers of Paul's letters. While
supposedly a stiff moral standard may lift its promoters out
of this world, Paul's summons is by no means a call to an
exodus. The saints already have been called out from the
estrangement, hopelessness, godlessness, and death which held
them captive "in the world" (2:12). They have been called
into the citizenship and the house of God, and they are enthroned in heavenly places with Christ (2:6, 19). But all of
this has happened "in Ephesus," on earth. Christ's descending
to the lowest places (4:9) has reached them where they are.
Christ's dominion over all and his power to fill all (1:23; 4:10)
gives them reason not to give up the world, but to stand their
ground. Therefore Paul exhorts them to "stand up" (5:14)!
They are encouraged not to withdraw, but to "stand" and

"withstand" whatever comes against them in their present position (6:11, 13, 14). Knowing the many varying, tempting,
threatening assaults the saints are exposed to individually and
as a community, Paul asks for wisdom: "Watch out carefully
how you walk; [do it] not as fools, but as wise men . . . for
the days are evil" (5:15-16).

How does the Church "walk worthily"? And what does it
mean for each of her members to walk as a "wise man" on
the evil days from which Ephesus is spared as little as any
other community? These questions have to be answered now.
The main passages, arguments, and key words of Ephesians
that are to be considered, are those that follow.

The Church is called "the fullness of him who fills all in
all" (1:23). This verse is often understood to say that Christ
is full only where the Church is added to him, in which case
the Church would *make* Christ *full*. But the notion that
Christ is "being filled," or "made full" by anything human,
or that he is imagined to be "only" the head of the Church
(as if he were but a part of the body, and not its life!) is not
supported by biblical evidence. In Eph. 1:23 the Church is
most probably designated as that community which is already
filled by Christ, this means that she consciously acknowledges
his dominion and lifts her voice and arms to praise him. But
Christ's dominion is wider than over the Church only; his
praise will be sung by all (cf. Phil. 2:10 f.). "All" men do
not know as yet that Christ is already "filling all." Only the
Church knows it both for herself and for the others. Therefore we may call the Church the first fruit, the beginning,
the example, the sign, or the manifestation of that dominion
and praise which are to be known universally and enjoyed
consciously by all men. The Church is but a preliminary,
transitory, and serving institution. For the time being she
is the only community on earth that consciously serves Jesus
Christ.

But more and more men are to join in giving Christ the glory! The Church is but a representative of those who are being "filled" by Christ, not their full number (Rev. 6:11). On their behalf she praises Christ for reconciling all. She is "giving thanks for all" (5:20). She praises God by making known to all what love and grace there are to acknowledge. The Church will be superfluous one day (cf. Rev. 21:22); but Christ and his praise by "all knees . . . and tongues" will not cease to belong together (Phil. 2:10-11). It is not the Church that is now filling "all in all," or that is in future time or eternity to fill "all in all." For the activity of *filling* with his love, will, and glory must be left to God. The Church can only be thankful and pray that she *and* all men live and will live by *being* filled (3:19; 4:13; 1:23; 4:10). Therefore the "full" or "whole Christ" is not (as is often said) "Christ and the Church," "Christ in the Church," or "Christ with the Church." The "whole Christ" is He who is filling all in all (1:23; 4:10).

"God gave him who is head over all to [be head over] the Church" (1:22). Even clearer than the utterances in Ephesians about the fullness of Christ, this verse proclaims that Christ is not restricted to being merely "the Church's head"; instead, he is "head over all." He is head over both the believers and the unbelievers. The way in which he is "head" is described in 5:23-26 by the terms love, self-offering, and salvation. Not only the Christians, but "the world" is "reconciled with God in Christ" (2 Cor. 5:19). "It pleased God . . . through him to reconcile all" (Col. 1:19-20).

Again, only the Church knows this reconciliation and proclaims it by her conscious "submission to Christ" (5:24). Still, her submission to Christ is not a private affair, but a public service. By her recognition of the "head" in words and deeds and attitude, she proclaims what Christ did for all men. His blood and word manifestly have purified only the Church (5:25-27); but "he preached peace to those that

are far, and to those near" (2:17). Therefore the Church
cannot exist without "making [the Gospel] known" to those
that are still far, and without going out to them "prepared
with the Gospel of peace" (3:10; 6:15).

God is not exhausted by having raised some people in
Ephesus and elsewhere. He is still saying, "Arise from the
dead" (5:14)! Consequently, the Church is not described as
a perfect or exclusive body. But she is the living "Christ's
body" (1:23, etc.) — a body that lives from the head only
where it is a "growing structure" (2:21; 4:15 f.). The Church
is not a closed circle of people, and it must not strive to
become an exclusive assembly of certain classes, races, or
religious individuals. As we have said before, the Church
is an ongoing (act of) gathering. She remains in the process
of formation. When she "grows into the holy temple" (2:21),
then she has the destination to be "a house of prayer for all
peoples" (Isa. 56:7). "All the flocks of Kedar shall be gathered to you" (Isa. 60:7). And she is not to be "a den of
robbers" (Jer. 7:11; Matt. 21:13) that claim for themselves
(by babbling of closed membership or closed communion)
the glory that is God's. The proclamation and manifestation
of "peace for those that are far, and peace for those near"
(2:17) forbid the erection of walls of separation. Israel's
true *raison d'être* is her election and destination to be "a
light to the nations" and mediator of a "covenant to the
[Gentile] people . . . that the Lord's salvation shall reach
to the end of the earth" (Isa. 42:6; 49:6, 8). This mission
is summed up in the words of Ephesians: "You are now light
in the Lord. Walk as children of the light" (5:8)!

So the Christians have been saved by grace alone (2:5, 8),
and they have heard and believed the Gospel of salvation
(1:13) not for their own benefit only. God's purpose was
"to show, by the kindness [exhibited] to them, the abounding riches of his grace in [or, among] the coming ages" (2:7).
And he revealed the mystery of Christ to the apostles and

prophets, and through the apostolate to the Gentiles, "in order now to make known through the Church to the rulers and authorities, his manifold wisdom" (3:10). Because of these very explicit passages, we deem it necessary to consider the "sealing by the Holy Spirit" (Eph. 1:13; 4:30) to be more than a guarantee of the future heritage of those who already are called saints. Rather, those who presently are members of the Church are made a sign and seal of God's claim upon *all* the world. God will use them as his manifest imprint upon earth.

We observe that in all of these passages God's will and ways, his love and might, do not end with the Church. The Church is not the end of all things. But the Church has its place and function between Christ and the world. She is not the mediator of salvation; she is not the savior of the world; she is not even a redemptive community. But she knows and makes known the Savior and salvation. By her very existence on earth, she is a manifestation of God's love for "the world" (John 3:16), of the "reconciliation of the world" or of "all" (2 Cor. 5:19; Col. 1:20), of the power of resurrection (2:5-7), and of God's will to create of Jews and Gentiles one new man for the praise of his glory (1:12, 14; 2:15).

What we have said of the Church applies also to the individual members of the Church. Even as the body of Christ is not called perfect, so the individual Christians are never called perfect in this epistle. All of us have still to "attain to the oneness of faith and knowledge of the Son of God, to the perfect man, to the full measure of the stature of Christ" (4:13). The saints "grow into Christ in all regards" only when they are joined and knit together, when they are being served and are serving as "parts" (or, members) of the whole body and structure of the Church (4:15 f.). No individual Christian can be any better or holier than the Church. Nor can he be relieved of any responsibility that is essential to the Church. There is no member of the Church that can

leave to "the Church" or to some Board of Missions or Department of Evangelism all contact with the world. No member of Christ's living body can enjoy quiet partnership with
the head without participating in the building and growing
that is willed and inspired by the head. Each one of the
saints in Ephesus is addressed in this epistle. Written "to
the saints," it deals with "each one of us" (1:1; 4:7); its treatment is not that of an amorphous mass, an ideal collection,
or a plantlike organism. The Gospel of peace which Christ
preached to those near and far, and the Church's life and
witness to the world are either a concern of each and all
Church members — or they are saboteurs of the perfect work
of God and dead members of a body that is destined to live.
Either they are made light and let their light shine (5:8), or
they are obstructors and deniers of their own salvation. No
one of them has other shoes to use for standing in the world
than those called "preparation for the Gospel of peace"
(6:15). No one of them can walk as a "beloved child" and as
a "child of the light" (5:1, 8) unless he is a "spotless child
of God in the midst of a crooked and perverse generation"
and a "shining light in the world" (Phil. 2:15). "You are the
salt of the earth. . . . You are the light of the world . . . that
they give glory to your Father who is in heaven" (Matt.
5:13-16). In all these statements the saints are saints and
children of God only if they stand, walk, and serve in the
world to the enlightenment and salvation of those who do
not yet believe.

We ask again and more specifically: How is this standing,
walking, and serving done? The "service" will only be honest
when done in lowliness. The "walk" will have to be directed
to one clear goal. The "stand" will presuppose a firm ground
and the decision to stick to it. Under the three headings of
solidarity, witness, and faith, we shall try to set forth the
answer which is given in Ephesians.

I. SOLIDARITY: SINNERS AND SAVED TOGETHER

When Paul explained that by Christ's cross the wall of partition between those far and those near had been "abolished" (2:14), and when he proclaimed that Christ is enthroned "above all" principalities and powers and is the head "over all" (1:20-23), he meant what he said. And when the Church hears this Gospel and believes it (1:13), she is to acknowledge its implications and consequences, whatever they may be. One meaning of Paul's message and one consequence must be pointed out at this place:

There is no wall between the Church and the world!

That there *was* a wall between the elect people and the nations is clear, and its removal must not be forgotten. But this wall is gone; it is no more. Christians who would still believe in its existence, or who would rebuild it or protect themselves by something like it, would only be proving themselves hopelessly antiquated, outmoded, outruled, and ridiculous. How could they admire, erect, or use for a shelter that which is "abolished" and "abrogated" (2:14 f.)?

Yet it has become characteristic of almost all assemblies of Western Christians to take place behind the walls of a church building — behind walls that are meant to keep out interference by the outside world, and that are sometimes adorned by paintings and somber stained-glass windows which enhance the feeling of security, seclusion, distinction, and separation from the world. When Christians meet outside such walls, in tents, stadiums, gardens, or on river banks, they make the headlines and become highly controversial. It has become unusual and surprising, both to themselves and to the world, for Christians to abstain from seeking privacy and seclusion behind protecting walls! Now we have tried to show that according to Ephesians, the Church is created and destined to be the visible, audible, tangible, and public manifestation of the life, love, and power of the risen

Christ. No apology can be made for a cult that stays behind stone, wooden, or steel-and-glass walls, when Ephesians, its author, and Christ, the head of both the Church and the world, are taken seriously. But are not the walls only technical conveniences and necessities for the creation of a beautiful sanctuary and of a worshipful atmosphere? They were, indeed, built by devoted people who were filled with the best of intentions. But in the light of what Paul says in Ephesians about the origin and the purpose of the Church, these structures, whether erected in the open country, on street-corners, or on other well-exposed sites, are striking examples of a general attitude in which Christians have become entrenched and to which they and the world have become accustomed.

Not only walls designed by more or less able architects and built by skillful craftsmen, but walls of statutes and ordinances, of rules and authorities, of respected names and sacred traditions, fence in today's congregations and denominations. All these walls are supposed to serve the separation of the Church from the world. But the same walls also divide Christians, congregations, and denominations from one another; and we are reminded by Eph. 2:14-16 that any wall which separates man from man in hostility means also and primarily enmity against God.

We had better admit that in flat contradiction to the Gospel of peace which Paul preached to the Ephesians in his letter, we have sought and still are seeking salvation in walls. Little wonder that the churches' talk of reconciliation and peace is discredited in the eyes of the whole world and of many Christians. A church that secures herself against the world and against fellow churches by walls of doctrines and traditions, declarations and "distinctive heritages"; a church that in her worship and common life keeps apart different races, nationalities, classes, and age groups; a church that ultimately believes in a limited salvation, and in hell rather than in God's love for the world — such a church can only learn from Ephesians that the world is right in treating it or bypassing it with the pity or contempt fit for the hypocrite. Paul and his letter to the Christians in Asia Minor stand on the side of those who cannot believe that the wall-church is a true or necessary manifestation of salvation from enmity, captivity, and death. The wall-worshiping church serves an idol. It serves but itself, and is blind to the fact that it makes of itself an almost insurmountable wall of separation between Christ and the men who are in need of Christ. We say "almost insurmountable," for the story of the paralytic who was brought by his friends (if not through the door of the building, yet through the roof!) to the feet of Jesus (Mark 2:1-12) prevents utter despair. This encouraging incident reveals primarily that Christ came to forgive and to restore the seemingly hopeless outsider; but it discloses also the devastating function which a wall-forming church can assume. Unless its structure is wrecked from above, it can only be an obstacle in the way of both the needy and Christ himself. In similar fashion, the Gospel of peace preached to the Ephesians is a double-edged sword. It extols Christ "our peace" (2:14) and cuts through the walls of pride, exclusiveness, and self-promotion which Christians are tempted to construct, to uphold, or to strengthen. In conclusion, there is, according to the Gospel of peace, *no* wall between the near and the far, between the Church and the world!

But what about the "great and high wall" that surrounds the "city that descends from heaven" (Rev. 21:10 ff.)? What the seer John was given to see in his vision was not an image of the Church on earth, but of the final and eternal presence of God among men (Rev. 21:3). No temple is in that city which he saw (Rev. 21:22). Therefore, the wall and the ever-open gates that nevertheless do not admit "dogs and sorcerers and fornicators and murderers and idolaters" (Rev. 21:12-27; 22:14 f.) into that city should not be understood

as a symbol of temple or church, or of walls and gates, which
men ought to build or to maintain. When in another vision
John saw Satan, together with Gog's and Magog's hosts, storm
against "the camp of the saints and the beloved city," no
walls are mentioned. This "camp of the saints" is probably
the community of those that are already raised and enthroned
with Christ (Rev. 20:4; cf. Eph. 2:5 f.); it is the Church.
According to what the seer saw, God defends this "camp" from
its enemies, not by walls, but by "fire descending from heaven"
(Rev. 20:9).

But there might still be a wall between those inside and
those outside the Church. The very distinction which Paul
makes between "those outside" and the saints that are "in
Christ" seems to point to it (see 1 Thess. 4:12; 1 Cor. 5:12 f.;
Col. 4:5; cf. 1 Pet. 2:12). That there is indeed a difference
between those that are still far and those that are already
near is obvious even in Ephesians. By the Holy Spirit, God
had made of the saints in Ephesus something which they
had not been before and which the Gentiles in their environment were not yet. Not all, but "you who once were far have
become near. . . . You are no more strangers and sojourners,
but fellow citizens and members of God's household"
(2:13, 19). Only the Church is "washed in the waterbath of
the word . . . to be holy and spotless" (5:26 f.). Of the Gentiles it is said that they (still!) "walk in the vanity of their
minds, darkened . . . estranged . . . delivering themselves to
the practice of every [kind of] impurity" (4:17-19). But
whatever distinctions between the Church and the world are
pointed out in these and other verses, it is typical of Ephesians
that *this* epistle does *not* use a name like "those outside" for
the description of those who do not yet "hear and believe
the word of truth" (cf. 1:13). If they were called outsiders,
then the existence of a wall, and of places in and outside that
wall would be tacitly presupposed and accepted. Then it
would be suggested that some sort of wall has still a right to

stand between man and man, and also between man and God. It is precisely this assumption, and all the attitudes, words, and works that flow out of it or contribute to it, which are warded off with all possible vigor by the author of Ephesians. And he is not alone in this issue.

In Hebrews, the same topic is treated in slightly different terms, but with the same result. "Bodies of [sacrificial] animals are burned outside the camp. So Jesus also suffered outside the gate in order to sanctify the people through his own blood. Therefore, let us go out to him — out of the camp! — bearing the abuse with which he was abused. For here we have no lasting city" (Heb. 13:11-14). This argument, as it moves from the Old Testament ritual, over Golgotha, to ethical conclusions, may puzzle us. But the intention is clear, and a strong point is made. The Hebrews are admonished not to consider the Church, or to establish the Church in its present form, as an "abiding city," but are to "go out [or, to make the exodus] to Christ, out of the camp"! There alone they will find him, because he chose to go where he would be abused. Equally in his commission to the disciples (Matt. 28:18-20; cf. Acts 1:8) Jesus Christ speaks of his full power over all the world and of his presence with his disciples "always, to the end of the age" and "of the earth." Therefore they have to "go," to be "witnesses." Instead of fleeing from contact with the wicked and disgusting world, and instead of cultivating unconcern, neutrality, or contempt for its drab or dramatic, sleek or tyrannical features and history, they have to go out and to stand, like witnesses in a trial before a court, outside, in the world. This is the Church: those who because of Christ's mission are sent out (John 17:18; Mark 3:14).

From where death and darkness, deceit, impurity, and greediness ruled, the saints in Ephesus were chosen, raised to life, and gathered. There God showed the power of his grace. There they can also "stand against the methods of Satan . . . and accomplish all things" (Eph. 6:11, 13). They do certainly need a good and solid armor to hold their place. But among the weapons which Ephesians enumerates in detail (6:14-17), neither soft, wall-like draperies, stained-glass windows, altar fences, private pews, nor sound- bomb- and earthquake-proof hard walls are mentioned. The Church stands *upon* walls; indeed, upon the foundation of apostles and prophets and upon Christ the cornerstone (2:20). But none of these walls separate the Church from the world. They were given by God. They support the Church so that she can stand, well "rooted and grounded in love" (3:17), in Ephesus or wherever else she is gathering. The man-made walls, however, have through the centuries done more harm to the manifestation of love and peace and the abolishment of "the wall" than they have done (alleged) good by stimulating feelings of belonging, of aesthetics, and of intimate fellowship.

Jesus Christ has brought salvation by entering "the deepest places of the world" (4:9). Only when we stand where he stood can we call ourselves Christians. "Access to the Father" we have only "in Christ" and "in the one Spirit" which is his gift (2:18; 3:12; 4:7). The Church does not live "worthily of her calling" when she remains inside and behind walls. But wherever a group of obedient and brave Christians bears some fellow man's burden, there is the place of the living Church — be it in the red-light districts of our great cities, in taverns and dives, in the hideouts of wild parties, in crooked political and business meetings, in Red China, in territories which are being commercially exploited, or in refugee camps, over-crowded and ill-equipped hospitals, and other areas of personal and social disaster.

No Christian will be capable of carrying the sin of the world. Christ bears that burden alone (John 1:29, 36). But the Christian can confess his own guilt by acts of concern, kindness, and help. No Christian can save the world or even a single soul from spiritual death. There is but one Savior and Mediator (Phil. 3:20; 1 Tim. 2:5). But being saved, as an example (or "type," 1 Tim. 1:16) of how the many shall be saved, the Christian can attest salvation in words and acts of solidarity. In this sense, Paul speaks of himself as trying to "save" some of his Jewish brethren (Rom. 11:14) and of a husband's or wife's chance to "save" his or her Gentile partner (1 Cor. 7:16). No Christian has the key to the solution of any of the great problems of politics and economics, of science and culture, of society and psyche. The keys for every abyss and for the sealed book are safely in Christ's hands (Rev. 1:18; 5:1 ff.). But the Christians can be intimates and associates with all who seek and err, who suffer woes and punishment far from the knowledge and consolation of the Gospel. Solidarity and association, inward and outward nearness to those that are still "far" — these are the signs of the holy Church and of the saints that are not ashamed, but are to live in the world "worthily of their calling" (Eph. 4:1).

An objection against such solidarity and association of the Church with those who are still "far" has to be met before we can proceed. In Eph. 5:5-13 Paul writes: "Be sure of this, that no fornicator or impure or greedy man — that is, an idolator — has any inheritance in the kingdom of Christ and of God. Let no one deceive you with empty words. For because of these things comes the wrath of God upon the sons of disobedience. Therefore do not become their associates. . . . Walk as children of the light. . . . Test (or, prove, try to learn) what is pleasing to the Lord. And do not participate together with them in the fruitless works of darkness. Much more, convince [or, expose, overcome]! For it is a shame even to speak of the secret things they do" (cf. 1 Cor. 6:9-11).

It is comparatively easy to guess what Paul meant in speaking of "secret things," and in calling deeds of immorality, etc., "idolatry" (cf. Col. 3:5). For the public and secret attitudes, passions, and actions, of which he thought are enumer-

ated at some length in Rom. 1:18-32 (cf. Gal. 5:19-21). Pederasty (homosexuality) figures prominently among them. In
the same passage of Romans, there is described clearly the
relationship which exists between idolatry and the many sins
committed between man and man. It is not as if immorality
made man an idolator! Paul argues that because God's revelation is not received with praise and thanks, men have substituted idols for God and idol worship for the "knowledge of
God" (Rom. 1:18-24). The acts which we would call acts of
moral depravity and decadence or which we would ascribe to
lack of religion, are by Paul described as the result of (idolatrous) religion. They are consequence and punishment, not
cause and source of man's "failure to acknowledge God"
(Rom. 1:28). Because men are making and worshiping idols,
"therefore," so Paul declares no fewer than three times, "has
God delivered them" to wicked desires, passions, attitudes,
and deeds (Rom. 1:24, 26, 28). It seems that in Rom. 2:17-24
a similar or even closer connection between sin against God
and sin against man is presupposed.

More difficult to explain are the statements of Eph. 5:5, 7,
saying that "no fornicator, impure or greedy man will have
any inheritance in the kingdom" (cf. Gal. 5:21; 1 Cor. 5:9 f.;
Rev. 21:8; 22:15), and that no association with evildoers must
take place (cf. 2 Cor. 6:14-18). Nobody could ever be saved,
least of all such men as the saints in Ephesus who had been
Gentiles "dead in trespasses and sins" (2:1, 5), if immorality
of one or another sort were to limit God's grace and power
to resurrect the dead and to save! We ask if Jesus' entering
into the house of publicans and his eating with them, and
his mercy shown to the adulterous woman and other sinners
(Mark 2:1-12, 14-17; John 8:1-11; etc.) should be ignored,
forgotten, repudiated, or invalidated by that moralizing,
pharisaical, zealotic Paul? Did the apostle ignore the fact
that those who are sick, not those who are well, are in need
of the physician, and that Jesus came to call sinners? Or did

Paul leave it to Jesus to associate with sinners, while he considered such association too dangerous for the saints?

It seems indeed as if Paul were promoting a sharp division between believers and unbelievers. He wrote to the Corinthians: "Do not be yoked in unequal partnership with unbelievers. For what common share have righteousness and iniquity? What community has light with darkness? What accord Christ with Belial? What part believer with unbeliever? . . . We are the temple of the living God. . . ! Therefore walk out from their midst; separate yourself, says the Lord; don't touch anything unclean! Then I will welcome you and be to you a Father" (2 Cor. 6:14-18; cf. Isa. 52:11, etc.). A high standard of moralism, but also a rather pharisaical attitude and a bolstered trust in the existence of a "pure" congregation, seem to speak from these vigorous commands. If they were applied without compromises, the Christians would not only have to seek refuge in no man's land; they would do better to leave the world altogether! We ask, did Paul really want his hearers and readers to draw conclusions which would mean nothing less than complete dissociation, isolation, and retirement from the world?

We cannot discuss or decide at this place whether Paul wrote the rigorous passage which we quoted from Second Corinthians before or after First Corinthians was sent off. Neither is it important now to follow up possible developments and changes in Paul's thinking and teaching. But a third extensive quotation must be heard, if any light is to fall upon the problem of the Christians' association or dissociation with the "unbelievers." That passage is 1 Cor. 5:9-13: "I wrote you in the [previous] letter not to mix up with fornicators. [So I wrote] *not* at all [meaning that you should not mix at all] with the fornicators *of this world* or the greedy, robbers, or idolaters. For then you would need to go out of the world. *But* now [actually], I wrote to you not to mix *if one who bears the name of a brother* is a fornicator,

a greedy or idolatrous man, a reviler, drunkard, or robber —
with such a one you shall not even eat! What have I to do
with judging outsiders? Is it not those inside whom you
[are to] judge? God will judge those outside! Remove the
wicked person from among you!" It is obvious that these words
give to us a specification and an interpretation of both the
rigorous passage (2 Cor. 6:14 ff.) and the seemingly ambiguous passage (Eph. 5:5-12). It is *not every* fornicator, impure,
and greedy man that is excluded from the kingdom, but it is
the "brother"; i.e., the fellow Christian and member of the
Church who is so threatened if he sticks to the life of one
who is "dead in sins." We conclude that what is said about
not associating with immoral men (Eph. 5:7) concerns association with a "brother" (i.e., a fellow Christian); conversation
with the sinners in the world is not prohibited.

What has to be "convinced" or "exposed" by the Christians
(5:12-13) is, therefore, not the sin of the world. As if the
Christians individually, and in their church agencies and
great assemblies, had nothing more urgent to do than to tell
politicians and economists, scientists and artists, and also
gangsters and prostitutes "how bad they are" and that Christians are "against sin"! Much more *in the Church,* "*among
you,* as it is fitting [to your reconciliation and resuscitation by
Christ], fornication and all impurity and greed shall not
exist, not even nominally (or, not even be mentioned)" (5:3).
"Shameful even to speak about" are the evil works therefore
not only because of their immoral character, but also much
more because they happen, though in secret, within the congregation! The solidarity of the Christians with all the sinners of the world does not involve or permit "participation
in the fruitless works of darkness" which blasphemous and
idolatrous Christians are committing under the name of "conformity" with the world's ways of life (cf. Rom. 12:2), or
with other more or less sophisticated excuses (cf. Rom. 6:1,
15; 1 Cor. 6:12; 10:23).

This, then, is the world from which the Christians are to separate themselves according to Paul: Not the world outside the Church, but the world that penetrated into and pops up in the Church, reappearing in the garment of "Christian" compromises, with the enticement of fashionable trends, with the allurements of personal "liberty" and necessary "experience," under the shallow excuse of "weakness," or under the pretense of existential exploration "of the depths of Satan" (Rev. 2:24). The world that makes itself broad inside the Church is the enemy to be fought, vanquished, exposed, and wiped out thoroughly. "Church in the World" — this is God's creation, the Church's God-given privilege and hopeful mission. "World in the Church" — this can only be "sacrilege of desolation" (Matt. 24:15; Dan. 12:11). The interest of Ephesians is centered so primarily upon the announcement of peace to "those that are far" that the steps of consolation, exhortation, warning, and "excommunication" (i.e., the features of what is commonly called church-discipline against the brother who is a fornicator, adulterer, thief, slanderer, apostate, heretic, idolator) are not discussed at any length. Matt. 18:15-17; 1 Cor. 5; 2 Cor. 2:1-11; 3 John 9-10 are some of the main New Testament texts dealing with that issue. From Ephesians we receive only this little hint: "All that is convinced [exposed] is manifested by the light" (5:13). An obscure, legalistic, pharisaical sort of church discipline could hardly be equated with a convincing "light."

But we return to the main issue: the association of the saints with the sinners of the world. The Ephesians are held by a double clutch to accept and to show this solidarity. On one side, there is God's work. It is the establishment of a peace which makes those who are far to become near (2:13). On the other side, are they themselves, the workmanship of God's hand (2:10). They were "in the world" themselves as deep and dead as any man could be. But they were raised.

So they hope for the world with good reason. They know that God is *for* the world. And they are themselves the evidence of God's power to create to himself out of those near and far one new man. They are called and enabled to live and to walk among Gentiles according to their knowledge. By them it is shown, and by them it is to be shown, what riches of grace God lets "overflow" (1:8; 2:7; 3:10). Worldly, estranged, inimical, foolish people they have been. And then, even "now," God's love did not let world be world, or death be death. As first representatives of "all," the Ephesians were saved and raised. They cannot give up, despise, or shrug off the world. They cannot even condescendingly or nobly stoop down to it. They will gladly associate with those who are also to be raised. The Christians will learn and recognize that none of today's unbelievers can be excluded from the power and grace of God. "What do you know, whether you save him" (cf. 1 Cor. 7:16)? Therefore, no Gentile is too bad, no pagan's life too putrid, no erring soul too far away, no miserable man too deep in the captivity of evil: the Christians can recognize in each and all of them their own likeness, even dead men to be raised by God, and men in darkness who have a right to see the light which God has kindled. There is no wall between Church and world. But there is solidarity. Because of God's work, there is hope. "Rejoice with those who rejoice! Weep with those who weep! Live in harmony with one another! Do not be haughty, but associate with the lowly" (Rom. 12:15-16)! There is also work to be done and words to be pondered — "in order that you have [something] to give to him who is in need . . . to impart grace to those who hear" (4:28-29). We conclude with two observations:

1. Solidarity between the Church and the world excludes the claim or pretension that the Church is better than the world. If not the public works, then certainly the hidden things done in the Church (5:12), even immorality, all im-

purity and greed (5:3, 5), are precisely the same things which also the Gentiles do, in whose midst the Church lives (4:17-19). What the members of the Church have done — "once," before they were called "no more" to walk in such deeds — are exactly those works of darkness (5:8), lying (4:25), theft (4:28), estrangement (2:12), etc., which are still typical of the Gentiles' walk (4:17-19). What we said in a previous section on God's judgment on the world was built almost exclusively upon passages in which the Ephesians' own past was described. So the world is not primarily something bad around the Christians but is what the Christians were and where they came from.

But even more must be stated. What the saints in Ephesus are tempted to do and are warned not to do is set forth, not because of some unfounded suspicions or malicious insinuations in the mind of the apostle who addresses them. On the contrary, the world in every one of its deadly forms and forces is still tempting them. Not some Gentiles, but the Christians are admonished "no more" to vagabond about in the shifting winds and waves of human doctrines, devices, and errors (4:14), "no more" to walk like Gentiles (4:17), no more to wear, but for good to throw off, the caricature and grimace of man: "the old man" (4:22), and "no more to steal, but to work" (4:28). It is they who need the reminder that the wrath of God strikes "the sons of disobedience" (5:6), that lies, foul words, bitterness, shouting, dirty talk, blasphemy, "with all badness" (4:25, 29, 31; 5:4) are "not fitting; but rather thanksgiving" (5:4) and mutual kindness (4:32). Bossy husbands, shouting parents, tyrannous masters, over-emancipated women, rebellious children, and hypocritical servants obviously were found even in the Christian congregation (5:21—6:9); else the practical exhortations gathered up in the so-called household rules would be spoken out the window rather than addressed to the saints in Ephesus. These saints have not only been dead in sins (2:1, 5). They need also to be called again to awaken and to stand up from the dead (5:14).

In short, whatever may have to be said about the world is said also to the saints. And whatever concerns the saints, whatever exhorts those who have (already) "become near" to "walk worthily of God's calling," this is also a call to repentance, conversion, hope, and new life extended to those that are (still) far off. If there is a difference between those far and those near in regard to life in temptation and sins, then it is only this: the Gentiles walk still far off from knowledge of salvation, while the saints are made to know, to acknowledge, and to admit God's grace and their sins. They confess the sins and the forgiveness of sins (1:7) as chosen representatives of the world in the world. There is no superior moral standard or performance to separate saints from sinners. But there is forgiveness of sins, a solid ground for solidarity between the believers and the unbelievers.

2. Solidarity between the Church and the world does not depend upon a friendly or even at least a tolerant attitude of the unbelievers to the saints. Solidarity is unconditional. There may be times when state and society recognize the usefulness and freedom of the Church, and when, as in America today, a favorable wind seems to encourage and uphold the Church's serving function. But the Church is not dependent on trade winds.

The writer of Ephesians displays an embracing doctrine of the Church and expects that his words will be heeded, even though the powers that be do not acknowledge their factual subordination to the enthroned Christ. Rather the Church of which Paul speaks finds itself in a continuous "wrestling match" (or, fight; but not, war!) with the powers that be (6:12). The days are evil; the available time is short (5:16); the present world is a "world of darkness" (6:12); the "bad day" (of general persecution, of trials, of tortures — or of a great apostasy before the end of the world, 2 Thess. 2:3?) looms before the door (Eph. 6:13). Satanic methods are used against the Christians (6:11; cf. 4:14). "Flaming darts of the evil one" shower upon them (6:16). Paul writes from the prison in which he is bound (3:1; 4:1; 6:20); and the Ephesians are urgently entreated to accept the exhortation not to lose heart over what he is suffering for the Church (cf. 3:13). So it certainly is not a friendly and sympathetic world; neither is it a "Christian world," with which the Church has to deal. The Church's solidarity with the world may be put to the test under more or less easy or difficult, alluring or disgusting, circumstances. But the Church cannot shift from its position. She is called and equipped to "stand" and to "withstand" (6:11, 13 f.). If she is so "prepared" by God and Christ himself (2:10; 4:12; 6:15) as to "stand glorious before him" (5:27) and to be "holy and spotless before God's face" (1:4), who will prevent her from standing courageously also before the powers that be? After Christ has abolished the wall, no one can force her to build or to recognize new walls of separation and to waver from solidarity. "I am convinced that neither death nor life, neither angels nor rules, neither present nor future, nor [any] powers, neither zenith nor nadir, nor any other creature, can separate us from the love of God" (Rom. 8:38-39). According to Ephesians, this "great love" is exhibited expressly to such men as were "dead in trespasses" (2:4 f.), alienated, hopeless, and godless (2:12).

Solidarity with the world because of God's love is by no means a giving in to the slanders, temptations, and pressures of the world. On the "bad day," solidarity may have to accept a militant character. Then it will mean "resistance" (6:13). Its tools are tough like a leather belt, hard like steel, and sharp like a sword (6:14-17). Whereas the armor of the old, divided, hostile, wall-worshiping man can only prove deceitful (4:22) and perish, the saints can "stand" whatever comes (6:11, 13, 14), "prepared for the Gospel of peace" (6:15). Such is their solidarity: invincible like a true mother's love and kindness, and powerful to withstand all attacks and insults like a well-equipped soldier's spirit.

The last-quoted passage compels us to proceed from this discussion of the Church's solidarity with the world to the testimony which the Church owes to the world.

II. WITNESS: LIVING AS THE BELOVED

Among the many things that have made the Epistle to the Ephesians unique and outstanding among the Pauline letters and other early Christian documents, there is one most remarkable, constantly repeated, unshakable element: the jubilation over the will, might, and grace of God to manifest himself and his perfect work through the Church to all men. He is Father of all and there is no fatherhood (or, family) in heaven and upon earth which is not "named from him"; i.e., given title, place, function, limit — and hope! — by him (4:6; 3:15). Jesus Christ removed the wall between all men and God, and was enthroned above all powers in order to fill all (2:14-16; 1:20 f.; 4:10). The Holy Spirit makes the mystery of Christ known by so enlivening, enlightening, gathering, building, and directing formerly dead men that the community of these privileged few becomes a seal and a light in and for the whole world (1:13; 2:7; 3:10; 5:8). God has already saved those that now are called "saints" or "Church," in order to show to coming ages the riches of his grace (2:1-7). Those who are given to know the mystery of God's will, readily acknowledge that through the Church the same mystery is to be made known to all powers and to more and more men (1:9; 3:10; 6:18-20). The nature and constitution of the Church is such that she is and remains to be a growing body and structure (2:21 f.; 4:15 f.).

Wherever we turn in this epistle, we find two thoughts repeated like a refrain or perpetual *ceterum censeo:* (a) In Christ, God's love works in heaven and upon earth for all.

(b) The Church, inspired by the Spirit, makes this work manifest upon earth to all. Upon these two sentences rests what, in the language of our day, is called "The Evangelistic Task of the Church," or, by an even less convincing term, "The Theology of Evangelism." Both of these resounding titles and catchwords are wanting in truth, warmth, and precision. For evangelism is not one among many tasks of the Church. It is of her nature, and it *is* her nature, if she is the One Church created by God. An extra theology of evangelism has as little need to be contrived as there is need for an extra philosophy, theology, or apologetic for preaching and prayer, for family and education, for church architecture, or for jazz and horses!

But despite the formulation and deficient and misleading character of these two often-heard catchwords, their very coinage shows at least that some Christians have again become aware of what Paul called "being debtor" to all the world (Rom. 1:14). The existence and devoted work of some Mission Societies, and the support given by the "home churches" to missionaries among Gentiles, Jews, and Moslems, obviously has not exhausted the meaning of the words: "You shall be my witnesses in Jerusalem, in all Judea and Samaria, and to the end of the earth" (Acts 1:8). Between Jerusalem and the end of the earth lie Judea and Samaria, the unbelievers of Jewish and Gentile origin. They have their equivalents today in the immediate neighbors of the Western Christian churches; namely, in Israel and in the dispersed Jews; in the people that live alienated from the Church, whether inside or outside the many walls which have been erected; in the communities of social, political, or economic character that wrestle for better or worse purposes; and in the misery or bliss produced by, and continued under, the management of the powers and principalities that be.

In the following pages we do not need to interpret what light, direction, or correction one or another form of the

"Great Commission" (Matt. 28:18-20; Acts 1:8) give to recent theory and practice of "evangelism." But we must point out the distinctive message of Ephesians on this topic. Five theses concerning evangelism impose themselves upon the reader of Ephesians. We put them at the head of our argument and let their exegetical foundations and their practical implications follow.

1. God is his own evangelist, and it is a pleasure for the Church to be used in his service.

2. The Church has no other destination and purpose than to live publicly to God's praise.

3. The members of the Church cannot give anything to the world, unless they receive it, together with the world, always and only from God.

4. The witness to God is borne in lowliness by the whole person of each saint, in every realm of life.

5. Only the true, full Gospel is good enough to be witnessed to the world by the Church.

1. God is his own evangelist, and it is a pleasure for the Church to be used in his service.

If God did not make himself (i.e., his love, might, fullness, mystery, and kindness) known, nobody would ever know of him. Yet "in Christ" he has made known the mystery of his will (1:9; 3:3, 5, 9 f.) and the riches of his grace (1:8-9; 2:7). He is still giving the Spirit of wisdom and knowledge that enlightens the heart (1:17 f.), and he makes the heart firm by letting Christ dwell in it (3:16 f.). So he reveals himself by the work perfectly done "in Christ."

Christ is the perfect evangelist. "He came and preached [literally, evangelized] peace to those that are far and to those near" (2:17). We have shown earlier that not only the words spoken by Jesus in synagogues or houses, on lakeshores or mountains, were meant, but also and primarily the work done on the cross, when the phrase "he preached peace" was used.

According to Heb. 2:3 (cf. Heb. 2:12), the Lord is the first to preach "salvation"; according to Heb. 12:24 (cf. Heb. 5:7 f.), Jesus' blood "speaks better" than anything else. So also in Eph. 2:13-17 it is pointed out that in Christ's (sacrificial, 5:2) blood and flesh and in his (crucified, 2:16) body, the evangel of peace was brought to Gentiles and Jews. The crucified Christ is "The Evangelist." He is "The Apostle . . . of our confession" — as "High-priest" (Heb. 3:1). In the resurrection of Christ, the power of this evangelist becomes manifest.

But Ephesians knows also of other evangelists. Under the crucified and risen Christ stand and work the apostles, especially Paul, as selected, authentic, authoritative, and universal "servant[s] of the evangel" (3:1-9). They can in no way compete with Christ — "or is Christ divided? Is Paul crucified for you" (1 Cor. 1:13)? The special authority, given under and by Christ to the apostles and foremost to Paul, is explained (in Acts 1:1-11, 22; 10:39-41; 9:3 ff.; 22:3 ff.; 26:9 ff.; 1 John 1:1-4; 1 Cor. 9:1 f.; 15:3-11; Rev. 1:9 ff., etc.) by reference to their election for eyewitnessing to the highlight of God's revelation: they saw the risen Lord! "Not from men or by a man . . . but by revelation of Jesus Christ" (Gal. 1:1, 11 f.), an apostle receives his commission. "I became a servant of the Gospel according to the gift of God's grace which was given me according to the energy of his power" (i.e., by the Spirit, 3:7). Not even angels know more or better about the Gospel than the apostle does (Gal. 1:8)! Therefore the apostles are a special, the "first," gift of God (4:7-12; 1 Cor. 12:28) for ministering the evangel which is preached by Christ himself. Paul is called "a chosen instrument (or, an instrument of election) of Christ to carry his name before Gentiles and kings and the sons of Israel" (Acts 9:15).

Again, the apostles are not left alone. "Prophets, missionaries (or, evangelists), shepherds, and teachers" were added to them. Such helpers are "given" to the Church as much as the apostles were "given" by the risen Christ (4:7-11), or as much as they were "appointed" (in the language used in 1 Cor. 12:18, 28) by God. The gift of the Spirit is indispensable for each one of them (4:7; 1 Cor. 12:3-11). Tychicus is among the number of such ministers; as a "beloved brother and faithful servant" he receives a citation in 6:21-22.

Evangelism, therefore, is not a more or less necessary invention, contrivance, or decision of man. As Paul's call into the service of Christ shows (Acts 9:1 ff., etc.), a chosen man of God is not even free to ponder or to decide whether or not he will take up or continue day by day the mission for which he is chosen. Paul says of himself not only that by sheer grace of God he became an apostle of Christ (3:7; 1 Cor. 15:10). He also emphasizes that the grace given to him, is "grace *and apostleship* for the purpose of (harvesting, cf. Luke 10:2; John 4:35-38) obedience of faith among the Gentiles" (Rom. 1:5). So grace *is* apostleship! Now the term "apostle" means "sent-out, missionary, plenipotentiary, commissioner, delegate," and it is used by Paul not only in an exclusive, narrow sense for himself and the twelve (as in Rom. 1:1; Eph. 1:1; 2:20; 3:5; 4:11, etc.). He can call "apostles" all the different ministers of the Gospel that have received a share in the commission to spread the Gospel abroad (1 Cor. 15:7, 9; Rom. 16:7; 2 Cor. 8:23). All — except the eyewitnessing and the special authorization depending on it — that Paul says of himself, can and must, therefore, be applied to all public witnesses of the good news. They have no personal knowledge or salvation that is to be enjoyed only by themselves. The grace given to them is identical in essence, cause, and purpose with their commission to serve to the obedience of faith among those who do not yet believe.

"To each the manifestation of the Spirit is given for the common good" (1 Cor. 12:7). "To each one of us is given grace according to the measure of Christ's gift. . . . It is he who gave [or, made] some apostles, some prophets, some missionaries, some shepherds, and teachers for the preparation of saints . . . for the building of the body of Christ" (4:7, 11-12). "I became a servant of the Gospel according to the gift of God's grace which was given to me according to the energy of his power. To me, the less than leastest among all the saints, was this grace given: to preach [literally, to evangelize] to the Gentiles . . ." (3:7-8). "When I preach the Gospel, I have nothing to boast of myself. For necessity is laid upon me. Woe to me, if I did not preach [evangelize]! If I do this willingly, I have a reward; if unwillingly, I am [still] entrusted with the commission" (1 Cor. 9:16-17). Both aspects are equally important: (a) that the commission to evangelize is privilege, grace, and gift granted by God, and (b) that the grace given by God is far from being lazy, inactivating, benumbing, or stupefying. The grace of God is a living and quickening gift. It makes him to whom it is granted "an instrument of election" (Acts 9:15); i.e., not a man who can feel well in private because of his election by God himself, but rather a herald of God's eternal election of many that are still far. To be an elect man of God means, according to Acts 9:15; 22:14 f.; 26:16-18, to be chosen as servant and witness for the opening of the eyes and for the enlightenment of the Gentiles. Election and salvation are never private. But out of his privacy and egotism, man is chosen and saved to be "a servant of the Gospel" (3:7); i.e., "a minister of Jesus Christ to the Gentiles, in the public [priestly] service of the Gospel" (Rom. 15:16). This concerns every Christian!

But is it sure that not the Church's first "office-bearers" only, not a "clergy" only, whether defined more widely or more narrowly, are given the grace of apostleship and the commission to attest the Gospel to "those that are far"?

According to Ephesians, evangelism indeed does not stop and end with "apostles," whether in the narrower or wider sense of that term. In 4:21 it is certainly presupposed that from the mouth of "holy apostles" (3:5 — including Paul?), and of prophets, missionaries, shepherds, and teachers, the Ephesians "did learn Christ, if indeed they heard of him and were taught in him that [or, as] the truth is in Jesus." So the Ephesians were reached by the evangelism of certain persons and they have profited from the work done by others. Yet this is not all. The missionaries which the risen Christ sent ("gave") to the Church are not only giving and leaving some information. The God-sent gift of preachers and teachers is destined and serves "to the preparation of [the] saints for the work of ministry, for the building of the body of Christ" (4:12).

At this point, a short digression into an exegetical detail cannot be avoided. Guided by many predecessors, the RSV in Eph. 4:12 adds a comma after the word "saints" — with a saddening result. The verse then means that only the special ministers, not all the saints, are called to do the "work of ministry" and to co-operate in the "building of the body." Clerics and laity then are kept apart by God, who gave to the Church only "some" for the ministry of building. Only four verses later, however, Paul says explicitly, according to the RSV, that "from Christ the whole body, joined and knit together *by every joint* with which it is supplied, *when each part is working properly*, makes bodily growth and upbuilds itself in love." This rather free translation of the infinitely complicated Greek sentence makes it sufficiently clear that not only all the joints, but also "each part" has to "work properly," if the body and building shall grow. Paul speaks in 1 Cor. 12:18 of an "appointment" given by God to *each* member, corresponding to the "appointment" of apostles, prophets, teachers, etc. (12:28; unfortunately the RSV uses, in 1 Cor. 12:18 and 28, different English words for an identical Greek original). It seems that in 1 Corinthians 12, as much as in Ephesians 4, the Spirit of ministering and the commission to minister is given to *"all"* (4:13) the saints and to "each" saint (4:7), not to a select clergy only. "To each one of us grace is given"; "to each is given the manifestation" (Eph. 4:7; 1 Cor. 12:7). So much by way of a digression.

In Eph. 4:11 f., it is stated that the ministers given to the Church are destined to prepare (all the) saints *for* the work of the ministry, so that they may "*all* attain to the oneness . . . of the fullness of Christ" (4:13). This means that no member of the Church is chosen or condemned to be either only an observer or only at the receiving end of evangelism. The congregation in Ephesus may have had as many unconcerned, neutral, lazy members as the average church has today. But Paul's epistle calls them to "wake up" (5:14). "By hearing the word of truth, the Gospel of their salvation, and believing it" the saints in Ephesus are "sealed" as God's property (1:13 f.), prepared for work of service (4:12) in the building of the growing body of Christ. They are called to be no more babes that are tossed around (4:14), but to "walk worthily of the calling with which they have been called" (4:1) and to "stand . . . empowered with the strength of God's might . . . their feet shod in preparedness for the Gospel of peace" (6:10-11, 15). We observe that in these verses reference is made to the following things: the true word and Gospel, the actual faith, the unmistakable seal of authority, the right calling, the right spirit, an erect stand, and a worthy walk; even the good shoes are mentioned. Now, the things enumerated are exactly those which we would wish a good (ordained!) minister to have! But the same essentials are named by Paul as the right equipment for each and every saint in Ephesus! All of them are called to be evangelists. The daring metaphor, "shod with . . . the Gospel of peace" (6:15), may indicate that they are carried abroad by the Gospel, rather than that they carry it. The Gospel which they hear (1:13) makes them be something which they were not before. It makes them move, go, dare, stand imperturbably. They are all commissioned and authorized by word and seal (1:13) to stand as well-equipped soldiers in the world (6:13 ff.). No exception is made for certain cases, times, or individuals. That the whole Church has no other function than to make known the Gospel to those who do not yet know it, is stated in 3:10. The mystery of Christ was revealed to the apostle and preached by him to the Gentiles "in order that now *through the Church* the manifold wisdom of God [should] be made known to the rules and authorities."

This is one of the reasons why sometimes the Church (with capital C) is not only called One, Holy, Catholic, but also "Apostolic" Church. The Church cannot possibly be one, holy, and universal, unless she lives as recipient and messenger of the evangel of salvation; i.e., unless she lives as an apostle of the Gospel. She serves the same Gospel which "began to be preached by the Lord, and was solidly attested to us by those who heard it [i.e., the eyewitnesses, or apostles], while God bore witness to it . . . by gifts of the Spirit distributed according to his own will" (Heb. 2:3-4). According to John 17:18-20, Jesus prayed in this sense for the apostles and for the Church: "[Father,] like as thou hast sent me into the world, I too have sent them into the world. I sanctify [RSV, consecrate] myself for them, so that they may be sanctified [consecrated] in truth. I ask not only for these, but also for those who [are to] believe in me because of their word." In Hebrews and in this Johannine text, as much as in Ephesians, the necessity of evangelism is rooted in Christ's evangelizing ministry, as performed on the cross (2:16 f.); and the power of Christ's own evangelism shows in the seizure of all disciples and later generations of Christians for carrying his work further by making it known. The evangel of peace does not come to an end; through the Spirit, God creates and protects the evangelizing, apostolic Church.

To be "saints" and to be the "holy" Church (1:1, 4; 5:27) means, therefore, to be set apart, to be called, to be gathered, to be cleansed and empowered — in short: it means to be consecrated (RSV) by God himself. For what purpose? In order to be a messenger of the Gospel of peace to those that do not yet know and praise God. "Holiness," or "sanctification," or to be called a "saint" — these great and strange terms do more than denote a relationship between God and the Church, or between God and individual men. Sanctification is call to a ministry, appointment, preparation, and equipment for a service which, in God's name, is to be rendered to many. To receive grace is to receive a public ministry. If somebody should doubt that God is any good to him — let him stop the quest for a private interrelationship between his soul and God! Perhaps he has not expected to hear God's good news to him in the many opportunities which he has always had to serve his brethren and to be a witness of grace to them. By refusing to accept the good news which God would give through him to some miserable little brother, he has deprived himself of hearing and believing what grace is — and from receiving grace! Grace and apostolate are inseparable (cf. Rom. 1:5; 2 Cor. 5:18-21; 1 Cor. 15:9-11, etc.).

If Paul, who persecuted and butchered the earliest church, and if the Ephesians, who were not only sick or weak, but also dead in sins, were reached by God, overcome by his love and might, and made saints — then there is no man too bad or too far away to become and to live as an evangelizing member of the evangelizing Church.

We sum up: All the texts which we have so far quoted in order to understand what witness to God's work in the world is (i.e., what evangelism might be) have pointed in one direction. There is not only what might be called an unbroken apostolic succession of evangelism, but there is a kind of Divine Hierarchy at work in one great mission. God, Jesus Christ, and the Spirit manifest themselves in the perfect work of reconciliation and resurrection, in order that sinning, hostile, deceived, godless, hopeless, dead men may be beneficiaries and recipients of life, peace, and revelation. Apostles, prophets, and other preachers and teachers carry the great news to Gentiles and do not labor in vain. There is (though under many temptations and threats from inside and outside) a Church in Ephesus, as in other places of the world. This Church is enabled as a whole and by the conduct of each of her members to be a "light in the Lord; [and to] walk as children of the light" (5:8), and to make known that God is Father of all, that Christ is reconciler of all, and that he rules above all by the gift of the Spirit.

Because of this intimate connection between God's own work and the saints' service, Paul can say, "We are God's fellow-workmen" (1 Cor. 3:9; cf. 2 Cor. 1:24; 6:1), and "Christ works through me" (Rom. 15:18; cf. 1 Cor. 15:10). More comprehensive and less prone to misuse are the following formulations: "The love of Christ controls us. For we make the conclusion, if one has died for all, all have died. And Christ *has* died for all. . . . This is all from God, who has reconciled us to himself through Christ, and has given us the ministry of reconciliation — that is, God has in Christ reconciled the world to himself. . . . So we are ambassadors for Christ; for God is exhorting (or, comforting; or, warning) through us. We beseech you [as ambassadors] for Christ: Be reconciled to God" (2 Cor. 5:14-20). The same concept of ambassadorship is used also in Ephesians and there is connected with hope for joy and boldness. "[Pray that it] be given to me . . . in joy [or, in boldness] to make known the mystery of the Gospel, for which I am ambassador in chains. [Pray that] I may become (or, be) joyfully bold in it! For thus I must speak" (6:19-20).

We may appear to formulate a meaningless paradox in concluding that, by the grace of God, the Church is forced, under Christ and with the apostles, joyfully and boldly to partake in God's own evangelism to the world. God's and man's work, grace and force, force and joy, seem to exclude each other mutually. But the combination of these terms makes sense when we think of the power and character which love has. And they are convincing, when rather than any sort of love, "the love of Christ controls us" (cf. 2 Cor. 5:14). This love is of immediate practical importance.

Again and again questions are raised today; Why is evangelism urgent? Why should it be really necessary? We can answer these questions in the shortest possible way by referring to an analogy which Paul himself uses in Eph. 5:22-33. True love between man and wife compels the wife voluntarily and gladly to show, through her attitude, words, and conduct, in private and in public, that she is "subject" to him who loves her. How much more is the love of *Christ* most urgent reason and necessity for showing the width and depth of *God's* love, and for singing its praise! Only when the Church is "rooted and grounded in love" (3:17), when she acknowledges "the love that surpasses knowledge" (3:19), when she "walks in truth in love" (4:15), when she "makes growth . . . in love" (4:16), when, in short, she "walks in love" (5:2); only then does she live as Christ's bride. The Lord's love and the corresponding bridal love make the Church jubilant. That nothing less than their "first love" had been abandoned or forgotten by the Church in Ephesus, is said in the letter to Ephesus contained in the Book of Revelation (Rev. 2:1-7). Therefore, Paul probably had special reasons to build everything on the preaching of love and the ambassadorship for love.

Ambassadorship beyond any doubt is a service. It involves "necessity laid upon me" (1 Cor. 9:16). But not every servitude and necessity is evil. Even as the apostle introduces himself with a certain ministerial consciousness as "servant of Christ Jesus" (Rom. 1:1 f.), so the Church is entitled to rejoice in her commission by a good Lord for a good purpose; namely, the praise of God's glory. It is the Church's joy and privilege to know and to praise in and before the world the love of Jesus Christ.

2. The Church has no other destination and purpose than to live publicly to God's praise.

It has been held, and it is still believed by many devoted Christians, that the Church is created and inspired by God to serve at least a dual purpose — worship *and* mission. Some have distinguished even more purposes in such passages as Acts 2:42-47, where worship, fellowship, service, and the preaching and teaching mission are carefully set apart and seen in their interrelation. All of these terms are biblical. Indeed, all that is indicated by the four equivalent resounding and impressive Greek nouns, *eucharistia, koinonia, diakonia,* and *kerygma,* belongs to the inalienable forms and tangible utterances of the living Church.

But we observe that this catalogue of essentials is certainly far from being complete. Ephesians would add growth and knowledge, the uniting of Israel and Gentiles, and the oneness in Christ which precedes, affects, and rules the most manifold gifts and the bold joy given to all the saints. Other New Testament books make further contributions to the list of fundamentals. Philippians, 2 Corinthians, 1 Peter, and Revelation emphasize suffering with Christ. The Gospels and Acts put much stress on confession in baptism and before princes. We may further ask why insights and experiences that were given to earnest Christians and awake churches in the course of 1900 years of church history should not also be appended to the list of requirements? If so, we might be more or less well entertained and kept busily at work by making endless distinctions, definitions, corrections, and changes. The maximum that could be so achieved would be a long list of duties which have to be inculcated and performed. We would be back where the well-meaning rabbis and Pharisees have stood since the time of Ezra. Pleasure in quibbling, rather than the "bold joy" or "joyful boldness" of access to the Father and of the evangelistic work to be done in the world (3:12; 6:19-20; Heb. 4:16; 10:35; etc.) would be displayed and would win the day. "The one thing needful" (cf. Luke 10:42) might easily get lost or be forgotten in the tangle of projects and prescriptions.

The testimony which Paul gives in Ephesians to the life of the Church is rich, broad, and deep. It treats of "the manifold wisdom of God [which is] to be made known through the Church" (3:10). But with incomparable clarity and vigor it also shows that the Church is created and gathered, enlightened and commissioned, sustained and equipped for but one purpose: "That we be for a praise of God's glory" (1:12; cf. 1:6, 14); i.e., that we be giving thanks always for all [gifts; or, people] in the name of our Lord Jesus Christ" (5:20).

For a student of Ephesians, it is a matter of course that the response to be given to God's work and revelation in "thanksgiving" and "praise" means true preaching and hearing, brave serving and withstanding, common building and growing, joyful singing and incessant prayer. The manifoldness of the signs of a living Church is certainly affirmed in a way which leads from the one thing needful; i.e., praise of God or thanksgiving, to a great freedom and variety of ways of giving praise and showing gratitude "for all things" or "for all men."

But it is less clear whether the Church, in all her acts and signs, is basically oriented toward two fronts, i.e., toward God *and* toward the world.

If the Church were engaged, certainly *not* in a two-front war, but in a two-front peace, then she would be entitled to feel secure on one side, in the peace with God. But she would be forced to feel worried without end about questions of "peace on earth" (cf. Luke 2:14) and between men. There have been times and there still are congregations in which the Christians have not been and are not now engaged in any evangelistic work in favor of "those far." And, though it is a shame to say so, the omission of all missionary work, the absence of awareness and openness for the task of evangelism, and the intentional seclusion from the world's challenges and miseries, have often gone and are still going arm in arm with a highly cultivated, deeply emotional, uninterruptedly continued liturgical life. Burning candles and scented incense, sacred music, movements, robes, and shrines, but first and foremost, thick and solid church walls give melancholic or sanguine expression to this division between worship in the church and mission in the world. Indeed, there are monastic orders which are a hundred times less guilty of this criminal division than is a schizophrenic sort of Protestantism.

But even where it is conceded and acknowledged that worship must be complemented, filled up, or extended by mission work, and that the axiom *ora et labora* ("pray and work") is obeyed only when prayer in the sanctuary and work in the world receive each their full due of time, concentration, and energy — there is still an underlying dualism at work which creates havoc of the Gospel of peace, of unity, and of the souls of men. Blatant signs of this dualism are the distinction which is still made between clergy and laity, even in Reformation churches, and the differentiation between "holy seasons" and other (unholy?) times.

When things come to the worst — as indeed they have a tendency to do — then the division between worship and mission entails, among other sorry results, the following sacrilegious dogmas: that the Church's liturgy is an end in itself, notwithstanding the disturbing cries of hungry crowds; that an individual's soul can enjoy peace with God, while concern and care for those who do not believe is a secondary affair; that the cleric's contemplative, administrative, scholarly, or pastoral work is more perfect than the layman's industry. As if anybody could worship and please God, when his neighbor is offended or starving (Matt. 5:23-24; Mark 7:9-13)! As if we could love God, who is invisible, without loving the visible brother (1 John 4:11-12, 20-21; 3:14-18; according to Matt. 22:39 the second "great" commandment is "like" the first)!

As if the disciples had first fed themselves to Jesus' glory before they distributed his gift to the thousands (Mark 6:30-44,
etc.)! The disciples certainly were not left hungry when
Christ provided provisions for the great and hungry crowd —
but no mention is made of any little private feast being held
first for them and the Master. According to Acts, even the
Lord's Supper had after Easter the form and meaning of
"breaking the bread" (Acts 2:42 ff.) in the name of the Lord
for the needy (cf. Acts 6:1 f.). Whether held in the Upper
Room (Luke 22:12; Acts 12:12) or in any house or situation,
it apparently was a love-feast (agapē, cf. 2 Pet. 2:13 in some
old manuscripts; Jude 12), rather than a ritualistic ceremony
or "closed communion."

We may yet ask whether or not the Christians are entitled, by the grace of God, to celebrate a particular fellowship between God and themselves, and among one another,
in which the world has no part whatsoever? What church
would that be that does not have, and foster and keep in
and for herself, an incommunicable mystery? What church
could exert any attraction, if it did not have some signs and
gifts, promises and places, "for believers only"? It seems to
be evident that not only the sacraments, but also all preaching
and praying, all teaching and singing, all fellowship and
sharing that belong to the sacraments, are mediators and
indicators of an exclusive intercommunion between God and
his own; i.e., of an intercommunion that necessarily implies
the actual or implicit "excommunication" of outsiders. Therefore, if nothing else, then at least the sacraments and the
sacramental actions and life of the Church seem to create
and to justify doctrines, policies, and practices of a closed
circle in which God and his saints are alone, at least for a
little while, and are unperturbed by the unbelieving world.
Why should it be wrong that the Christians attempt first to
be fed themselves with spiritual food, before they try to feed
others?

The vocabulary, structure, and contents of Ephesians are equally dominated by references to prayer, to the Church, and to worthy conduct in the world. We may expect from this epistle, therefore, more than from other New Testament books, some clear-cut information about the exact relationship between the Church's service to God (worship) and her service in the world (mission or evangelism). Our question at this point is: Does Paul in Ephesians, in the most Churchly of all of his letters, dictate, promote, or encourage the formation and cultivation of a sacramental concept of the Church? In other words, what role has the sacrament in the Church, and what character does it give to her? The term "sacrament" is obviously the very core and criterion of the double issue: worship and mission.

Ephesians uses as little as the rest of the New Testament a term that would be equivalent to the patristic or scholastic, Lutheran or Reformed, concept of a "sacrament." Roman Catholic interpreters give unconvincing reasons for translating "mystery" in Eph. 5:32 by sacrament, thereby making even marriage a sacrament. But though the term "sacrament" is missing, a sacramental ground, structure, core, and nature of the Church might be presupposed or proclaimed. Seven observations can be made by the reader of Ephesians. Their sum will provide an answer to the questions concerning any sacramental nature and dual purpose of the Church.

(a) Of the two sacraments (baptism and the Lord's Supper) that are celebrated, with very few exceptions, in all Christian communities, only baptism is mentioned in Ephesians. The occurrence of the terms "blood . . . flesh . . . body of Christ . . . cross . . . Spirit" in 2:13-18 is hardly proof enough for assuming that Paul wanted to ascribe to the Lord's Supper, rather than to the Cross and the Spirit, the reconciliation of man. The noun *eucharistia* is found in 5:4 (cf. the corresponding verb used in 1:16; 5:20); but the context shows that it means "thanksgiving" in every possible form, and not only

in the shape and act of celebrating or receiving "the Euchar-
ist." Whereas in the first three Gospels (Mark 14:22-25, etc.),
in 1 Cor. 10:14-22; 11:20-34, and in Rev. 3:20; 19:6-9, the
Lord's Supper is the very heart, center, criterion, and summit
of all that is said about the Church, Ephesians does not even
mention it. This does not mean that Paul and the Ephesians
did not know or celebrate it. But the silence of Ephesians in
regard to the Lord's Supper shows that the greatest, the most
important, and the most comprehensive things may be said
about the Church without the construction of a "eucharistic
mystery."

Baptism is mentioned but once. In Eph. 4:5, Paul (in a
creedal formula?) mentions "one baptism" together with "one
Lord" and "one faith." Recently attempts were made to
demonstrate that the term "one baptism" includes more than
the ordinance of Christ as performed by the minister and the
congregation. Christ's descent and ascent (cf. 4:9), the
Church's birth out of the Spirit (Acts 2), and the saints' incorporation into the body of Christ, are all supposedly included in the words "one baptism." But such a sweeping
interpretation of "one baptism" is convincing to but few.
What is more likely is that Eph. 4:5 refers indeed to what is
usually called the sacrament (or, ordinance) of baptism; i.e.,
to that baptism into the name of Jesus Christ which derives
its oneness and weight directly from the "One Spirit . . . One
Lord . . . One Father," and which is received by the One
Body (the Church) in One Faith and One Hope (4:4-6).
Now, since the days of the Church Fathers, other references
to baptism have been read between the lines of 1:13 f.; 4:30;
and 5:26. But that the "sealing by the Spirit" and the "cleans-
ing by the waterbath of the word" are done only and punctu-
ally in and by baptism, has rather been guessed than demonstrated. If Paul had wanted to say that the Spirit of God and
the blood of Christ have bound themselves to the water and
to the ritual which the minister and the congregation use, he

certainly would have done so emphatically. Then he would have put the "institution of the sacraments" beside or above the constitution of the Church. It is both astonishing and important that in his most "Churchly" epistle he does *not* do so.

(b) The places left vacant by the omission of any reference to the Lord's Supper and by only one mention of baptism seem to be filled with utterances of vital concern respecting many other liturgical elements. Prayer and benediction (1:2, 3 ff., 15 ff.; 3:14 ff., 20 f.; 5:4, 20; 6:18 ff., 23 f.), even prayer on one's knees (3:14), preaching and hearing (1:13; 4:11, 21, 29; 6:19 f.), hymns and odes and spiritual songs (5:14, 19; 1:6, 12, 14), a confession of faith (4:5-6), reference to the Scriptures (2:20; 4:8; 5:2, 31; 6:2 f.; etc.; the origin of the hymnic call to "Arise . . ." quoted in 5:14, is unknown), reverence for the ministers whom the risen Christ "gave" (4:7, 11; 3:1 ff.; 6:18 f.), the concept of a house, a people, and a temple of God (2:19-21) — all such elements appear as essential to the life of the Church. As has been pointed out, the language and diction of Ephesians as a whole has a thoroughly liturgical character. Paul is certainly for liturgy and not against it. It is all the more noteworthy, therefore, that the many features of the Church's worship which are mentioned again and again do not allow us to sketch an ideal or, at least, an "Ephesian order of worship" which has only to be recovered, completed, or enforced, in order to make the church the Church. Paul makes it clear enough that there will be prayer and preaching, singing and giving to the needy (4:28), baptism and thanksgiving, when the congregation assembles. But it is by no means a certain series of motions to be performed during certain seasons by certain persons only that the apostle has in mind when he refers to the indispensable elements of worship. He is neither a liturgical reformer nor a legalist disciplinarian.

(c) Paul presupposes that his readers know as well as he

does that there is a fallacious concept of worship not only in the air but followed after with care and precision. There is a people who put Word and Sacrament above all other things. Their Word is the "Law," which they watch, explain, and apply in commandments and statutes (2:15). Their sacrament is circumcision. "Uncircumcision" sounds to them as bad as prostitution, paganism, or excommunication may sound to us. But they use that word for "the others," while they feel that they themselves are under God's care; for they accept and bear his sign and seal (cf. Rom. 2:17 ff., 25 ff.; 4:11). They have a holy book and stick to it. They have a temple and build on it. That they keep traditions, seasons, days of fasting, order, at great expense of devotion, speculation, time, and health (Col. 2:23), may be learned from Galatians, Colossians, Hebrews, and Acts 7. All that they have cannot be swept away merely by cheap labels, such as external, artificial, unnecessary, ceremonial, and rigmaroles. For together with the "giving of the Law and the cult," they have "the sonship, the glory, the covenants . . . the promises, the fathers — and Christ according to the flesh" (Rom. 9:4 f.). But those who have and preserve all these things are *the Jews*. Whether it be irony, grief, or triumph that is shown by Paul when he speaks of the "so-called" circumcision and of the "abrogation" of the Law interpreted by statutes (2:11, 15), certainly he does not intend to lead the saints of Ephesus back into Judaism. The devoted Jewish legalist and liturgist was for Paul as much "dead," "hostile," and "old man" (cf. 2:3-5, 14, 16; 4:22) as the Gentile who lived in the "lusts of the flesh." "We walked . . . like the others" (2:3).

(d) "But now" something had happened and been revealed (2:13; 3:5) which had neither been present nor real in any other form of worship or religion. A mystery — the mystery of Christ (3:3-4) — was revealed that was not unveiled to former generations of men, but hidden from (for?) ages (3:5, 9). It became plain that even the sacrament of Israel, circumcision, was only "in the flesh, handmade" (2:11), while God had performed a work (2:10, workmanship) whose effects prove powerful "in the Spirit" (2:18, 22; 3:16; 5:18), in the hearts (1:18; 3:17; 5:19; 6:6 f.), and whose power overcame even the influence of angels and demons whom the Jewish worshipers feared, despite all careful motions and precautions (cf. 1 Cor. 11:10; Eph. 1:20-23; 6:10 ff.; Col. 2:8 ff.; Heb. 1:6 ff.; Rev. 19:10; 22:8 f.). In his negative hints, Paul in Ephesians does not go so far as the author of Hebrews, who briskly declares the priesthood, liturgy, worship, sanctuary, and sacrifices of the Old Covenant "antiquated, senile, near disappearance" (Heb. 8:13), "worldly . . . according to the flesh" (Heb. 9:1, 10, 13), a solemn "remembrance," but not "forgiveness of sins" according to the conscience and heart (Heb. 10:2 f., 17 f., 22; 9:9, 14). But the distinction between worship "in the Spirit" (Eph. 2:18, 22) and worship "according to the flesh" (Eph. 2:11) is made by Paul also. What he says in Ephesians about word and sacrament, i.e., law and circumcision, points straight in the same direction as Hebrews. John's Gospel contains a similar passage in 4:22-24 (cf. 7:37-39). In consequence, it is unlikely that Paul wanted to promote or to strengthen among the Ephesians a concept and a practice of worship similar to that of "Israel according to the flesh" (cf. 1 Cor. 10:18). The "new man" created of Jew and Gentile in Jesus Christ (2:16) cannot approach God in the way the old man did while living behind the wall of his "Law . . . in statutes" (cf. 2:15).

(e) But what replaces the carefully developed and transmitted, explained and observed, teaching and sacrament and ceremonies of the Jews? Paul is far from writing that there is now "no more" sacrifice, access, or worship to God. Nor does he suggest formless, be it silent or tumultuous, meetings. He reproached the noisy, informal Corinthian exuberance (1 Cor. 14), even as he might today disagree with the quiet, formless Quaker meetings. There is a sacrifice of which he speaks in

Ephesians: "Christ gave himself for us as offering and sacrifice to God, [for] a pleasing odor" (5:2). A solemn act of reconciliation by sacrificial blood and flesh took place: "Through the cross he reconciled both [Jew and Gentile]" (2:13-16). An act of preaching is indispensable: "He came and preached peace" (2:17). The dramatic act of a descending and ascending priest is not missing: Christ descended to the lowest and ascended to the highest places (4:9). A culminating finale sets the last accent: "He sat at God's right hand in the heavenly places" (1:20). And the co-operation and response of the people are not missing: "We have . . . joyful boldness . . . and access to the Father in one Spirit. . . . Be filled with the Spirit! Speak to one another with psalms and hymns and spiritual songs, singing and praising in your hearts, giving thanks always for all. . . . Pray at all times in the Spirit" (2:18; 3:12; 5:19-20; 6:18).

This is the sacrament, the worship, the liturgy which Paul proclaims — even the death and resurrection of Christ, the ongoing operation of the Spirit, and the gathering of a singing and praising people that is called to stand holy and pure before God and Jesus Christ (1:4; 5:27). Because there is one Priest officiating and one Spirit enlightening, strengthening, and directing the saints, there is but one movement, one worship, one liturgy, one common access to the Father — wherever and whenever the saints meet or live. The sacrament around which the Church gathers, the priest's movements and words which she watches, the Spirit's direction by which she is moved to take courage and to rejoice — all of this keeps the Church alive, together, on her ground (2:20; 3:17) and on the move to "walk worthily," and not to "sleep" (4:1; 5:14). Here are indeed visible appearance and signs of the invisible grace. The people gathered to hear from Christ, to let him dwell in their hearts, to follow his call — this is the worshiping assembly according to Ephesians. We note specifically that their worship follows no fixed rule except this one: that it be worship in which Christ officiates, in which his death and resurrection are accepted as the saving and revealing sacrifice, and in which his Spirit is not resisted. This worship has no limits. It is not an affair of one hour of one day a week only, or of special seasons, or of people of certain social standing or race, or of the feeling, the mind, the bodily presence only. The worship to which Paul calls the Ephesians is enjoyment of an open access to God wherever they walk. This will entail, as we shall see later, that their whole conduct in every sphere of life belongs to their worship.

(f) Another observation is necessary. It is sometimes believed and said that the Christians should have as fixed and consistent elements of sacred worship as the Jews had at one or another time. Those holding this belief are postulating only that the Law be replaced by the Gospel, circumcision by baptism, the Passover by the Lord's Supper, the name Israel by the Church, the rabbi by the preacher, etc. Paul makes in Ephesians no such analogies. Interpreters of Paul and promoters of liturgical movements who believe they have found them (in Col. 2:11 f.; Luke 22:14 ff.; Gal. 2 ff., etc.) should be warned by Ephesians. The new man which the saints are called to put on daily (4:24) and to take up as the God-given, unfailing armor (6:11, 13) is created of (or, in the place of) Jew and Gentile (2:15). He is a *new* creature. And in his access to God he rejoices in hearing the good *News* of the *New* Covenant. Conversation and solidarity of the Church with Israel are bypassed hypocritically and actually denied, when in our days Protestant Christian worship — as much as Roman worship and theology since the second century A.D. — is "reformed" after Old Testament and Jewish patterns. To both Jews and Gentiles, the Church obliterates the evangel when she tries to return to the fleshpots of the earthly Jerusalem. Ephesians, with its outstanding liturgical interests, does not invite us behind the cover or into the boundaries of any liturgical wall.

(g) How, then, shall the Ephesians worship God? The answer can only be, publicly! What has to happen "through the Church" is that the mystery be made known to the "powers that be" (3:10). The "work of service" to which the saints are prepared by the ministers given by God (4:11 f.) is the "walking in the good works" of God (2:10) — in Ephesus, and in whatever place, plight, or personal relation the Christians find themselves. To walk among Gentiles "not like the Gentiles walk" (4:17); to be a light where darkness ruled (5:8); to be lowly where pride divides and suppresses people (2:9, 11 ff.; 4:2); to bring the Gospel of peace where enmity is ruling (6:15); to give to the needy from the results of one's labor (4:28); and to abstain from joining in angry, dirty, silly, blasphemous talk (4:31) — of such kind is the "service" to which we are "made," "called," and "prepared" (2:10; 4:1, 12; 6:15).

James goes so far as almost to identify true religion or cult with social service: "Religion that is pure and undefiled before God and the Father is this: to visit orphans and widows in their affliction and to keep oneself unstained from the world" (James 1:27). It may indeed be more pleasing to God to sweep the poor neighbor's kitchen floor on a Sunday morning than to consider participation in liturgical exercises a pleasing odor to God.

In Ephesians, worship in the form of "always giving thanks in the name of Jesus Christ" is mentioned in the same sentence that speaks also of the mutual submission of the Christians to one another (5:20-21). The "psalms and hymns and spiritual songs" to be sung "in your hearts to the Lord" (5:19) do not primarily imply a private, self-edifying process in the individual. "Heart," in Hebrew anthropology and terminology, is the center of will, that which makes the whole man move steadfastly and with undivided attention and devotion in a specific direction. The Ephesians, accordingly, are not told to swallow their songs; rather, they are encouraged to let will and action be concentrated upon only one thing: on the manifold ways of praising God. May they sing when they are working or resting, on "bad days" (5:16) and on easier days; in short, "always" (5:20)!

Correspondingly, a slave's service shall come "from the soul" (6:6). Each word a Christian utters shall be "thanksgiving" (*eucharistia,* 5:4) and "for edification . . . so that it imparts grace to those hearing it" (4:29). The whole life of the saints is designated as "service for the building of the [growing] body" (4:12; cf. 4:16). The words "in the name of the Lord" (5:20) do more than call for special hours of devotion in closet or sanctuary. Indeed, Paul says, "whatever you do, in word or deed, do everything in the name of the Lord Jesus, giving thanks to God the Father through him" (Col. 3:17).

"That we should be for a praise of his glory" (1:12)! These words bid farewell to any comfortable refuge in a man-made house-of-the-Lord. They affirm that the whole and undivided existence of the Church and of each Christian on earth has but one purpose: that God's love and might be manifested to those near and to those far. Witness to God's glory is not one among other essential signs of the Church. But the worship which the Church owes God is a public witness to all men with whom Christians have to deal daily. And the witness of praise is worship to God. To put it in simpler terms: There is only one "service" to be rendered by those that are sanctified. It is service to God in the world, before the world, and for the benefit of the world.

Paul makes this clear when he speaks of the slaves; i.e., of those Christians who appear to have more reason than any others for saying: Only in the meetings of the congregation, only in a sanctuary, only in prayer can we serve God; for in our daily life, we have to toil miserably in the service of other masters and other rules. "You servants," writes Paul, "be obedient to your earthly masters . . . as to Christ . . . as servants of Christ. . . . With enthusiasm be servants — as to the Lord, and not to men" (6:5-7). What Paul says of the slaves' work applies to all Christians. There are not two lords to be served, two yokes to be borne, or two absolute claims to be satisfied. Fellow man does not compete with God in the claim and right to be served. Even if obedience to men is hard, even if men seem not to deserve service and respect, even if the Christian would like to run away from a distasteful position in life and society (cf. Paul's Epistle to Philemon), God still wants to be served by and in the service we render to our fellow men. There are limits of obedience which will have to be discussed later; but even the misuse of human authority does not relieve the saints from the appointment to witness by serving for the benefit of men. They know that there is but one Father over all, one love that will fill all, one Spirit that is stronger than all powers and principalities. Accordingly, the Church and every Christian will always serve God and man at the same time. They will so serve God that what they do is good for fellow men; their service of God thereby becomes "public service." None other than public service is true service to God.

The concept of "liturgy" seems to imply the exact opposite of all this. The term itself is not used in Ephesians, although the epistle bristles with references to acts of worship. We may add at this place that the word "liturgy" has both a proper and an improper sense. The improper, degenerated sense is rampant today; private service of and among Christians only is its nucleus. May it burst! The original and proper meaning of the term liturgy presupposes a relationship, not between two partners only (i.e., God and the Christians), but between three; namely, an employer, an appointed servant, and the people to whom the servant communicates his employer's will. Liturgy is "public service" and has to be sharply distinguished from private or house service of a chambermaid or valet. In the New Testament, the angels, for example, are called "liturgical spirits," not because they stand before God without any care or concern for men, but because "they are sent out [by God] for service on behalf of those that are to be saved" (Heb. 1:14). The same is true of the Church's liturgy. True liturgy is not what it has become behind smokescreens and thick walls, where saintly egotists seem intent upon nourishing their own souls. Instead, it is the public service of those who are commissioned to serve their Master before and among those who do not yet know how good is his will and how mighty is his love.

The public servants of God will have to go to and fro between prayer and the work of evangelism. Even when on their knees before God, they will ask for those to whom they are sent: "I bow my knees before the Father from whom every fatherhood . . . is named, that he may grant *you* according to the riches of his grace to become strong" (3:14-16). And when chained in prison or engaged in hard work, they will rely on the prayers offered before the Lord on their behalf (6:18-20). Worship and evangelism are not two different things, not one inside and the other outside of the Christian's life, not one first and the other second in rank and necessity. But they are one — even as the servant's service to his earthly master is actually rendered "as [by] a servant of Christ . . . as to Christ, to the Lord" (6:5-7). We observe that Jesus Christ's high priestly prayer (John 17) and also Paul's prayer of thanks and intercession for the Ephesians (Eph. 1 ff.) are fully directed to God; yet these prayers are also good news, instruction, exhortation, and help for the disciples, for the many who believe, and for those who still are to become believers. Christ's, and Paul's, service to God was and is actually a service for the benefit of men. The whole Church, that is, every saint, is called to serve, to worship, and to work in this way only.

To say it in other words: Worship is the heart, while witness, mission, and evangelism are the hand and mouth of the Church. Heart and hand are not parts, but functions, signs of the life of the body. According to Ephesians, Christ shall dwell in the heart (3:17), eyes shall be opened by the Spirit (1:18), hymns shall be sung (5:19), singleness shall rule (6:5), consolation shall be received (6:22). With the hands, the good shall be wrought in toil and labor (4:28). And from the mouth only such words shall proceed as are good for the need of building (the growing body), and convey grace and thanksgiving (4:29; 5:4). Every other use of hand and mouth would "grieve the Holy Spirit of God" (4:30). There is no lifting up of the heart to the Lord which does not lift up the hands and voices, too, to work and prayer. And there is no lifting up of hands and voices from evil moods, laziness, sleep, and despair, which can dispense with the direction and energy given from the heart. It is the same one body living from the same one Spirit (cf. 4:4) that manifests its life in giving thanks to God publicly "with heart and hands and voices" for the wondrous things which God has done. Worship and witness can never be separated; one without the other would be dead. The living Church is always and fully both at the same time: a praying and an evangelizing community. Worship is what the Church does in the world and for the world. If all people do not thank God for his work, yet the saints are called "to give thanks always for all" (5:20).

Now the Ephesians might object that the world is too large, the method of Satan too shrewd, the heart of the saints too shaky and weak, their equipment with knowledge and techniques too inadequate for the venture of a public praise of God's work. By raising such objections they would only show that they do not know or love God. God, who did a perfect work in Jesus Christ, does not urge them to make unchangeable plans, to invent earthshaking schemes, to produce virtuosos of martyrdom or public speech, to gather huge crowds of people, or millions of dollars first, or to create some-how an atmosphere convenient and favorable for later preach-ing and evangelical witness, before they set out to worship Him in obedience to their commission. What Paul asks of them in his brotherly and pastoral exhortation is much simpler. He asks only that they shall not resist, "not grieve the Holy Spirit" (4:30), i.e., God's own ongoing work of self-glorification by the Gospel which is preached to the Church (1:13) and is to be "made known through the Church" (3:10; 2:7; 6:15, 18-20). They need not walk on their hands or per-form miracles in order to worship God in acts and sufferings of evangelism. Let them be, simply and plainly, the holy Church to which they were called and gathered, at all times hearing the word of truth and learning, in attitude and in acts, in gratitude and confidence. They are not to let go of the "hope of God's calling" (1:18; 4:4).

As has been said already, they cannot and are not expected to save the world. They are not asked to bear its sin. They cannot make the light shine. But they can bear testimony to salvation by grace (cf. Rom. 1:16; Eph. 2:5-10); they can take here and there, and again and again, a burden from another's shoulders (Gal. 6:2; Eph. 4:28 f., 32); they can let the sun shine, the sun which God makes rise on the evil and on the good (cf. Matt. 5:45). They must not quench, veil, or betray the light which they are made to be and in which they are called to walk: "You were once darkness, but now [you are made] light in the Lord. Walk as children of the light" (5:8)! "Your light shall shine before men that they may see your good works and give glory to your Father who is in heaven" (Matt. 5:16). This is the spiritual worship (Rom. 12:1) and the praise of God's glory (Eph. 1:6, 12, 14) to which the saints are called.

But we ask, How can some men, or a community of men, even when they are "beloved of God, called [to be] saints" in Rome (Rom. 1:7), in Ephesus (Eph. 1:1; 5:1 f.), or elsewhere in the world, be "the light of the world" (cf. Matt. 5:14)? And we may add at this point another question. What good do the Christians receive for themselves when the worship to which they are called is not an exercise for their own sake, but is for the benefit of the many that are near and far? "What then shall *we* have" (Matt. 19:27)?

3. The members of the Church cannot give anything to the world unless they receive it, together with the world, always and only from God.

Nowhere in Ephesians is the Church called high, rich, wise, or mighty. The congregation in Laodicea appears to have made such a claim, and it did not have to wait long for a reply: "You say, I am rich, I have prospered, and I need nothing. And you do not know that you are wretched, pitiable, poor, blind, and naked" (Rev. 3:17). The Epistle to the Ephesians speaks of abounding riches, but those riches are God's or Christ's alone (1:7, 18; 2:7; 3:8, 16). The Church is given knowledge of a mystery that was hidden before the world (1:9; 3:5, 9), but she does not master or marshal it. She is the first that needs to be reminded of it and to learn more about it; she needs still to be "filled for [or, into, with?] all the fullness of God," and to "attain to the oneness of faith and knowledge . . . the fullness of Christ" (1:17 f.; 3:18 f.; 4:13, 21 ff.; 5:18).

The Church is neither called nor equipped to be the world's prophet, shepherd, or teacher. But apostles, prophets, missionaries, shepherds, and teachers are given to her by the risen Christ that she may be prepared to become "wise," to "understand what the will of the Lord is," to be "shod with . . . the Gospel of peace" (4:11 f.; 5:15-17; 6:15). The "preparation" which she receives does not make her a master, but she is prepared "for the work of service" (4:12) and the life of a "beloved child" (5:1). Not for private enjoyment and pursuit of happiness in a quiet corner or in the clouds, but "for the Gospel of peace" is she given the whole armor of a heavy-infantry man (6:14-17). She does not even own her own harness; for her armor is God's and remains God's property (6:11, 13). It has not grown to her skin; for it is not by her own thick pelt, her sharp claws, her weight around the waist, or her cleverness in warding off attacks and insults that she is to "stand" in the world against whatever comes. But in order to be "renewed day by day" (2 Cor. 4:16), she has to "put on" what God has "created" and "made": the one new man (4:24; 2:14 f.), the perfect "workmanship of God" (2:10), even the "whole armor of God" (6:11, 13) "in order to walk in them" (2:10). There is a glory to be gained by the walk in this equipment; but it is not the Church's or some individual's glory. Only God himself (1:6, 12, 14) and his workmanship (2:10) will deserve to be praised ". . . that, seeing your good works, they give glory to your Father who is in heaven" (Matt. 5:16).

The weapons given to the Church and the "good works which God has before prepared that we should walk in them" (2:10) are, according to 6:14-18, truth, righteousness, readiness for the Gospel, faith, salvation, the word of God, and prayer. All of these weapons and "works" are distinguished from individual virtues in a Greek sense, or good works in a Pharisaical sense, by a common feature. They describe a living relationship between God and man which cannot remain hidden. No one of them can be defined so narrowly, or be so squeezed, as to become only a religious, only a social, or only an individual virtue. No one of them can be handled, mastered, or secured. All point to God, who acts in revelation, salvation, and inspiration. All are gifts of God to formerly erring, unrighteous, egotistical, tottering, dead, and hardened men. Only by receiving these gifts and by "taking them up" can the saints stand and withstand what rushes against them. They have no works of their own of which to boast (2:9). Whatever access to God and joyful boldness before God and men they may "have," they have been given "in Christ" who "through the Spirit will dwell in their hearts by faith" (2:18; 3:12, 16-17; 6:10).

It is impossible to determine whether the Ephesians were more tempted by a saturated, self-assured attitude in regard to the world around them (and within them, 5:3-13), or by despair in regard to the littleness and futility of what good a handful of saints might do in "this present darkness" and on the "evil days" (6:12; 5:16). Ephesians seems to be written for both sorts of failures as witnesses, for the proud who preach but themselves, and for the desperate who feel so empty that they never undertake to do or to say anything "more . . . than publicans . . . and Gentiles" (cf. Matt. 5:46 f.). And both sorts of failures in worship and evangelism are still characteristic of many churches today. Paul's message to both of these groups, therefore, needs to be pointed out in somewhat greater detail.

(a) Those who are too shy, too humble, too fearful, too empty, or too disgusted by the world to live as witnesses, are not despised or scolded. Paul knows that they are tempted "to lose heart" over what he suffers (3:13); that the "inner man" — even Christ who will dwell in their hearts by faith (cf. Gal. 2:20) — and the power of the Holy Spirit must again and again be given to them; that they need more strength than they have shown so far (3:16-17); that they have not yet been able to understand the breadth and length and height and depth of the love of Christ and of God's will and power to fill all (3:18-19). Paul is well aware of the desperate, cynical, or merely lazy resignation to "walk like the Gentiles," after the pattern and in the uniform of the "old man." He understands their daily temptation (4:17-22; cf. Rom. 7), especially in "these evil days" (5:16). He realizes even better than they that they must contend against cosmic and psychic, cultural and economic powers that are stronger and more dangerous than anything "flesh and blood" might be to them (2:2;

6:11-12). Paul is plain and frank and honest with the saints in Ephesus, for he is one of them (2:3; 4:13; 6:12; etc.).

Now, in Ephesians, Paul does not call those tempted by many fears, troubles, and inimical forces, the "weak ones" — as he does indeed in Romans, in the first Corinthian epistle, and elsewhere. Rather, he has only a positive message: I pray to the Father "that according to the riches of his glory you [may] be strengthened with power" (3:16). "Be renewed in the spirit of your mind! Put on the new man" (4:23 f.)! "Be strong in the Lord and in the strength of his might! Put on the whole armor of God that you can stand against the methods of the devil" (6:10-11). Paul knows that the Spirit of God is operating powerfully in men that were dead, and that God can and will use this energy "to work within us . . . far more abundantly than all that we ask or think" (3:20). Relying on this power, Paul speaks encouragingly, consolingly, brotherly, and vigorously to the fearful: "Be strong!" (6:10). You can, because God is able to make and keep you strong!

God is asked and trusted to make the Ephesians strong — not for standing or sleeping in a corner, but — to "stand up" (5:14), "to walk (around) worthily" (4:1), and to "stand" in the world (6:11, 13-14). They are being equipped for service. And if only they will step from service to service, from thanksgiving to thanksgiving, from receive and give to receive and give, they will discover in their own experience that the power and the equipment of God are great, sufficient, and good. According to Rom. 1:12, Paul expects to be "comforted" not alone, or for himself first, but "together with" those to whom he is sent. How great and mighty God's love is, will be learned by the saints only when they walk as witnesses for the "Father over all" (4:6), for the Gospel of that peace which was made for those far and those near (2:17), for the resurrection of the dead (2:1-5). Knowledge of salvation grows only when we dare show to this world what we believe. This is what we learn to accept: that every depth is visited by Christ (4:9);

that every captivity is taken captive by him (4:8); that no death is too dreadful, no sleep too deep, to be reached by his upraising call (5:14). Christ was in the world and for the sinners before we became concerned or began to work. And he is even greater and reaches farther than we can comprehend (3:18-19).

The Christians need not worry about their own salvation and edification when they care more than for themselves for those who are not yet of their number. Moses and Paul (Ex. 32:30 ff.; Rom. 9:1 ff.) put their own life and salvation at stake in order to entreat God to save those that had sinned. So unselfish was their ministry! They did not lose anything by thus offering themselves, for God was with them in their labors and sufferings. Similarly, a church that spends itself in the work of mission and evangelism is precious in God's eyes and will receive what it needs. By losing its life, it will find it. The same is true of the church's members. Many have had the experience that the understanding of a Bible passage, of a theological doctrine, or of God's love, does not come when they as individuals have sought it for themselves. But they have been given surprising, refreshing, and enriching insights as soon as they attempted to read their Bible to others and for the benefit of others. When believers seek to explain the Good News to those who have never believed in the Savior — whether they do so by teaching in the church school, by preaching, by conversation with a worried neighbor or colleague, or whether it be by lending a hand where there is need, on the workbench or in the home — always they will be "comforted together" (Rom. 1:12) with those whom they serve.

"Under the test of this service [to the poor], you will glorify God by your obedience in acknowledging the gospel of Christ, and by the generosity of your contribution for them and for all others" (2 Cor. 9:13, RSV). When God is thus glorified, the Christian will not be left empty-handed. "Outside the gate," they will be where Christ has gone (Heb. 13:12 f.). To their own surprise, they will have visited, fed, and clothed him by caring for prisoners, and for hungry and naked people (Matt. 25:44 f.). In the "deepest places of the earth," among "the spirits in prison" (Eph. 4:9; 1 Pet. 3:19), their joy will be greatest. For they will find that there Christ himself is the preacher of peace. Their service among others is a joy and privilege for themselves!

It is in this service which is worship, and in this worship which is service to others, that the Christians gain individual distinction and what is called personality. Up to this point, following the trend of Ephesians, we have been concerned, first of all, with the Church as a whole, and only secondarily with individual Christians; for if they are "saints" (1:1, 4; etc.), then only as members of the "holy" Church (5:27-30). Yet we cannot be unaware of the fact that Paul speaks in Ephesians of "the Church" relatively seldom, while the more personal noun "the saints," and the pronouns "you" and "we" are used much oftener. We may learn from this observation that salvation and revelation by God, that creation of one new man and growth of the body of Christ, and that the worship and mission of the Church do not depersonalize man so as to make of him a mute particle of some collective plant or process. A saint is not an impersonal instrument; neither is he merely a trading post or exchange place, between God and the world. Neither the Church nor its equivalent, the new man created in Christ, is a uniform to be worn, or a nameless, lifeless, senseless, and otherwise mortifying and stupefying pattern to be adopted and cherished.

Instead, the "grace given to every one of us" (4:7) creates *varied* witnesses of Christ. Different profiles are shaped by grace. Some men become apostles, some prophets, some missionaries, and some shepherds or teachers (4:11). Husbands and wives, parents and children, and masters and servants do not abandon the station and place where God's call has reached them. But in the different and changing needs and opportunities to which their eyes were opened by God's calling, they serve God for the benefit of their fellow men, each in a special way, "according to the measure of the gift of Christ" (4:7). "To each of us the manifestation of the Spirit is given to the common good" (1 Cor. 12:7).

Thus, the Church is not a pail of water or a box of sand, in which each drop or grain is identical with every other, and each exchangeable for any other. It is a body having many members which, in their manifoldness, are indispensable for the whole (1 Cor. 12:14-30). It is a building whose growth depends upon a solid foundation, a reliable chief cornerstone, and the addition and function of different materials (Eph. 2:20-22; 4:15-16).

It has been argued that the list of greetings which is now found in Rom. 16:1-16 may have belonged, originally, to the Epistle to the Ephesians. It was in Ephesus, not in Rome, that Paul would know, and wish to greet so many individuals personally. However that may be, the warm recommendation of Tychicus (Eph. 6:21-22) and the character of Paul's greetings in all of his epistles show that his knowledge of the almighty grace of God caused him to respect and recommend individual persons. What makes him remember them? When he gives any reason, he never calls them "good," "pious," or "virtuous"; neither does he give them any title that would indicate a purely individual perfection. He greets and recommends them personally and distinctly because of what they are in relation to God and to their fellow men. He who is a servant of God before many, always gains a noteworthy profile and name. He will be remembered personally. "A man sent from God . . . who came to bear testimony . . . that all believe through him" (John 1:6-8) will never claim any honor for himself (cf. John 1:19-23; 3:28-30). But he will be given some distinct and personal honor, such as is due (and prominently attributed in the New Testament) to a man like John the Baptist. Not by celebrating a cult in a far-off corner, nor by busybodying among crowds, but by worshiping God in the work of service and mission to many, a Christian is raised out of the anonymity of the mass. God gives his servants and evangelists the right to be somebody; to be children, citizens, and persons whose names and achievements are worthy to be remembered.

(b) We turn now to the other group among the Ephesians which Paul addressed with his exhortations. There are those who may eagerly take up the call to be "shod . . . for the Gospel" (cf. 6:15), because they pretend or claim to know the truth, to possess forgiveness, and to be able to mediate and grant salvation to the poor and pitiable outside the haven of the Church. Paul certainly does not fight with windmills, but he makes a necessary and well-aimed stroke when he exhorts the Ephesians "with all lowliness and meekness, with patience, forbearing each other in love . . . to keep the oneness of the Spirit in the bond of peace" (4:2-3). He must have had good reason to place "mutual submission in the fear of Christ" at the head of his counsels for the daily walk in house, society, and community (5:21–6:9). Nobody is a soldier of God (not to speak of an officer or ambassador) unless he is equipped with the armor *of God* (6:11-17) and the cloth of the *new* man (4:23-24). Might it be that already in Paul's time, the Church's evangelism was discredited, because its representatives actually still walked in the ways of the old man (4:22), and showed little knowledge of the "truth in Jesus" (4:21)? Furthermore, they apparently were displaying with loud, angry, bitter, and coarse words (4:31) little "grace to those hearing them" (4:29) and little "thanksgiving" (5:4). Surely, they caused much "grievance to the Holy Spirit of God" (4:30). Such people and their evangelism are not what is meant by "receiving while giving." They reveal rather a preposterous distortion and misunderstanding of the words, "It is more blessed to give than to receive" (Acts 20:35).

On more than one occasion, individual Christians, congregations, denominations, and church councils have brought into disrepute their own public pronouncements. They spoil their witness by undertones and overtones of all-wise counsel, by harsh self-righteousness, or by the attitude of a misgiving plaintiff, a prosecuting state's attorney, or a final judge. To "expose the works of darkness" (5:11) which individuals, society, and economic and governmental authorities commit, appears to some to have become the major task of the Church. All the while, Paul has been writing of "convincing" (or overcoming) first of all those evil works done in the Church by Church members (5:3-13). When Paul reminds the Ephesians of what they have "heard" and "learned" (1:13; 4:21), he means the Gospel of salvation (1:13), the creation of the new man (2:10, 15; 4:24). When he tells them what does convince and what is revealed, he speaks only of "light" (5:13). Christians who scarcely know, or listen to, what apostles and prophets preach to them; writers, boards, and conferences that agree in disliking the terms "revelation," "atonement," and "sanctification"; churches who want to grow in numbers rather than in knowledge — all of these may easily, and do profusely, produce words, declarations, and stratagems for improving the world. They ignore the fact that the Church of itself possesses neither truth nor salvation. She is but a servant to the revelation of truth and the Gospel of salvation. Service means hard labor, toil, repentance, and humility. We may apply to the whole Church what Paul says of the thief: "He who is a thief shall steal no more, but rather labor and work what is good with his own hands, in order that he may be able to give to those in need" (4:28).

It is important to note that pity for those far, in need, and in darkness does not appear among the arguments which Paul uses in Ephesians. To be sure, compassion with the "harassed and helpless," the "hungry," the "sick," and "the crowds" was felt and shown by Jesus Christ (Matt. 9:36; 14:

14; 15:32), and nobody is saved unless by "the mercies of God" (Rom. 12:1). But the gracious love of God is one thing. It saves the sinner by calling him to life and enthroning him with Christ in heavenly places (Eph. 2:4-6). Compassion, or pity of the saved for the lost, is another thing. Human pity is a poor starting-point for the Church's evangelism. It involves the pretense that the Church is like God, or is a substitute for God. But probably there are few people left in the world who care for being pitied by condescending Christians of the Western hemisphere. What in Ephesians is called "kindness to one another, compassionate . . ." (4:32) has nothing to do with condescension. What is called "lowliness and meekness" (4:2) has nothing in common with an enacted display of humility. The self-appointed, big-mouthed, denunciatory or patronizing evangelist is put to shame by Ephesians. He is invited to learn that the Church and her members cannot condescend, because the Church is already "down" as deep as can be, and the Church's service is only done "down here" on earth. We have no right to pity others when the state of the Church itself, despite all assertions to the contrary, is "pitiable" (Rev. 3:17). Instead, we have every reason to confess that our death in sins was like that of "the others" (Eph. 2:1, 3, 5), and that the love, the work, and the power of God are able to raise the dead wherever and whoever they are (1:19; 4:8 f.; 2:1, 5-6; 5:14).

Instead of a haughty pity, God gives his witnesses the "oneness of the Spirit in the bond of peace" (4:3), which proves effective and rich in manifold services (4:7, 11 f.). In a previous section we described this oneness as solidarity in the confession of sin and in the hope for salvation.

The members of the Church can only "give to those in need" when and while they receive the Spirit which makes Christ dwell in their hearts (cf. 4:28; 3:16 f.). The receiving heart and the open hand are inseparable. The hands of an evangelist will therefore labor and toil to receive grace and knowledge from God in order to be able to give faithful witness. As for every man, so for the evangelist, the promise, "Whatever good anyone does, the same he will receive from the Lord" (6:8), is solid, encouraging, and heartening.

4. The witness to God is borne in lowliness by the whole person of each saint, in every realm of life.

The second half of the Epistle to the Ephesians bristles with imperatives. We hear the friendly tone of "I admonish you . . ." (4:1). The Greek word translated in the RSV by "I beg" also means "I exhort," "I warn," "I comfort." We hear also the formal tone of "I affirm and testify in the Lord" (4:17), the brisk tone of command (4:25 ff.) and of warning (5:15), the pastoral tone of encouragement (6:10), and the hymnlike tone of what apparently is a fragment of a "spiritual song" (5:14, 19). In each tone the Ephesians are distinctly told both what to do, and what not to do. "Walk worthily. . . . Let us no more be babes" (4:1, 14). "No more like the Gentiles. . . . Put off the old . . . put on the new man" (4:17, 22, 24). "Put away the lie. Speak the truth. . . . Do not sin. . . . The thief shall steal no more, but rather he shall labor. . . . No putrid word. . . . All bitterness . . . away from you, with all badness. Be kind. . . . Become imitators of God. . . . Stand up, sleeper, arise. . . . Watch out," etc. (4:25-32; 5:1-20). Each affirmation and command seems to entail a distinct negation and prohibition. The life of the saints is directed by "Yes" and "No," by "This" and "Not that," and it suffers no neutrality and no compromises. There is no third way between or around obedience and disobedience.

This great number and intensity of imperative commandments and exhortations has led to several interpretations. (a) It has been said that man must be basically and naturally good and capable of doing good, else he could not be expected to fulfill such commandments, and he would never have been given them. (b) It has been said that the rule of

God over man's life is a great and wonderful possibility which becomes actual only when man obeys the law, accepts God or his grace, and builds his kingdom. So the kingdom was delivered into the hands of man, or divided between God who wills, designs, and prescribes it, and man who has to make it real and actual. (c) It has been said that the imperatives contain desirable goals of perfection, but that perfection is unattainable by mortal man. Therefore, the commandments were considered to be like a mirror in which we see our deficiencies, and are brought to our knees. Or they were esteemed to be directives, less for actual and possible deeds, than for the heart's mood and intention. (d) It has been said that the imperatives mean "absolutely" what they say, and that they do not permit any caviling. They were considered so essential that moral renewal and rearmament of man was sought only in "absolute obedience" to them. Christianity then was looked upon as a conglomeration of legalist statements to the people; i.e., statements that begin uniformly with the words, "You must . . . ," "You must . . . ," "You must. . . ."

None of these four, or of other similar interpretations, does full justice to Ephesians. (a) Paul writes that all men were dead in sin, "by nature children of wrath" (2:1, 3). Therefore, the imperatives cannot appeal to "natural" goodness. Rather they are appeals that gratitude be shown for the workmanship of God and the "new creation" made in Christ (2:10, 15; 4:24; 5:4, 20). The good works which they describe are "fruits of light" (5:9), not of unregenerate man. (b) For Paul, the rule of God and Christ "over all" (5:5; 1:19-22; 4:5-6) is the reality from which all thinking and talking of God and man start and flow. God is Father and King, independently of man's obedience. But he chooses and makes us to be living, beloved, and loving members of his household, and citizens of his realm (2:5 f., 19; 5:1 f.). The Kingdom of God is God's own kingship over all. We cannot "build," but duly proclaim it by our witness in word and deed. The Church is "being built" by God himself (2:20, 22). Only while being built "from the head, the whole body [the Church] . . . makes growth . . . toward the building of herself in love" (4:16). So the Church receives what she is and does, but she does not make herself, or the kingdom.

Furthermore, concerning (c) and (d) above, Paul does not convey exhortations to the Ephesians in order to crush their souls in despair, or to puff them up in conceit. He shows them that God has sent Christ to the lowest places of the earth and raised him above all, in order to save them from Spiritual death in both the lusts of the flesh and alleged righteousness by works (2:1-9). It is God's will to empower them by the Spirit (3:16; 5:18 f.; 6:10 ff.) to live "no more like the Gentiles" (4:17), but "as beloved children . . . in love" (5:1 f.), and as "enlightened . . . children of light" (1:18; 5:8); i.e., as those that "give thanks always for all" (5:20). Nothing is "absolute" in Paul's commandments and prohibitions. All is "relative" to the "workmanship of God" and the "good works which he has prepared beforehand that we should walk in them" (2:10).

This, then, is the meaning of the commandments contained in Eph. 4—6. They show that God, by his work and revelation, calls the whole man, unconditionally, really, and effectively, to a new life. God's eternal will and counsel of grace, the salvation wrought out by grace, the gift of knowledge, and the call to obedience, are uncompromising and unlimited. Every fiber of man, every step of his walk, every thought, emotion and impulse of his heart is destined and called "to be [for] a praise of God's glory" (cf. 1:12). Without the imperatives, no man could really know, or would ever recognize, that his whole existence is renewed by God and saved from death in sins.

It is God's "pleasure" (1:5, 9), "love" (2:4; 5:2, 25-27) and "might" (1:19; 3:16, 20; 6:10) that his eternal "will" and "counsel" be revealed to us (1:9; 3:9-11). The same "will" is also to be "understood" (5:17), and "done from the soul" by the "servants of Christ" (6:6). The question of man's "free will" is not discussed in Ephesians. Free will cannot be discussed as an eventual capacity of those who are "dead in trespasses and sins." Dead is dead. Neither mind, nor will, nor bodily functions and actions are exempt from death in sin. But the resurrection with Christ creates a new man that is neither without a will nor unwilling in regard to God's will. The resurrection shows that God's will is done from heaven for the benefit of earthly man, in order that it might also be done on earth. What was "dead" is called to life. What was captive is liberated. Especially in Galatians (4:21 ff.; 5:1, 13), the whole Gospel is summed up under the keyword, "freedom." To be a "slave of Christ," (Rom. 1:1), to be a "prisoner of Christ" (Eph. 3:1; 4:1), to be bound to Christ's will totally (cf. Gal. 2:20), does not exclude, but involves the privileged position and task of an active "servant" of the Gospel (Eph. 3:7) and of a "beloved child" of God (5:1). God makes man free from the captivity of death (4:8; 2:1, 5 f.) in order that he may walk as a [free] child and [free] citizen (2:19; 5:1 f.) in God's service (cf. Rom. 6). "Freedom of will" is indeed preached by Paul. It is the freedom to stand and to walk as an elected, saved, adopted, and privileged child of God, "in love" (3:17; 4:2, 15, 16; 5:2). An ancient variant reading of 3:12 speaks instead of the "confidence" of "our liberation" through Christ's faith.

The Ephesians' calling is to live as God's beloved, in love (5:1 f.). We should also note that there is no other "call of God to which you have been called" (cf. 4:1). But other doctrines of vocation or calling are still being spread around the church and in the world. Is there not a divine call to the ministry; i.e., to the occupation of a preacher and pastor? Are there not different calls for different people? Is there not a divine call to some to get married, and a divine call to others to remain single; to some to be a carpenter, to others to be a teacher; and to still others to hold out in a subordinate position, whereas others are called upon to bear the responsibility of a superior position? Such different calls or vocations, if all of them came from God, would certainly relieve some members of the Church from any direct responsibility for the "preparation of the Gospel of peace" (6:15); i.e., for evangelism, mission, and witness. What about some "dispensation of the call" which would imply, for the huge majority of the Christians, release *from* the call to bear witness?

For supporting the theory of different vocations, a passage from 1 Corinthians has been frequently used. In 1 Cor. 7: 17-24 we read, "Thus shall every one walk, each as the Lord has dispensed to him, and each as God has called him. . . . Was anyone called when already circumcised? He shall not remove the marks of circumcision. Was anyone called in uncircumcision? He shall not be circumcised. . . . Everyone shall stay in precisely that calling [vocation] in which he was called. Were you called as a slave? Never mind! But if you can become free, take the opportunity. For he who is called in the Lord as a slave, is [yet, or, at any rate] a freedman of the Lord. Equally he who is called as a free man, is a slave of Christ. You were bought with a price. Don't become slaves of men. Brethren, in whatever [status, or station] each was called, there let him remain before [or, with] God." From this passage many interpreters have derived both the comfort and the challenge to consider Jewish and Gentile religion and culture, the married and the single status in life, the subordinate and the higher positions in society, the economic and the political, and perhaps even the distinction of different races, a "calling" or vocation of God. If this were true, the saints in Ephesus would have been exhorted in Eph. 4:1, 3 to "walk worthily" of these distinctions, and to "strive to keep" them alive, rather than "to keep the oneness of the Spirit."

Also it would follow (and, indeed, it has been so concluded

by some) that not only God's saving work and revelation in Christ, but also the place to which we find ourselves assigned by the providence of God the Creator, is an end in itself for a Christian's conduct. It is not only some Lutheran theology which makes the distinction of different vocations and of the equal right of a "theology of creation" to exist beside a "theology of redemption." But far beyond Lutheran churches and theologians, there are found in almost every denomination zealots for different unalienable rights and duties dispensed to different men. The color, the race, the social or cultural standing, and other features of creaturely distinction are then declared sacrosanct. Anything else but "mutual submission in the fear of Christ" (cf. 5:21) and "the bond of peace" (4:3) gains then the upper hand, allegedly in the name of the creator God.

The actual meaning of "calling" or "vocation" in Ephesians, in 1 Corinthians 7, and in the other Pauline letters is entirely different. References to their calling remind Paul's readers that wherever they stood or stand in creation, history, or nature, they have heard the calling of God. Their natural status and occupation did neither extend nor convey, neither did it exhaust, their heavenly calling. Mere observation of the rules or natural laws prevailing in education and society, in economics and among races will not help them to "walk worthily" of God's calling. For if the high calling were identical with the requirements of the place which the saints occupied before the Gospel reached them, thriftiness might be declared the divine vocation of a businessman, shrewdness of a lawyer, total warfare of a soldier, vanity of a scholar, and bossiness of a foreman! But the Corinthians were not called by God either to be circumcised or to be uncircumcised, to be slaves or to be masters, or to be married or single. They were called *in* whatever state, status, or station they were. Their occupation was and is the place or the occasion, not the goal and purpose, of their high calling. The same thought

appears also in other epistles of Paul. Whether the Christians were in Rome, in Galatia, or in Ephesus, whether they
were Jews or Gentiles, men or women, owned or owners, cul-
tured or barbarians (1 Cor. 12:13; Gal. 3:28; Col. 3:11), they
were called with one calling only, with God's call (Eph. 4:1).

This call comes in only one way, and points to only one
goal. It is "through the Gospel" (2 Thess. 2:14), "in one
hope" (Eph. 4:4; cf. 1:18), "in one body" (Christ's! Col.
3:15), "in Christ" (1 Cor. 7:22; Eph. 1:11, variant reading),
and "in the grace of Christ" (Gal. 1:6). It is a "holy [not a
creaturely or secular] calling" (2 Tim. 1:9). It is both from
"above" and for "above" (Phil. 3:14; Heb. 3:1). The saints
were called by God, not into this or that occupation, sex,
color, or social status, but "into his kingdom and glory" (1
Thess. 2:12), to salvation (2 Thess. 2:13 f.), "to eternal life"
(1 Tim. 6:12), "for freedom" (Gal. 5:13), and "for peace"
(1 Cor. 7:15; Col. 3:15). In short, they are "called [to be]
saints" (Rom. 1:7). There is but one call — extending through
the life-span of a man. Different vocations are never mentioned.

How, when, and where do they walk worthily of this calling? The answer to this question, given in Ephesians and
elsewhere, is as clear and emphatic as it could possibly be.
Not by running away from the texture of society or economics,
or from their racial, or marital status! Not by denying that
the saints are "in Rome," "in Ephesus," or in any other location or state! Not by disavowing this world and trying to
escape from it! Not by cursing it, and by repudiating any
participation and solidarity with its woes and joys! But rather,
by being God's holy people who live indeed *in* the world, and
who nevertheless are ever mindful of their appointment to be
holy servants of God, whether married or unmarried, whether
as parents or children, whether as a manager of large estates
or as the last worker on the production line (5:21-33; 6:1-7).
Why should Christ have descended to the lowest places of

the earth, and have ascended to be head over all and to fill all (4:9 f.; 1:20-23), unless it were for the giving of new life everywhere, to people in any and every plight?

A saint is called and enabled to be a saint, not by detachment from Ephesus, or from the tasks, tensions, and joys of co-existence with people to whom he is bound by providence, nature, history, compulsion, or choice. But he is called to be a saint in the very place in which he finds himself. There he is appointed to be "servant of Christ" by "doing what is good" to and among his fellow men (6:6, 8). Whether or not he likes his status and place, and whether he chose it or was forced into it, do not matter. He is given a call which the Gentiles have not yet heard, and according to which, consequently, they cannot be expected to walk (4:1-4, 17). He is warned not to fall back into imitation of their values, standards, and pleasures (4:17 ff.). Whatever his predicament in life, he is not to give up hope, but rather to "know what is the hope of God's calling" (1:18), and to stick to "the calling in one hope" (4:3 f.). The place of living in hope is in this world. The environment of hope is "this present darkness" (cf. 6:12). The strength of God is promised and given to the man who does not run away. It is strength to "stand" and to "withstand" on earth, "in Ephesus," "on the evil day" (6:11-14). The harness given by God is designed to fit and to protect not angels, supermen, or inanimate tools, but the tempted, wrestling, and suffering children of God on earth.

Paul wants to show that in every thought, word, and deed, in every hour of every day, in every earthly position and responsibility, the Christians are called and enabled to bear witness to God by acts of gratitude. Therefore the apostle speaks distinctly of the relationships between man and wife (5:21-33), between parents and children (6:1-4), and between lords and servants (6:5-9). It is a basic mistake to consider these passages merely a collection of "household rules," and to criticize Paul for not adding advice, commands, or prohibitions for the wider realms of labor, politics, culture, and history, for it is not a small part of man's life in the world (the "family-life"), but rather the totality of the Christian's involvement and entanglement with the sunny and seamy sides of daily life that here is daringly and directly brought into focus. Paul discusses, in 5:21-33; 6:1-9, three familiar dimensions of *every* man's life; he treats of these dimensions that are typical and representative of the *whole* of earthly life.

Common to all of them is that man is seen and understood, not as an insulated individual, but always and only in relation to his fellow man. To speak of man's actual life in the world means to speak of his factual and inescapable relation to others. This life-in-relation has the following three aspects.

(a) Man is a *sexual* being. Before Dr. Freud or Dr. Kinsey had put their fingers on this fact, Paul had begun his discussion of actual life with this topic (5:22-33). The numerous references to impurity, wicked thoughts, dirty talk, fornication, harlotry, and pederasty (4:19, 29; 5:3-5), bear this out.

(b) Man is a *temporal* being. He is tied to the generation to which he belongs. He is older or younger; he will be no more, and he is not yet. He claims the right to have time for some one thing, and he pretends to have no time for other things. He is understood or misunderstood; he is an asset or a great problem; he is ripened by years or is still a babe that is tossed around. Not only the days of old age (cf. Eccl. 12:1), but all "the days are evil." A man has to "make the best of [his] time" (5:16). Paul has all of this, and more, in mind when he speaks of parents and children (6:1-4). He knows that it cannot be "well with you" and that "long life on earth" is impossible, unless men, who are entangled in the passing-away time, are given a "promise" from God (6:2-3). Long before the problems of seniority, of gerontology, and of Christian and general education were brought into the light by psychological and sociological studies, Paul saw and respected their urgency.

(c) Man is a *material* being, and part of an economic structure. Honor to whom honor is due! What Karl Marx said, and what many more or less dialectical materialists have said before and after him, has, despite all that may be held against it, a good and solid foundation in Paul's thinking and teaching. Paul speaks of lords and slaves, of owners and owned, of management and labor, of fake value produced to please the eye, of enthusiasm for good service, and of just wages (6:5-9). "Threatening" bosses and the "soul" of the worker are before his eyes (6:6, 9). What he says is applicable to both agricultural and industrial enterprises. He knows what prominent roles greed, laziness, and theft play in man's life (4:19, 28; 5:5).

So this is man: a sexual, temporal, and material being, who, without exception, is enmeshed, and, as it seems, hopelessly trapped in the structures of these three dimensions. Each of these realms appears to have its own constitution, laws, rules, and authorities. Physiologists and psychiatrists, sociologists and historians, and economists and leaders of industrial and rural groups do their best to analyze the laws of those realms in which they are expert, and to show how to move rightly and successfully in them. Paul does not pretend to be all-wise in his understanding of facts, rules, and potentialities, or in his giving of guidance in the solving of all the problems with which man is faced. But one thing he does do. He shows that Christians cannot consider these realms as limiting God's calling, as if they were out-of-bounds for worthy conduct, or hideouts or excuses for letting "bitterness, wrath, anger, clamor, cursing, and all evil" (4:31) govern. Rather the saints are always and everywhere "sealed by the Holy Spirit of God for the day of redemption"; there is no excuse for "grieving" this Spirit (1:13; 4:30).

Indeed, these realms are angelic or demonic in nature (1:21), not tangible and manageable, like "blood and flesh" (6:11). They usually appear to us in the form of necessary,

sacred or cursed, well used or misused institutions, each fostering its own tradition and prospects. The Christians can yet
"stand" in them, and if need be, "withstand" against them
(6:10-13). There is no need, and certainly no call from God,
to run away from them, or to accept their rules and authorities
with holy awe, or to waste time and energy in denouncing
them as diabolic. On the contrary, the Ephesians are called
to be "saints" and to "walk worthily of God's calling" as male
or female, as members of a certain generation, as farmers or
farmhands, managers or laborers, only and precisely within
the social webs and textures. What is unnatural in the Church
is not that there are but few full-time preachers, missionaries,
and evangelists, while most of the members follow "worldly"
occupations; that which is really paradoxical and absurd is
the supposition that a "call to the ministry" is extended to,
and heard by, a few "full timers" only! Ephesians teaches that
all the saints are "prepared for the work of service" (4:12)
and are "to be shod with the preparation for the Gospel of
peace" (6:15). All the saints are "destined and appointed . . .
to be [or, to live] for a praise of God's glory" (1:11 f.). Each
one of them is meant to be a full-time saint and servant of
God, even "in Ephesus," in his respective occupation.

We conclude, therefore, that the opportunity and main
front of evangelism is not to be sought in extraordinary assemblies, enterprises, and methods; Paul mentions nothing of
that sort. The necessity and really great chance for witness
is in the daily life, when and wherever male and female, older
and younger people, rich and dispossessed folks, are con-
versing, meeting, working, toiling, and suffering.

One exception must be mentioned. The realms of profes-
sional theft (4:28), immorality (5:3), and organized lying or
blasphemy (4:25, 31) are such that the Christians can in no
way "take part in their fruitless works of darkness" (5:11). It
is not that the assignment to remain in, to stand in, and to
witness in the world is limited by this radical prohibition.

The exception made by Paul's words reveals that, despite all solidarity with the world, the saints do not participate in sowing for death. As a witness to the "life of God" (4:18) and to man's calling to participate in it, the Church is sent to "stand" in the world and not to succumb!

How do the saints bear a testimony to God under these circumstances? Paul answers by making a series of statements, some general and some specific. Both kinds must be considered.

(1) We have discussed already most of the *general* exhortations: "Become imitators of God as his beloved children. Walk in love" (5:1-2). "Be kind to one another, compassionate, forgiving" (4:32). "Walk as children of the light" (5:8). Do "what is fitting to [or, among] saints"; omit what is "not fitting" (5:3-4). "Stand up, O sleeper, arise from the dead" (5:14). "Walk not as fools, but as wise men. Make the best of the time" (5:16). "Understand what the will of the Lord is" (5:17). "Give thanks always for all" (5:20, cf. 5:4). "Be subject to one another" (5:21).

All such key words and calls may surprise the reader by their general, unspecific character. "Is this all the help we get from Paul?" we may ask; for if so, we feel rather lost among the factual complications, ambiguities, exigencies, and possibilities of daily coexistence with our fellow man in house and shop, in the office and on the street, in school, and in political life. We should not assume that the pressures and lures of daily life in smaller and in larger realms were any' easier to bear in Paul's time than they are today. General malaise and cynicism flourished in the Hellenistic Mediterranean World as creepingly and sometimes as boisterously as they do almost everywhere today. Political threats from the East and North, decay of morals, business, and politics, burden of taxes and pressure of conformity were felt and resented as keenly as they are today.

Why then does Paul give so many generalized exhortations? The reason is simple. In none of his epistles does the apostle have at his disposal a definitive set of values, principles, or patterns; and nowhere does he attempt to master life, to marshal personal decision, to regulate Christian existence by casuistic prescriptions. The life of a Christian is the life of a free child, not of a marionette or a well-made watch. When he obeys God, then he obeys personally the personal Lord, not regulations or eye-pleasing devices (6:6). When he lives as a saint, it is from a heart in which Christ dwells (3:16 f.; 6:6 f.), and not because he has swallowed a stick or pressed himself into a uniform. The life of a Christian is a matter of freedom; a matter of free will, of free decision, of free choice, and of testimony to redemption from statutes and prescriptions of a Pharisaical kind (Gal. 5:1, 13; Eph. 2:15; etc.). May this Christian not become again a servant of fleshly desires (1 Cor. 10:8), of religious exercises (Galatians; Col. 2), or of any "man," after he has been "bought for a price" by Christ (1 Cor. 7:23)! Paul is far from inviting the Ephesians to become his slaves. This is why he must abstain from giving detailed rules for conduct.

All of his general remarks are summed up in the two words, "in Christ." "In Christ" God has in eternity chosen to make the saints a holy and spotless people (1:4 ff.; 3:11). "In Christ," also, not only was a perfect work for those dead in sins completed (2:6-22) and revealed to God's messengers (3:1 ff.), but also "in Christ" the Ephesians are to walk! Thus, God's eternal will, God's work, and the daily life of the Ephesians are held together by a oneness, unity, and bond which bears but one name: Christ. The so-called household rules may resemble, in many of their external features, the kind of moral advice given by Jews and Gentiles of Paul's time; but the references to "the Lord," or to "Christ," are indicative of a great difference.

"Women, submit . . . as it is fitting in the *Lord*. . . . Children, obey . . . for this is pleasing in the *Lord*. . . . Servants, obey . . . fearing the *Lord*. . . . Lords, do the right thing . . . you have a *Lord* in heaven." These words of Col. 3:18—4:1 have a parallel in Eph. 5:21—6:9. They are summed up by Eph. 5:20-21: "Give thanks always for all in the name of our *Lord Jesus Christ*. Be subject to one another in the fear of *Christ!*" What is the "name" and "fear" of Christ, in which we shall walk? To "walk" in, or to "live in Christ Jesus" (cf. Rom. 6:11) may mean that the saints are to think, speak, and do those things which (a) come out of, and show gratitude for God's work of salvation, and give glory to God always (1:12; 3:21; 5:20); (b) show reverence for Him who holds the last judgment (5:21; 6:8-9); (c) are recognized as the pleasure and will of the Lord (5:10, 17; 6:6); (d) are analogous to ("alike as") Christ's own work; i.e., to his love shown in his death for sinners (5:2, 23, 25, 29); (e) treat one's neighbor as a representative and protégé of Christ (5:22; 6:5 f.); (f) manifest that saints are members of Christ's body, the Church, and that they treat each other as such (4:25; 5:30); and (g) let the light given to the Christians shine in darkness (5:8).

This list might be extended, but these seven representative meanings of "walking in Christ" are sufficient to show that even the one strict ruler and rule of the Christians' conduct, Jesus Christ, comprehends a wide field "in" which the saints can walk joyfully, not a small pipe through which they can only crawl. While in other passages (e.g., 1 Cor. 7:10; Acts 20:35) Paul refers to commandments given by Christ, in Ephesians he mentions no other utterance of Christ but that of his "preaching peace" (2:17). It is evident that in this epistle Christ is not depicted as lawgiver, but rather as bringer of peace. The Christians' life is lived under his throne (cf. 1:20), in awareness of his judgment (6:8 f.), and in hope for the day of redemption (4:30). But the "fear of Christ" mentioned in 5:21 cannot mean a slavish, pedantic, ritualistic attitude. This expression can point only to the "joyful bold-ness" of Christians, with which they have access to God (3:12) and an open way into the world (6:20). By their works, words and attitude toward their neighbors, they thank and praise God. They respect and fear Jesus Christ; therefore they fear nothing else in the world.

(2) We are now ready to turn to some of the *specific ex-hortations* which Paul gives. What he says about the common life of man and wife, of parents and children, and of masters and slaves, is preceded and dominated by the call, "Be subject to one another in the fear of the Lord." This one sentence sums up three statements that are vital for our understanding of Paul: (a) a rightly understood submission is pleasing to God; (b) this submission is more than an external attitude; and (c) Jesus Christ is honored by such submission. These three elements will be considered in turn.

(a) When describing the fundamental relationships of sex, age, and economics, in which every man finds himself, Paul always begins with exhortations addressed to the one who is sometimes considered the "weaker" partner. The wife, the child, and the slave are admonished to accept, to keep, or even to enjoy a position which, if judged by common human stand-ards, seems to be dishonoring, inferior, humiliating, and dis-graceful. "Be subject. . . . He is the head" (5:21 f.). "Obey . . . for this is right" (6:1). "Obey . . . from the [depth of your] soul. Serve with enthusiasm" (6:6-7). We gather from these calls to obedience the same impression as that which is conveyed by other literary documents of Paul's time; that is to say, that autocratic women, rebellious children, and hypo-critical servants were not rare exceptions, but were in the majority wherever man and his fellow man lived together. Paul did not express commonly held views; rather he was swimming against the tide of his time when he exhorted the saints to "be subject to one another" (5:21), and to respect the ties and responsibilities between man and fellow man.

But why did he ask for submission, rather than for education, correction, counseling, or guidance of fellow man? Why
should obedience and submission be the primary marks of a
Christian's faith and witness? The answer is simple. It is
because of Christ. The Lord of whom the Christians know
is the Lord who offered himself to God for us (5:2). In his
letter to the Philippians (Phil. 2:3-13), Paul presents an extensive argument showing why, for Christians, the attitude
of "selfishness or conceit," of reluctance to obedience and
humility is impossible, and why each Christian should "count
others better than [or, superior to] oneself" (Phil. 2:3). He
argues that Christ was and is, in all eternity, equal in rank
to the Father ("in the form of God"). Yet Christ does not
treat this equality as a robber treats his prey (Phil. 2:6).
Rather, he works with it. How? By "taking on the form of
a servant," and by obeying God totally and unselfishly in the
midst of men and for the benefit of men, "even . . . on the
cross" (Phil. 2:7-8). Because of this service and obedience,
"therefore," he is exalted above all by God, and "therefore"
he is to be praised by all "knees . . . and tongues"; i.e., by
the deeds and words of all men and all creatures (Phil. 2:9-11).

This is the reason why the Philippians should "always
obey" and "work according to their salvation" (or "work out
their salvation"), for it is in their obedience and service to
God and each other that "God is at work in them" (Phil.
2:12-13). What is it then, to "have the same mind . . . as in
Christ" (Phil. 2:5)? It is to live as willing servants for the
good of men, not although, but *because* the saints are saved
by God alone and made "his children" (Phil. 2:12-15)!

We may sum up the strictly theological core of this argument by stating that, in God's judgment, submission, obedience, and service rendered to God for the benefit of sinners
in no way discredit him who thus humiliates himself. On
the contrary, if dominion, rule, commandment, and superiority are characteristic of the One who is "God," then in

Christ it was revealed that humble service is equally divine, i.e., as "equal to God" as the obedient Son is. God himself sees to it "that all knees . . . and tongues" shall join in the recognition of how high the humiliated One is. His name is above every name, for the salvation of men was wrought out not by a god who is incapable of serving, but by this God who revealed his majesty and might in the mission and work of the Servant-Son. It lies in the majesty peculiar to God that he can humbly serve us. God sustains no loss of dignity by being humble. Moreover, it is precisely our God's unique dignity to prove himself to be holy by saving those who are unholy.

Now we can also sum up the application of Paul's argument. So-called Christians, confessors of Jesus Christ the Lord, use and bear Christ's name in vain, unless by their words and deeds, they live to the praise of the *lowly Servant's* triumph. They know that Christ showed his equality to the Father in the very act of his free submission to God, to obedience, to death, and to the cross, for the sinners' sake. Without ceasing to be divine, he served the sinners' best interests. He made them children. Through him they can show that submission and service are not a reason for shame, but are exalted before God, and should be respected by all men. They trust and labor and wait not in vain. God has promised and will make them receive the same "good" that they do to their fellow men (Eph. 6:8). In Ephesians, Paul exhorts his readers expressly to become "imitators of God" (5:1) and to "walk in love," even as "Christ loved us and gave himself up for us" (5:2, 25). It is futile to ask anyone to be voluntarily and gladly subject to a fellow man, unless he knows of the mystery of God's majesty and love as it was revealed in Christ. But it is equally futile to learn and to make known the mystery of Christ by any other means than by "following in his [Christ's] footsteps" (1 Pet. 2:21). The saints will be "shod with the preparation for the Gospel of peace" (Eph. 6:15) only when they are subject to one another out of "reverence for Christ" (RSV, 5:21).

Anyone willing to decry Paul's call for "submission" as old-fashioned, authoritarian, or reactionary, should realize that the classical Greek and Roman gods — to the extent that they still had believers in Paul's time — did not require that their worshipers should become servants (slaves), either of the gods, or of each other. The Greeks and Romans saw in the Oriental religions a sort of religious slavery, and they despised it. The stories told about the Western gods instilled in men a yearning for liberty, heroism, and power equal to that of the gods themselves. These gods were, in most cases, unable to love otherwise than sexually, and incapable of humiliating themselves except in escapades of rather disreputable character. They had neither reason nor right to inspire a willingness to "be subject to one another." On the other hand, the deities which, in Paul's time, were imported from the East to succeed the ancient gods of Greece and Rome, promised and effected a wonderful uplift of the soul of man. They were believed to convey participation in heavenly being, wisdom, and rest, and they made the discredited life in the body at least temporarily tolerable. Still, there was little necessity or mission "to be subject to one another." Individuals and religious societies cared primarily for their own salvation.

What Paul wrote about God, about Christ, about love, and about submission, was a startling novelty in the first century A.D., as much as it is today in places where the Bible is no more or is not yet known. To refuse to be subject to one another in any realm of life, would amount to the same as a flat refusal to witness to the Gospel, the Christ, and the God whom Paul proclaimed. Nothing else but submission in service for one's fellow man is a praise which is a "pleasing odor to God," and an authentic and distinct sermon to all men, whether they be near or far. If evangelism is the Christian's mission and service to his fellow man, then submission is the way to carry it out. His fellow man has a God-given right to hear and see a testimony of the Servant-Messiah.

(b) Submission has no value when it is an eyeservice, rendered out of hidden arrogance or slavish calculation. "Obey . . . with fear and trembling, in singleness of heart, as to Christ, not in the way of eyeservice, as men-pleasers. But as servants of Christ do the will of God from the soul. Be servants with enthusiasm" (6:5-7). We observe that the references to Christ imply references to reverent, voluntary, joyful, and undivided service. The single heart, the soul, even enthusiasm (RSV, "good will") are mentioned as the seat, source, and character of this service. In Rom. 13:5, a similar statement is made regarding the political responsibility of the saints: "It is necessary to be subject, not only because of the wrath, but also because of the conscience." The "conscience of God" (i.e., the consciousness of God's will and work) is also mentioned in 1 Pet. 2:19. James lashes out against doubt and double-mindedness (James 1:6-7; 4:8), which are the opposites. What is it that makes the conscience, soul, or heart ready for service and submission?

Ephesians speaks of a heart in which Christ dwells (Eph. 3:17), which knows of Christ's mystery (1:17 f.), and which sings to God (5:19 f.). It is the heart filled, enlightened, and made strong by the Holy Spirit (5:18; 1:13; 3:16), a heart whose hardness (cf. 4:18) was overcome. Paul does not promise the Ephesians salvation of their souls, success in their lives, or a miraculous reduction of the world's miseries. No motivation for submission is given other than knowledge of God's work, reverence for Christ, and inspiration by the Spirit. This knowledge, reverence, and inspiration are powerful enough to move and carry the saints from inside. They have a consciousness, they seek and find strength from the inner man (i.e., from Christ, cf. 3:16 f.; Gal. 2:20; Rom. 7:22), and they are sealed (1:13) with a certainty and conviction of which they need not be ashamed (3:12). No one need apologize for acting according to his conscience. Conscience means, literally, both in English and in Greek, co-knowledge. Aware of God the Father of all, of Christ the reconciler of all, and of the Spirit's irresistible power, the Christians are free to serve, to bear, and to stand. Of course, they still need to be strengthened (3:16; 6:10). But if they know anything of God, then they cannot deny, but only acknowledge in gratitude and joy, that God's "power is working in them" (3:20). They will never be masters of the situations which they encounter, but they are so "prepared for the work of service" (4:12; 6:15) that they can be servants to their fellow men "with enthusiasm, as to the Lord" (6:7).

(c) To whom do the saints submit themselves for service when they hear the call to "walk worthily" as husbands or wives, as masters or slaves? Whatever a man's predilection and actual status may be, he finds himself confronted not only by men, but also by institutions and orders. There is the institution of marriage and the family; there are also the political and economic necessities and structures. Such institutions and orders may be considered fundamental and representative of all the ramifications of individual and social life. Whether we prefer to declare that man is moral and society is immoral, or choose some other way of stating the distinction between the individual and society, the question must be answered as to whether the saints, by their submission, render service to men, to institutions, or to both. Who is for them (like) "as Christ," so much so that they are subject to him "as to Christ" (5:22; 6:5, 7)?

The answer given in Ephesians is clear. Husbands and wives, parents and children, and masters and slaves are called to *mutual* submission. "Be subject to *one another!*" (5:21). Direct service to fellow man, rendered "from person to person," from the I to the Thou — this is their calling. But they are *not* expected to submit to some law, rule, or idea of perfect marriage, family, economics, or society. They need not submit to any such "It"; not even to "true being," or the

"power of being." God freed men from death in sin in order
that they might serve *him* for the benefit of *men;* he did not
free them so that they might enter into a new slavery under
institutions and orders. We remember that Paul had in mind
such things as ideals, institutions, orders, and necessities, when
he spoke of "principalities and powers." He comes nearest
to an explicit reference to our concept of "family" in Eph.
4:15, when he states that every family (or tribe, clan, kin,
or lineage) in heaven and upon earth comes from God. But
we note that Paul bows his knees before God, who is *above*
all angelic or demonic, political, racial, and economic clans
and clubs. He does not bow before any one of the latter.
Correspondingly, in Rom. 13:1 he teaches that all powers
that be are "from God," which means "under God" (cf. 1 Cor.
15:24-26; Heb. 1:13; etc.). Does he command that Christians
obey the impersonal institution and order of the state? The
unfolding of Paul's political exhortation begins indeed with
references to the impersonal and institutional "authorities"
(Rom. 13:1-2). But Paul proceeds by calling the authorities
"rulers," "servants of God for your good," *"leitourgoi* [i.e.,
public servants] of God" (Rom. 13:3, 4, 6). He ends the argument with the call for distinct, individual, and personal respect for each one of the many political office-bearers: "Honor
to *whom* [not *which*] honor is due" (13:7). The frame around
this whole argument contains the two key phrases, "peace with
all men, even the enemy," and "love for the neighbor" (Rom.
12:18-21; 13:8-10).

In Romans 13, as well as in Ephesians, striking examples
of how to deal with myths, demons, and ghosts are put before
our eyes. The entire New Testament is directed against the
ancient and modern mythological imaginations and fears.
Man is haunted by the demands which institutions, orders,
authorities, rules, rumors, traditions, and laws make upon
him. He gives them a religious halo. "Family," "marriage,"
"economic necessities," "our way of life," and other similar

expressions, all want to be recognized as absolute values, as realms having their own laws and rules, and as totalitarian claims upon man's devotion. They become idols. It is little wonder, then, that between the conflicting demands (e.g., between business and family, or between liberty and conformity), man is being chased to death, or at least, to mental breakdowns or frivolous cynicism.

The Gospel which Paul brings concerning man's life in the realm of these idols is that man need *not* serve even the best of these institutions, laws, orders, or authorities. A man is called to serve his fellow man; the husband, the wife, the parents, the child, the manager, the laborer — each is to serve the person with whom he is mated or associated in the realm of institutions. As to the institutions, powers, and principalities themselves, Paul acknowledges fully that they exist and raise claims. They have the "names" of "authorities, rules, and dominions." Indeed, they seem to have something religious about them, and they seem to be nearer to God than we are. Yet they are *under* Christ and *under* God (1:20-22; 3:14-15). All of them "have been given One head," even Christ (1:10). "Nobody is God except One. There are many so-called gods in heaven and upon earth, as there are indeed many gods and many lords. But for us, there is 'One God,' the Father, from whom are all things and for whom we exist; and 'One Lord,' Jesus Christ, through whom all things are and through whom we exist" (1 Cor. 8:5-6; cf. Eph. 4:4-6). The knowledge of the One God and One Lord destroys the myth that man must serve institutions, principles, realities, or necessities first, in order to be related to his fellow man. Even ideal institutions, or dreams of ideal institutions, such as those which might be concocted in books and conferences on "a theology of the family," "of the state," or "of the social order," actually tend to separate man from God and from his fellow man. But the saints are called to serve God and man, directly and personally. Both Christians and non-Christians are talking of communism and capitalism, of ideal democracy and absolute conformity, of holy traditions and juvenile delinquency, of ideal marriage and the perfect family. This talk is nothing less than idol worship and creation of new walls between God and man. Paul is not of the party of such idol worshipers, and he warns all saints not to join them.

But what if present institutions, and ideals produced by perfect institutions actually do not recognize that there is only one God, one Head? What if pagan persecutions and pseudo-Christian programs and statutes actually do create a barrier between the saints and God, and between the saints and their fellow men? Paul knows fully that this not only may happen, but that it is the daily experience of the saints (Eph. 2:2; 6:12). The Book of Revelation contains a whole chapter that deals only with this topic (Rev. 13). The answer is that Christians need not be hypnotized or blinded by the pseudo-religious and totalitarian claims of principalities and powers. To be sure, these things are stronger than "blood and flesh." The saints have to wrestle with them daily (Eph. 6:12; 5:16). But the saints are given a power and an armor sufficiently strong to "stand" before, and to "withstand" them (6:10-14). The very commission of the Church is to let "rules and authorities *know*" that the "wisdom of God" has placed them under God and under Christ (1:10, 20-22; 3:10). At their assigned place, under God, the institutions and ideals, the statistical facts and the current public opinions, even all rules and principles, have a right to be, and a function to fulfill. Christians are not enjoined to fight them, unless they are attacked or harassed by them (6:10-14). But the Christians "stand" in the service of *God* for the good of *man,* and not in the service of institutions. Firm in faith, they "resist" those institutions that belie the dominion of Christ (cf. 1 Pet. 5:9).

The saints will learn that institutions, if made "to know" their place, can change. A state can cease from open or secret persecution of the Church. It can change from a tyrannical and chaotic order to a more dignified one that respects the freedom and right of both society and the individual. The institution of slavery has fallen in most countries. Segregation is finding it hard to stand against the demand for equal civil rights for all men and women. Frantic fear, and treatment of Eastern nations as made up of incarnate devils, will not produce any good, and will one day stop controlling Western politics. The belief in arms and just wars is not likely to survive the beginning of the atomic age. City renewals will do away with the institution of the slums. As one form of institution follows another, it seldom can be held that each time the newer is better in all respects than the older, or that it will remain any better in the future. But at least, what was old and wicked and foolish had obviously and publicly to yield, to give in, and to change. And the newer institutions and orders will change, too, when signs of rebellion prove them to be against Christ's throne.

Why are such changes possible? It is not because the Christians can or do make the institutions "good," or that they can bring authorities and rules into subjection to Christ. It is because, through the resurrection, Christ is already head over all principalities and powers, and because the witness of faith which the saints bear in direct service to fellow men who are subdued by wicked institutions, cannot fail to impress and change the authorities and rules. When faithful servants of God "let them know" their stand and place, even demonic powers will be compelled to give up their flat denial of Christ's lordship, a denial which they dared to uphold in foolishness and with pitiable results.

So much about the common elements of Paul's specified exhortations to male and female, old and young, rich and poor (5:20—6:9). We have seen that submission, rendered from the heart, to one's fellow man (not to principalities), is the service which pleases God and for which we are prepared. Such service is actually rendered to God himself (6:5-7).

(d) We proceed by making only the briefest possible remarks on the *individual* exhortations given in particular to husband and wife, to parents and children, and to masters and slaves.

The counsel given to *husbands and wives* (5:22-33) does not include the sentence: "Husbands *must* be heads or bosses over their wives." In ancient times, as much as today, husbands always attempted to be chiefs. They have done so with little enough of success. No one needs the apostle Paul's opinion and advice for beginning or continuing in that futile enterprise. What Paul actually says, by drawing an analogy between Christ's saving work and the husband's headship (5:23-32), is that a husband shall be head in the way in which Christ is head over his own people. Christ exerts a headship of a very particular character. He gives himself up for his chosen partner; he does everything to make the partner (of the New "Covenant," 1 Cor. 11:25) stand "glorious before him" (5:27); he saves the whole man ("the body," 5:23) from loneliness and estrangement, guilt and contempt, and misery and vagabondry. A "great mystery," incomparable love, is the bond of peace between Christ and his beloved (5:32). Christ is the one, and he is the only one who shows what it really means to "love your neighbor as yourself" (5:28 f., 33; cf. Mark 12:31; John 15:13).

Now the *husband* cannot be the savior of his wife; he cannot make her "holy and spotless." What Christ did for his chosen partner, he did out of sheer love; the husband's love for his wife will always include a considerable amount of self-love (5:28 f.). God's and man's love are not identified by Paul, either mystically or sacramentally. Neither the husband nor the church teachers who attempt to counsel him are called upon to consider marriage in its sexual, social, and spiritual dimensions as a "mystery" in the sense of a "sacrament." For, says Paul, what the Scriptures seem to say in that regard, "I interpret as referring to Christ and the Church" only (5:31 f.), not to man and wife. Still, the husband shall be head over the wife in such manner that love and only love is the essence and sign of his rule. May he rule, but after the analogy of Christ! Likewise, may he be subject to his wife, after the analogy of Christ's giving himself up! May the wife be reminded, by her husband's humble love, of Christ's love! The responsibility which the husband is called to bear is so to live in marriage that his love is a witness to Christ's love, and that even the sexual relationship points to the covenant and peace which God has granted. This is what his wife is entitled to expect. God gave her no less a right in Jesus Christ.

It appears that such exhortation was as necessary in Paul's time as it is today. In Eph. 5:22-33, the bossy husband who treats his wife with contempt receives much longer and much more incisive commands and advice than the wife. The obvious presupposition is that there were husbands who only used, clothed, fed, and promenaded their wives — much as farmers do their prize cows at a fair. Such husbands are called to be heads of their wives by loving them with a love that responds and corresponds to Christ's love. Therefore not only the wife, but also the husband is called to "be subject one to the other" (5:21). Whether or not the wife is a Christian and "walks worthily" of God's calling, the husband is honored with the call to be head; i.e., to "go ahead" in loving her!

The submission to, and respect for, the husband, to which the *wife* is specifically admonished (5:22, 33), is by no means the submissiveness of a pussycat or a crouching dog. The translators of the Revised Standard Version made an unfortunate choice when they used the word "submissive" in 1 Pet. 3:1. Paul (and Peter also) is thinking of a voluntary, free, joyful, and thankful partnership, as the analogy of the relationship of the Church to Christ shows. Partnership in a covenant and under the bond of peace — that is marriage in Paul's teaching. The words "be subject!" imply that the wife is to be a "subject" in the sense of a person, a fellow citizen, a full member of God's household (cf. 2:19). By following freely the man who chose her, and by becoming one flesh (or body) with the husband (5:31), the wife enters upon a ground on which she can stand and be somebody. She finds a root upon which she can grow, even as the Church, rooted and grounded in the love of Christ, can stand and grow (2:21 f.; 3:17; 4:12-16; 6:11, 13 f.).

Again it appears that such exhortation was as necessary in Paul's time as it is today. Paul speaks to women seeking emancipation and trying to build up their personalities on other grounds than their husbands' love, and who thus were about to separate themselves from the root of solidarity and partnership with their husbands. And he equally addresses women who have stopped striving, seeking, and growing after reaching the haven of wedlock. The form of witness and evangelism to which they all are called, is readiness to serve without any selfish interests, upon the ground of love. In many cases a husband will need to learn from his wife what it means to "give oneself up" for the service of a fellow man. Too easily and vainly he excuses himself with the pretense that he is serving institutions.

Parents are not admonished to impose their will on the children (6:1-4); neither are children told to swallow blindly the will of the senior generation. "Breaking the will of the youngsters" is as little the gist of responsible parenthood as servile submissiveness is the ideal behavior of children. Paul reminds fathers and mothers that they themselves have to walk "in the discipline and instruction" of the Lord. If any angry will has to be broken while they engage in "bringing up" children, it is their own (6:4; Col. 3:21). They are to bear public witness to Christ by showing their children that they accept not some educational theory or materialistic philosophy, but the direction given by Christ when he "gave himself [up] for" those dead in sin.

Paul reminds the children that to have and to honor parents is equal to having a promise from God. The parents have already lived longer upon earth than the children. They have already received blessings of which the children have had no experience as yet. But the children, too, shall live long under God's blessing (6:2-3). Unable to choose, they were given their parents. It is only "right" that each child should respect and obey the gracious will of God as represented by his father and mother (6:1). However much parents may fail in not submitting themselves first to the "discipline and instruction of the Lord," the children's behavior shows whether or not they, as children, are willing to live as children of God, by being obedient and of service to fellow man. Freedom is not found in arbitrariness, in the alleged choice to serve or not to serve fellow man, to murder or not to murder, to curse or not to curse, or to let starve or to feed the hungry. The freedom to which God has freed his children (cf. Gal. 5:1) is the ability and power to stand for and to do "what is right."

According to Eph. 6:5-9, *masters and slaves* are not bidden to maintain, either by force or with a fatalistic attitude, the institution of slavery. Philemon is admonished by Paul with almost irresistible pressure and arguments, legally to release his runaway slave Onesimus (see the Epistle to Philemon). But "running away" is not the solution of social problems or of factual misery; nor is it the sum of Christian ethics. Paul had written about slaves: "Were you called as a slave? Never mind. But if you can become free, take the opportunity" (1 Cor. 7:21). Onesimus must have misinterpreted the second half of such counsel. In the case of the marriages of which Paul wrote, one partner was not a Christian (1 Cor. 7:12-16). Similarly it is probable that among the masters and slaves in the same house, only one of the partners, be it slave or master, was a member of the Church. In either case, Paul did not preclude, but rather opened the possibility of a separation of the ties. But in the case of divorce, as much as in the case of the liberation of slaves, Paul asked for a voluntary agreement of both partners. When it did not exist, when Christians remained inextricably chained to powers stronger than their wishes for freedom, he saw that there was still a way — indeed, an even clearer way — to bear witness to Christ.

The testimony of laborer and master to the love and rule of Christ is "singleness of heart," enthusiasm for work that serves one's fellow man, and awareness of the final and just judgment of the Lord himself. Such singleness, enthusiasm and awareness are gifts of the Holy Spirit. They are given despite man's entanglement in traditional social and economical textures and structures. Actually, they are granted especially to the saints that are under such pressure. "Whatever good anyone does, the same he will receive from the Lord" (6:8). Consequently, there is no situation so bad or so hopeless that in it Christians cannot give a witness for the faith, and give an "account of the hope that is in us . . . with gentleness and reverence, having a good conscience. . . . Who is there to harm you when you are zealous for what is good? But even if you do suffer for righteousness' sake, you are blessed" (1 Pet. 3:13-16).

The ways of giving witness to Christ and giving an account of the faith that is in us are as many and as varied as the different necessities, opportunities, and chances of the Christian's daily contact with his fellow men. The Epistle to the Ephesians shows distinctly that the attitude, the words, and the deeds of each and *every* Christian count significantly for witness and evangelism.

But now God has given the Church some members that serve primarily by *preaching*. In Ephesians they are called apostles, prophets, missionaries, shepherds, and teachers. We shall call them "ministers of the Word." As a "gift" of the risen Christ (4:7, 11), they are respected and some are given the title, "holy apostles and prophets" (3:5). A man like Tychicus is recommended for friendly and trusting reception

(6:21-22). For the preaching of the Word, the congregation is asked to pray and intercede before God (6:18-20). A solemn act of laying on of hands is mentioned in other books of the New Testament (Acts 6:6; 13:1-3; 1 Tim. 4:14; 6:12 (?); 2 Tim. 1:6; cf. Rev. 1:17). Imposition of hands by members of the church did not make those men ministers, but it recognized them as a gift of God. What we call "ordination" is an act of intercession comparable to the laying on of hands upon sick people, and upon those who had been baptized, but had not yet received the Spirit (Acts 8:15, 17; 9:12, 17; 19:6). We now must ask if the witness to Christ given by gifted preachers is in any way qualitatively different from the mission which every Christian carries out by his attitude, word, deed, and suffering?

In Ephesians the witness by the preached and taught Word has indeed an outstanding function to fulfill which cannot be left behind, and for which not even acts of love, devotion, and service done between Christians and fellow men can be substituted. Paul shows the unique role of the (preached) Word on every page of his epistle, for the Church is dependent on the preached Word in all phases of its life. The Ephesians' "hearing and believing" the Gospel is mentioned before their "love toward all the saints" is acknowledged (1:13, 15). Christ's "preaching peace" opens our "access to the Father in one Spirit" (2:17 f.). The Church, "built on the foundation of apostles and prophets" (2:20), will have members "rooted and grounded in love" (3:17). In the Gospel which was made known to Paul, which is being made known to the Church, and which is to be made known by the Church, the mystery of Christ was and is revealed (3:3-10). The ministers of the Word and their service "for the preparation of saints" (4:11 f.) are mentioned before the witness of husbands, wives, children, and slaves (5:21—6:9) are discussed. The sins of the tongue (such as lies, foul words, clamor, curses, filthy, and silly talk) are weighed as heavily as immoral deeds. It is surprising, but revealing, that Paul refers to these sins of the tongue again and again (4:25, 29, 31; 5:3 f., 12). To put it more briefly, words spoken to a fellow man are as much deeds as services rendered to him by hand. To "walk in truth, in love" is indeed, as the traditional versions say, an act of *"speaking* the truth in love" (4:15).

Should the witness by words compete with the witness by works? Should it be of higher value, so that Church members equipped with the gift of speaking the "word of truth" (cf. 1:13; 4:15) form a class of their own; i.e., the "clergy" as distinct from the "laity"? It is indeed surprising that in 4:11 only ministers of the Word are enumerated. In contrast with other similar passages (see 1 Cor. 12:28; Rom. 12:6-13; Phil. 1:1; Acts 6—7; 20:17; 21:18, etc.), church administrators, such as bishops, presbyters, and deacons, and other church workers, such as healers, helpers, miracle workers, visitors, and hosts, are passed over in complete silence. In Paul's most churchly letter, that to the Ephesians, no one else but ministers of the Word are honored by the recognition that they hold an outstanding place in the Church. Neither a pope nor a historical episcopate, neither a synodal-presbyterian nor a democratic-congregational church constitution, but only God's gift of Gospel preachers and teachers make the church the Church! There is no mention of the ritual by which these ministers are ordained, but, instead, the intercession of all saints is mentioned. In their prayer (6:18-20) and by their "preparation" (4:12; 6:15), all saints have a part in the preaching and spreading of the Gospel of peace (6:15). All of them have been "appointed [literally, made clerics, or, put into the clergy] to live for a praise of God's glory" (1:11-12).

Does this mean, then, that each Christian must preach in order to be a full member of the congregation, a gift of God to the Church, and a servant for the benefit of those who are still far off? In 1 Peter this question is explicitly answered in a statement referring to the married women. "You wives, be subject to your husbands so that some, though they do not [yet] obey the word, may be won *without word, by the conduct* of the wives, when they see your reverent and chaste *conduct"* (1 Pet. 3:1-2). Though less explicitly, the same exhortation is given in Ephesians. "Shod . . . with the Gospel of peace" are husbands and wives, parents and children, masters and slaves, not only when they "talk" of Christ, but also when their conduct is different from that of the Gentiles (4:17); i.e., when they display at home and abroad what is "right" and "fitting for saints" (cf. Eph. 6:1; 5:4). There had better be no words at all than words of lying, bitterness, anger, silliness, or denouncement of misdeeds" (4:25 f., 29, 31; 5:3 f., 12). "Let not many of you become teachers," warns James, "for you know that we who teach shall be judged with greater strictness" (James 3:1). It is not given to everyone in the church or on other public occasions to "speak" the truth in love. But every one is called to "speak the truth with his neighbor" (4:25). "Walking in truth" is the genuine meaning of the word Paul uses in 4:15; that he *walk* in truth is commanded of each saint. Not all saints may presume to be able to *talk* worthily in public, but all the saints shall on all occasions *"walk* worthily of the calling with which they have been called" (4:1).

Not to every Christian is it given to perform exactly the same works of love. Therefore also the public testimony by words is a gift or task given to only some of them. But "to each one of you grace is given according to the measure of Christ's gift" (4:7). This can only mean that witness by word and witness by deed have the same origin and purpose, and are equal in rank and dignity, though different in function. The work of none of the body's members is dispensable. When toe, tooth, stomach, or heart are really sore, the mouth will hardly be able to speak very well. Onlookers will declare that the whole man is a patient when just one member of his body exerts a laming influence. Heart, hands, and mouth are an indivisible wholeness and unity. So the Church lives only when the specific dignity and need of service by conduct and by preaching are respected by all of her members.

The distinct functions of word and behavior, and the equal dignity, necessity, and purpose of witness by mouth and hands, have led to some strange procedures on the home and foreign mission fields. We may mention the soap-soup-slate-and-salvation tactics that were and are frequently applied to "prospective converts." By giving them the benefits of hygienics in hospitals, food in CARE packets, and education in schools, Christians have endeavored to get at least a foot into an otherwise closed door, hoping that ultimately salvation could be whispered or shouted through the opening. Should the door opened by soap, soup, and slate really be identified with the "door of the Word," "of the mouth," or "of faith" of which Paul obviously liked to speak (Col. 4:3; Eph. 6:19; Acts 14:27; 1 Cor. 16:9; 2 Cor. 2:12; cf. Rev. 3:8, 20)?

Those things which Western Christians have considered and used as door-openers are gladly accepted by many nations and individuals. Yet an attempt to smuggle a cake with a letter inside into a prison is considered dishonest, and is justly discredited as an infamous trick. Paul estimated the Gentile world higher than to use methods that actually humiliate and treat as subhuman the fellow man to whom the Good News is to be brought. God and the Gospel are given their due honor only when one's fellow man, be he Jew or Gentile, is considered, welcomed, and visited as one for whom Christ has died, and who has, first of all, the right to hear what great work was done and is valid for him. Medical missions, evangelism by education, and witness to God's grace through charity, must and will go on at home and abroad. But the church would attempt to deprive God of his glory, herself of her election and commission, and the world of the light it needs, if she persisted in considering the Gospel but an appendix to her humanitarian commission. The ministry of the Word is given to make known the truth everywhere. If this ministry is despised at home and neglected abroad, the Church actually repudiates her knowledge of the mystery revealed to her for the sake of the whole world. The one, true Church is a well-functioning body (4:16) that both speaks and acts from the heart and "in singleness of heart." She was not created to be dumb or lame. We conclude this section with the interpretation of one last statement.

5. Only the true, full Gospel is good enough to be witnessed to the world by the Church.

God is Father of all (4:6; the RSV reading "of us all" has no basis in the better Greek manuscripts). He loved the world so much that he gave his Son (John 3:16). In Christ he reconciled the world to himself (2 Cor. 5:19; Col. 1:20). This world has a right, therefore, to the Gospel — a right given by God himself. The world is not to be short-changed, cheated, duped, or fed with *Ersatz* products. The Ephesians were privileged to hear "the word of truth, the Gospel of salvation" (1:13). They were "taught that the truth is in Jesus" (4:21). We hear of no detours being taken by Paul or by the teachers. They did not first wait for the right moment of approach, then create an atmosphere favorable to the Gospel, then make excuses for the bold intrusion into the inner and outer life of the Ephesians, then present rational proof for as many of the Christian dogmas as possible, and then, finally, apologize for talking at all of the crucified and risen Christ!

The "saints in Ephesus," who lived in the atmosphere of the profitable Diana cult of Ephesus, were "raised from death in sin" (2:1-5). They were "sealed" by the Spirit, who works effectively despite all rulers "in the air" (1:13; 2:2; 6:12). They were given to know the love that surpasses knowledge (3:19). It was the preached Word that "prepared" them to be saints (4:12). They were not first prepared with soap, music, and religious dramas for some later opportunity of hearing the Gospel of salvation. How could they ever think that those who seem to be still far off would fare better, if approached in some other way!

"For the Gospel of peace" (6:15), not for playing any sort of tricks upon the world, have the saints been elected and prepared. Nobody can stand and proceed "in joyful boldness," and at the same time use shrewd methods, wait for better weather, and prepare apologetic devices or sophisticated flashlights. Christians wisely will leave the shrewd methods to their inventor and master, the devil (4:14; 6:11). They know that the time available for witness is both short and evil (5:16; 6:13). They are by no means astonished to find that darkness is still the result of rebellious principalities and powers which harass the Church from outside and inside (6:12; 5:3-12). They know that there is light only "in the Lord" (5:8) and only by the operation of the Spirit (1:17 f.). They have nothing else to say and nothing else for which to serve than "the Gospel of salvation" and "of peace" which they have heard (1:13; 2:17; 6:15). Joyful boldness is only possible where the confidence reigns that in and to this dark and deceitful world the light and "mystery of the Gospel" can and shall be preached.

Therefore, the saints can bravely and gladly resist the temptation to appear as all-wise teachers of the world and as omnipotent magicians for curing the world's woes. "When I came to you I considered to know nothing among you except Jesus Christ, and him crucified." So writes Paul (1 Cor. 2:2); and no reader of Ephesians has reason to claim that he is any wiser than the apostle. The Gospel of Christ is the only thing of which the Christians need "not be ashamed," and the only thing which they owe to the world (Rom. 1:14, 16). They will never exhaust its breadth and length and height and depth. Although they do not fully understand it, they can trust that it will carry them. Their own insight into the mystery's dimensions will grow while they show that no depth of darkness and no height of conceit is left outside or empty of Christ's fullness.

All of this would be trite and platitudinous, if groups and individuals today, as well as in Ephesus long ago, were not time and again caught and seemingly trapped without hope of escape in one or more of three ways: in attempts to change, adapt, and modernize the Gospel; in despair over the insufficiency of the Church's power and authorization; or in the pride of possessing a private fullness which does not reach beyond the Church's walls. Paul alludes to the attempts to change the Gospel when he speaks of the babelike individuals who are "tossed to and fro and carried about with every wind of doctrine [contrived] by the cunningness of men" (4:14). The despair of the "realists," who are aware of the sin and weakness that still rule in the Church, is met by his call, "Be strong!" and by the reference to what the Spirit of Christ does in men's hearts (3:16 f.; 6:10, etc.). He dispels the pride of the self-content by reminding all of the saints of their solidarity with the Gentiles in sin. Hope for all lies only in forgiveness of sin. Changing winds of doctrine, despair, and haughtiness are all features of the world. If the Church yielded to them, she would become nothing more than another religious club and social gathering.

By not trusting the Gospel and by conforming to the world in matters of message, methods, and standards of success, Christians do no good to anybody — neither to God, nor to the world, nor to themselves. Whether preaching is done from carved pulpits, fancy television studios, upturned soapboxes, or from one kitchen chair to another, the uncurtailed message of the great work of God is the message that must be preached. Whether the witness by works and deeds is rendered by man or wife, adults or juveniles, rich or poor, it is the peace of *Christ* that is to be attested; for Christians know of no other peace that could unite in mutual submission and love Jews and Gentiles, saints and sinners, those near and those far.

Everything else — such as apologetics for the superiority of the Christian religion, a moral and social code for those willing or in need to climb up, and a promised gain in self-esteem and public prestige — is not the Gospel, and its propagation is not the Church's business. When a man needs bread and fish, the saints must not try to feed him with stones or snakes. Only the Gospel of Jesus Christ is the "power of God for salvation" (cf. Rom. 1:16).

The "word of truth" (1:13) is the "treasure" with which the Church is entrusted. She and all saints are but "earthen vessels" (2 Cor. 4:7) that seem inadequate to hold God's riches. Nevertheless, as contents are often more valuable than the container from which they are poured, so God is free to use earthen vessels. He makes them holy and gives them the strength to serve the purpose of his glorification. We shall speak of the core, nature, and effect of the Church's sanctification in the next section.

III. FAITH: STANDING AT THE ASSIGNED PLACE

All that has been said so far about the Christian's life in the world may be summed up in the statement that the saints are saved only through faith (2:8), that they can be strong only through faith (3:16-17), and that they shall stand in faith and make use of faith in order to meet what occurs to them in the world (6:16). Without faith, they would not be what they are by God's election and calling. Moreover, apart from the witness of faith, they have nothing to say and nothing to do in the world.

Although it has become customary to talk, and talk, and talk more or less wildly of "faith" (this practice seems to have become established in earliest times; see James 2:14-26), Paul, in Ephesians, uses this term only with great care. The noun is used eight times, and the verb "to believe" only twice. It is not *talk* of faith which fills the pages of Ephesians. Paul, however, gives witness to the *work* which God does in Christ, and he gives exhortation to a *life* worthy of that "workmanship." The keyword and doctrine of "justification by faith" is not explicitly made the central theme of this epistle. But in surprising metaphors (such as "wall," "far" and "near," "commonwealth," and "house"), and in very practical counsels (such as those concerning married life, the tensions of generations, and of social classes), Paul announces what peace was brought and preached by Christ, and what is the right and good thing to do where this peace is made known. Faith is nothing else but the joyful acceptance of the proclaimed Gospel of peace (1:13), and a conduct of life among fellow men in that love with which the saints were loved. In Eph. 1:15 and 6:23, Paul treats of faith and love as inseparable.

Therefore we may call faith both "acceptance" of Christ who is our peace, and "conduct" in the love with which we are loved. With this double description, we have once again touched upon that unity in diversity which we observed in such relationships as those between the headship of Christ over the world and over the Church; between the election of Israel and that of the Gentiles; between peace with God and peace among men; between knowing God and making him known; between worship and mission work; between receiving and giving consolation; between testimony by word and by deed; and between the distinct witness by the husband and by the wife. In each partner of these pairs there was always the same dignity and necessity of election, function, and purpose. There was always growth "toward the head" taking place in "growing from the head" (4:15-16). Correspondingly, faith is not a relationship of only a part of man, e.g., of his feeling or of his mind, to God. Faith is the right relation of the *whole* man to both God and fellow man. The source and standard of what is "right" is the peace made through the cross. Faith is faithfulness both to God who made the peace, and to those with and for whom the peace was made.

The Old Testament root and meaning of faith shows that

the right relationship between God and man, and between man and fellow man is steadfastness on the ground of the covenant which God has made. "Knowledge of God" means reliance upon God and obedience to him in all dealings with men. This is the core of faith.

That which makes the relationship between God and man stable and firm is always God alone, never a capacity which man has apart from God. Because the human heart is "deceitful above all things and desperately corrupt" (cf. Jer. 17:9), it is not firm and solid enough of itself to produce, to contain, or to reach faith. But when the heart is made firm by God, solidly rooted, unwaveringly concentrated upon what God says, then there is faith. Therefore, in the Old Testament, faith is basically firmness, stability, and solidity.

Several statements in the New Testament likewise show and underline the identity of faith with firmness. "Stand firm in faith! Be men! Be strong!" (1 Cor. 16:13). "We are not of those who shrink back and are destroyed, but of those who have faith" (Heb. 10:39). Christ "has reconciled you . . . provided that you continue in faith, [well] grounded and steadfast, not shifting from the hope of the Gospel which you have heard" (Col. 1:23). "Walk in Christ Jesus — as you have received him as Lord — rooted and built up in him, and made solid by faith" (Col. 2:7). "I rejoice to see . . . the firmness of your faith in Christ" (Col. 2:5). Paul prays to God "that he may grant you to be strengthened with might through his Spirit . . . that Christ may dwell in your hearts through faith, that you be rooted and grounded in love" (Eph. 3:16-17).

The opposite of such solidity, strength, and firmness on a sure ground is found where people are "like babes, tossed to and fro and carried by every wind" (Eph. 4:14; cf. Heb. 13:9). According to other texts (Mark 5:36; 9:24; Rom. 3:3; 2 Tim. 2:13, etc.) fear, unbelief, and unfaithfulness are the opposites of faith. Opposite faith and solidity is found the trembling, erring, and stumbling behavior of one who does not know how and where to stand before God and man. The contrasts between Faith and Reason, Faith and Sight, and Faith and Opinion, which since the second century A.D. have been so minutely, endlessly, and fruitlessly discussed among Christians and non-Christians, were not unknown in the time of the New Testament (cf. 1 Cor. 1:18-29; 3:18-23; Eph. 3:19; 2 Cor. 5:7; Heb. 11:1; 1 Cor. 15:17, 19, etc.). But they contribute little to the elucidating of what is the essence and nature of faith, as presented in the Bible in general, and in Paul's epistles in particular. Basically, the opposite of faith is unfaithfulness, lack of reliance upon, and lack of obedience to, God's covenant with men. The closest analogy to faith is the faithfulness of a bride or wife. Her faithfulness is shown by her behavior to both her fiancé or husband and all people with whom she converses. Such faithfulness is contrary neither to reason, nor to sight, nor to opinion. But "not all have faith" (2 Thess. 3:2). It is a "good" gift of God when "the heart is made firm, by grace" (Heb. 13:9).

Among the many biblical utterances about faith, the witness of Ephesians is outstanding by reason of its many references to the rooting and grounding of the people of God. The eternal will, the love, the might, the work, and the revelation of God provide the ground upon which the author and the recipients of the epistle stand. They may appear to be but a shaky congregation, being still surrounded by the legalistic Jews and the erratic paganism from which they had but recently emerged (2:1-3, 11-12; 4:17-19), and tempted by ever-changing doctrines (4:14, 20 f.) and the unspeakably bad behavior of their own members (5:3-12). Yet the Church is solidly founded on the reliable ground of Christ and his apostles and prophets (2:20). There is no member of the Church who does not need to be strengthened and enlightened by the Spirit, encouraged to be strong, and reminded of the function of living members and stones (1:17 f.; 3:16 f.; 4:15-16, 25; 5:30). Yet the promise and the heritage warranted to every one of them is not shaken (1:14; 4:30). Many principalities, powers, and names influence them from "heavenly places" and try to make them afraid (6:11 ff.). But their confession, "One God, One Lord, One Baptism," and what they are made to be, "One Body" (4:4-6), is a oneness which cannot be divided, split up, or exchanged for anything else. Whether or not they are always aware of it and walk worthily of it, they are upon solid, unshakable ground.

In the kingdom of God something better than democracy, progress, productivity, or ever-changing fashion holds the rule. Comparable perhaps only to the realm of mathematics, "One" is, in this kingdom, the ground and the ultimate mystery and purpose of all things. All manifoldness — the display of God's "manifold" wisdom (3:10) in his perfect work, the gift of various ministers of the Word (4:11), the calling to distinct obedience and witness in all walks of life (5:20–6:9), the different pieces of the whole armor by which the saints are equipped to ward off assaults (6:14-17) — reveals this: the *One* God carries, meets, and supplies all the needs of all men.

Do the Ephesians really "have" the "One Faith"? Was their "One Baptism" a firm and confirmed public confession of the Lord? Do they live as "One Body" in "One Hope," and do they show to all generations and powers that God is the "One Father of all, over all, through all, in all" (cf. 4:4-6)? Such questions may indeed be raised, and they could drive every honest man to despair, for where on earth is there found that solidity, steadfastness, and firmness which is the nature and essence of faith? Paul gives an answer worthy of an apostle of Jesus Christ. He says that the Spirit given by the risen Christ is alive and still at work "for the preparation of [the] saints . . . *until we all attain to the oneness of faith* and knowledge *of the Son of God,* to the perfect man, to the measure of the stature of Christ's fullness" (4:12-13). Three things need to be emphasized.

1. Oneness of faith is not a Platonic idea, a fanciful dream of enthusiasts, or a program whose realization is dependent on the strength and good will of men. But "one faith," i.e., true faith and saving faith, has become and is real among men. Where is that faith? It is seen in Jesus Christ. His faith in God is the solid, saving, manifest faith of which the Bible speaks, and which is, according to other statements of Paul, instrumental for our salvation (cf. Rom. 1:17; 3:22, 25, 26; Phil. 3:9; Gal. 2:16, 20; 3:26). In Ephesians, Paul writes, "Through Christ's faith we have with confidence bold joy and access to the Father" (3:12). It is an error when current Bible translations speak only of "faith in Christ" and forget what is written in such passages as Heb. 2:17; 3:2; 4:15 and 12:2 and what is narrated in the Gospels about the faithfulness of (the Servant and Son) Jesus Christ himself. Without the "perfection" of the "merciful and faithful high priest . . . appointed [by God] on behalf of men for the things concerning God" (Heb. 2:14; 3:1 f.; 5:1, 7-8) there is no access to God, and no faith on the part of the many servants of God is possible. For before faith is a commandment and promise to man, it is a reality in Jesus Christ. Unshakably and solidly he alone is "the perfect man" (4:13). Faith does not become "one" by a mixture of man-made formulae and by compromises. Oneness of faith is attained only when we "attain to Christ." Therefore we read in 4:13, "attain to the oneness of the faith . . . of the Son of God"!

2. No saint has this Oneness of faith either in his pocket, in his creeds, in his experience, in his brain, or in his feelings. The words, *"We* all *shall attain* to the Oneness of faith" (4:13), show that all Christians are still pilgrims on the way to firmness and steadfastness of faith. Tired or loitering pilgrims, sinking Peters, doubting Johns in prison, fathers who can but cry out, "Help my unbelief!" need not despair. They are taken under their arms and supported by Paul when he writes: "Not that I have already grasped it or am already

perfect; but I pursue [it to see] whether I may get hold [of it], because by Jesus Christ I am taken hold of. Brethren, I [myself] do not reckon that I have already taken hold of it. But one thing [I do] . . . straining forward to what lies ahead, [having] the goal before my eyes, I pursue [to the end] for the prize of the high calling" (Phil. 3:12-14). These words show that Paul stands in the line of those who are aware of the imperfection of their faith. As for those who have gone to sleep, or those who attempt to behave again like those who are dead in sin, and even those who are still dead, Paul calls them by quoting (singing?) a hymn: "You sleeper! Stand up from the dead. Christ will give you light" (5:14). We conclude that the Oneness of faith is still to be attained, but there is no reason for assuming that anyone is excluded from the invitation to join the company of "the perfect man." It is noteworthy that Paul writes to saints, rather than to unbelieving Gentiles, that they still have to attain to the "fullness of Christ." May they stop believing that some immorality, impurity, or greed can be excused and made compatible with their future heritage (5:5). May they be "faithful servants of Christ and stewards of the mystery" (cf. 1 Cor. 4:1-2), while they are still pilgrims. Then they will not withhold the Gospel of peace from those that are still far off.

3. Paul writes that we are "prepared" by the ministers of the Word, "until *we all* attain to the oneness of faith." He may have in mind party divisions or schisms, which may have split the Christians in and around Ephesus as much as they divided the Church in Corinth (cf. 1 Cor. 1:10-17; 3:1-9, 18-23). Or he may have had in mind that the fullness of Christ (i.e., the love of Christ which already embraces those near *and* those far) is not really "acknowledged" (Eph. 3:19), until we see the house of God filled with all the prodigals who are still estranged, and all "the poor and maimed and blind and lame" from the highways and hedges, that are still to be "compelled to come in" (cf. Luke 14:21-23). It is also

possible, and indeed most likely, that Paul thought of both; namely, what we call today the problem of ecumenical unity, *and* what today finds expression in the work of the World Missionary Council. In either case, faith is described by him as "One faith" or as "Oneness of faith" (4:5, 13). Unity of faith is dependent on the Oneness and truth of faith. Only the faith *of* Jesus Christ and *in* Jesus Christ can unite. But what we may call "true faith" is a faith that does not seclude or secure itself behind walls. True faith is work for unity and work in mission. Its confession praises God as the Father *of all* (3:15; 4:6), Christ's mystery that is embracing and filling *all in all* (1:23; 4:10), and the Spirit that proves stronger than *all* principalities (6:10 ff.), including even death in sin.

We conclude that to live in faith is to live upon the firm ground of God's love, work, and power. Life in faith is a movement of gathering together and a movement of going out. It is the life of those who grow to the head and from the head, even Christ. It is radical turning away from the past and a straightforward walk to the goal. It is both learning from God and witnessing to God. It puts the churches and the Christians to shame because of their scandalous disunity. There is a bright spot in the world wherever the power of God is reaching, embracing, gathering, and raising people who were in darkness and alienated from the household of God. Faith is the stand which Christians are to take and to hold in this world. It prohibits and makes superfluous attempts to run away from the responsibilities of living in this world. The Christians, whether among friends or foes, Jews or Gentiles, members of their own or of other congregations and denominations, have a good purpose, a distinct call, a sufficient strength, and a vast field of labor. When they "hear the word of truth, the Gospel of salvation, *and believe it*" (1:13) then they will know what to do.

They have nothing to be afraid of, even when powers stronger than flesh and blood harass them from the inside and the outside. Precisely when the world (i.e., the psychic, cultural, social, and political "Ephesus" in which they live) shows its darkest face and makes its ugliest grimaces, they will feel that they are "in the right element," even in that world which God has loved, into whose deepest places Christ has descended, and from whose dungeon of death resurrection has taken place and shall take place. Christians can "take it," for they realize that God, in his patience, wisdom, and love, knows how things are. He knows also what is yet to come. The saints, therefore, need not fear the future. The days may be bad; but still they are not too bad. The Christians may be cowards; but there is still good armor for them at hand. "Put on the whole armor of God, so that you can *stand*. . . . Take it up, in order that you can *withstand* on the evil day, accomplish all, and *stand*. *Stand*, therefore . . .!" (6:13-14). This, even this, is faith, to "stand" at the place "in Ephesus" to which God has assigned his children "in Christ." It is the stand of a soldier, the stand of one who is well "prepared" (4:12; 6:15) to be witness to all men and all powers "for the Gospel of peace."

IV. THE GOSPEL FOR ALL

In nearly every one of the preceding sections of our interpretation, it may have seemed to the reader that a ghost was following him; following him as persistently and faithfully as ever Sancho Panza followed his master. What if this ghost should prove that the Church, despite its equipment with the whole armor of God, is but a Don Quixote engaged in futile excitements, pursuits, and battles? This ghost bears the name of "universalism," and Christians cannot really understand their place and mission in the world unless they possess some clarity of thought in regard to this issue.

Universalism has been discussed among Christians and has divided them, since at least the second century A.D. There always were those who seemed as much (if not more!) concerned to see hell filled with justly punished reprobates as they were devoted to calling sinners into the house of God. Some combined the preaching of heaven with the preaching of hell, and attempted to scare the prodigals into the arms of the Father. Despite all assertions to the effect that "mercy triumphs over judgment" (cf. James 2:13) they have insisted that it is a true axiom that "there must be somewhere a place for unbelievers." For they read with both horror and satisfaction what the Bible says about the "burning pitch" that "shall not be quenched day and night; its smoke shall go up for ever. . . . They shall name it, No Kingdom There" (Isa. 34:9 ff.; cf. Rev. 14:11; 19:3; 20:10). And they are aware that even the Gospels speak of people thrown into "outer darkness." Indeed, the Bible tells them that there is a "worm that does not die, . . . a fire that is not quenched" (Matt. 8:12; 22:13; 25:30; Mark 9:48), and a sin that is unforgivable "in this age or in the age to come" (Mark 3:29; Matt. 12:32; cf. Heb. 6:4-6; 10:26-31; 12:17; Rev. 21:8, 27; 22:15).

Others did not rely on Bible quotations, but lifted their voices for the defense of human freedom or for some principles of absolute righteousness. Legalists argued that the idea of a righteous God demands (like the Roman law) that the criminal has to bear his punishment, and that the debtor must remain captive without any limitations. Idealists reasoned that human dignity and the very idea of freedom demand the right for man to resist or to decline grace; to hold otherwise, they said, would be to conceive of God as a mechanical, irresistible, and ultimately deadly and deadening power. Again, other Christians pointed simply to what they called the "facts" of common experience. They claimed for themselves the title of "realists," and declared that there were innumerable examples to show that the conversion of a Jew or Gentile (or Moslem!) simply was impossible.

Of such sort are the proofs deduced from Scripture, reason, and experience, for condemning the idea of an ultimate salva-

tion of all men. We observe that all three — the Bible, reason,
and experience — appear to agree fully in their repudiation of
universalism. To be sure, devoted mission work is by no
means discouraged where the "particularist" position is held,
and where some people are considered to be eternally lost.
But failures of missionary achievement are borne with a certain equanimity when it is understood and agreed beforehand
that only *some,* but not *"all* shall attain to the Oneness of
faith" (cf. 4:13). God's "will that all men be saved and come
to the knowledge of the truth" (1 Tim. 2:4) is then viewed
(as the RSV translation of this text shows) as a mere "desire."
From this attitude there arises inevitably a certain fatalism
or cynicism in regard to missionary and evangelistic work.
One hears, both whispered and shouted, "The power of unbelief is too great. I told you so. In fact, the Bible itself
states this. The obstinate unbelievers are too wicked to be
saved."

But not all Christians joined in the repudiation of salvation for all. Likewise from Scripture, reason, and experience,
other arguments were compiled that were supposed to prove
the opposite of particularist redemption; that is to say, the
salvation or "restitution of all" (cf. Acts 3:21). It was pointed
out that "God so loved the world" (not only the saints) as
to give "his only Son" (John 3:16); that "the darkness did not
overcome the light" that shines in the world (John 1:5); that
the darkness is passing away "because the true light shines"
(1 John 2:8); that according to Col. 1:20, "the whole," "all,"
are reconciled to God through Christ; that according to 2 Cor.
5:19-20, "God has in Christ reconciled the world" so that
nothing else is left but to preach and to believe. You are reconciled, therefore, "be [i.e., live, give thanks, and witness as
those] reconciled with God." From the Old Testament, passages such as Isa. 2:2-4 (cf. Mic. 4:1-4) were cited: "It shall
come to pass in the latter days that the mountain of the
house of the Lord shall be established as the highest of the

mountains . . .; and all the nations shall flow to it. . . . They shall beat their swords into plowshares and their spears into pruning hooks; nation shall not lift up sword against nation, neither shall they learn war any more." All such Scripture texts were believed to say but one thing; namely, that God's love is powerful enough to overcome all the sin and foolishness of all men. And it was rationally and emotionally argued that a perfect divine kingdom is irreconcilable with vicious places, dungeons, or torture chambers that exhibit the most deplorable hygienic and social conditions.

The repudiation of "eternal hell" went arm in arm with an energetic practical attack on places of misery in this world, as they are found in slums and jungles, in alcoholism and prostitution, and in lack of food and education. Nothing and no one was "too bad" to be helped to a worthier way of life. Some universalists have gained a great name for the practical way in which they evangelize for their conviction. Those among them who continued to worry about what might be after death, and about the fate of people who had never accepted what God's love brought to them, found various answers. It either was believed that there would be a second and last chance after death to hear and to accept the Good News, or it was held that, together with all atheism and immorality, the obstinate sinners would simply be annihilated. So, over against the views of the particularists, the universalists put forth the idea of a possible experience of salvation after death or of obliteration. Gnostics and other heretics, Mystics, Pietists, Pantheists, and many outsiders or border figures of "normal" Church life provided the leadership for universalism. Many of them were slandered, persecuted, burned, or pushed into inconspicuous corners. But the issue they raised has not died.

This is not the place to discuss and to answer all of the arguments used by those who are for, and by those who are against, universalism. But the Epistle to the Ephesians imposes upon its reader the question as to where, if at all, he takes his stand in this age-old universalist controversy. Not only the character, vigor, and hope of the missionary and evangelistic work of testimony to Christ, but also his own prayer, worship, and oral witness will be deeply influenced by the answer which he gives. Four considerations may lead toward an answer.

1. The words "fullness," "fill," "one," "oneness," and "all," are used in Ephesians so frequently and so prominently that the message of this epistle may be summed up in the sentence, "The One God fills all with his love." Among other New Testament books, only Colossians, the Gospel of John, and the Revelation of John (each in its own way) come near to emphasizing God's being "One for All" as much as Ephesians does. In 1 Cor. 15:28, Paul says about the purpose and end of all things, "God will be all in all." In Ephesians the future dimension is not denied, but the accent is placed upon the fact that God is in Christ already filling "all in all" (Eph. 1:23; cf. 4:10). As One body, in One faith and hope, the Christians confess but One Father, Christ, and Spirit (4:4-6). They strive to keep the spiritual Oneness in the bond of peace, and to attain to the Oneness of faith (4:3, 13). This confessing and striving is not for the sake of adding something to God or to his work; rather, it is to magnify now in the Church the same glory which is God's in eternity (cf. 3:21). The life to which the Church is called is a movement "toward the fullness of God" and "into the fullness of Christ" (3:19; 4:13).

As has been shown earlier in the interpretation of Eph. 1:23, the Christians are privileged already to be filled with Him who is free, willing, and powerful to fill all. As the Ephesians are "filled" by receiving knowledge, so the "all" is to be filled by the spreading and deepening of knowledge. It was God's will and (good) pleasure (1:5, 9) to elect, to save, to bestow privilege, and to equip the Ephesians in order that, in the kindness exhibited to them, all coming generations should

THE GOSPEL FOR ALL

see and be given to know how rich his grace is (2:7; 3:10; 6:15, 19). We conclude, therefore, that the Ephesians cannot speak of the One God and thank him for his work, without instantly thinking of the overflowing riches of his grace. These riches overflow on people who are dead in sin, trapped in darkness, and alienated from fatherland and fatherhouse, as the Ephesians know by their own experience. Hence, they can think of the Gentiles around them only as persons who are "no more far" from the overflow of the love and life of God. They too must be "saved"; i.e., must "come to the knowledge of the truth" (1 Tim. 2:4). That the making of peace, the reconciliation, includes them from the beginning, is never in question. But what good is it to them, and what glory do they give to God, if they do not "know" it?

2. Another characteristic feature of Ephesians is the frequent and prominent use of the words "love" and "might," and of their equivalents, "grace," "mercy," and "kindness," on one side, and "strength," "power," and "energy" on the other. If God were depicted first as omnipotent or Creator, and only later incidentally as also a loving Father and Savior in Christ, the Ephesians might be permitted to believe in the power of God to love some and to hate others. In Rom. 9:6-29, Paul seems indeed to argue along that line. But he certainly does not do so in Ephesians. As the cross and the resurrection of Christ are not reversible, so the act of love (i.e., the removal of the wall) and the use of might (i.e., the resurrection of the dead) are not reversible. What in his love God decided to do, that he carries out omnipotently. The beloved and loving Son (1:6; 5:2, 25) was put by the loving Father (4:4) on the throne "above all" (1:20-22). So the love (of God) was shown to be mighty above all other powers that be. The might of God is his might to subjugate *all* to his *love*. It is not a might which allows either his love or his wrath to govern over all, or to divide the "all" in such a way that only part of it should enjoy and glorify his love. Does

this mean that God limited his freedom by favoring man only "in Christ," i.e., only "in love"?

Far be it! For God's concept of freedom (if not yet every philosopher's) is to be "all in all" loving Father, and not to let any murmuring, foolishness, and rebellion of his chosen ones interfere with his love. Even in the Old Testament, God's wrath against covenant-breaking Israel is not an alternative to, but rather the temperature of his love. The Ephesians know from their own experience what God does with men that are "by nature children of wrath." "We were children of wrath like the others. But God who is rich in mercy, because of the great love with which he loved us, has made us alive with Christ when we were dead in trespasses" (2:3 f.). We conclude, therefore, that the Ephesians do not know a Gentile who is too dead, too bad, or too far off to be raised, saved, and gathered to God's house. But they do know that they themselves are the proof (from 2:7 we could derive the term, "the showpiece") of the omnipotence of God's love.

3. A further feature which is typical of Ephesians is the thoroughgoing interrelationship between *receiving* and *giving*. There is the emphasis on knowledge, which was discussed above. "Knowledge of the mystery" implied both further penetration into it by deeper understanding, and communication of it by "making it known" (1:17 f.; 3:18 f.; 5:10; 6:19). Correspondingly, what the Ephesians give to the needy, and what good they do as servants of others, they are promised to receive themselves from the Lord (4:28-29; 6:8). Their worship is designed to be thanksgiving at all times for all, intercession for others, words of truth spoken to others, humble service to fellow man, and a brave stand against the powers that be (5:20 f.; 4:25; 6:10-20). They are made light, so that they can walk as children of the light (5:8). At no point have they anything, unless they receive it from God. In no instance are they given something, unless it is for serving as a light and an example for all that have not yet received it. It is

manifest that the Ephesians do not know any gift of God, or any relationship to God, which does not make them servants and witnesses to their fellow man. They are prepared "for the work of service"; they are appointed to be public servants; they are equipped to stand as brave soldiers in the world (4:12; 5:21; 6:14-17). The world is full of people who are living in darkness, deceit, and misery, but who are given the right from God to be served by the Christians.

4. In Ephesians, Paul has put more emphasis than in most of his other epistles upon the *order* of God's eternal plan and his work in history, the *order* of the Church and the saints' ministry, and the *order* of the words and deeds done by men in their daily lives. The words "in Christ" describe the common core, means, and frame of God's, the Church's, and the servants' order of household. Now, as we have shown, the plan and institution of one distinct order did not negate the freedom of man. But true freedom was created, founded, and sustained just because love is the order in God's house, and because God wills all his children, even the prodigal son *and* his brother to enjoy it. The Ephesians, before they were saved, were not free, but dead in captivity, in horror, and cringing before principalities and powers (2:1-5; 4:8). Now the Gentiles in their environment, as well as the backsliders in their midst, are not enjoying, like the saints, the privilege of "walking in good works" (2:10, 12). The Gentiles' minds, their words, and their actions produce but "fruitless works of darkness," shameful even to speak of (4:18-20; 5:3-12). Unbelievers are not free, but are captives of vanity and death. But to stand before God and Christ "holy and spotless," to be made the bride of Christ and beloved children of God, to receive power for standing and walking as children of light in the present darkness and evil days (1:4; 5:2, 8, 16, 25-27; 6:12) is freedom and joyful boldness!

Were the Ephesians free, or is anybody free to accept or to reject God's gracious order? Impossible! A dead man is not free. A blind eye cannot see. A stony heart cannot know God. Freedom that is worth its name is not what the snake promised Eve; neither is it what the prodigal enjoyed while he was far from home and dead; and it certainly does not find expression in the grumblings of the older brother against the returned and feted prodigal. Freedom rules only when man "in singleness of heart," "from the soul, with enthusiasm" (6:5-7), lives in the Father's house and order, and when he always has access to him. The prodigal was given such freedom. The older brother, representing the Jews, is invited to join the party. The Ephesian saints received this gift of access, joy, and singleness of heart when they were "called" and "sealed." The Gentiles around them need it bitterly. It must be made known to them that they too are invited. The Ephesian witnesses need not be ashamed to impose a strange yoke upon those whose doors they enter "shod with preparation for the Gospel of peace" (6:15). As God's ambassadors they bring the call and message which is "God's power for salvation" (cf. Rom. 1:16), which raises from dumb sleep and spiritual death, and which makes "free." They have no reason to fear that they demand impossible things either from God or from their fellow man when they believe, expect, and work that each one of their fellow men might be awakened and raised. A Christian will get acquainted with the "fullness" of God's love and might only when he experiences the fact that this neighbor, this child, this mate, or this boss can resist the call of God as little as Paul or any one of the saints in Ephesus could.

We summarize by stating that the words "fullness," "oneness," and "all," the irreversible relationship between the love and the might of God, the interrelationship of receiving and giving, and the emphasis which is laid upon receiving life, freedom, and joy in the order of Christ are typical elements of Ephesians. They all describe an indissoluble bond that unites God, the Church, and all people. Common to the four points are, among other things, these two: the relation of God to "all" men and of "all" to God is never described without reference to God's *workmanship,* the Church; and this same relation is never mentioned without reference to the Church's *mission* among all men. In these two common elements lies the reply to both the warmhearted and openhanded universalist who wants to have the world saved, and to his often ice-cold opponent who relies upon a stiff dogma of double predestination, and who considers it "just too bad" (but still necessary!) that to God's greater glory some people "go to hell."

With or without Bible quotations, predestinarians and universalists are in temptation to replace by a human scheme that which, in Ephesians, is described as the ongoing, perfect work of the living God. Particularism and universalism are both of the family of the many "isms" that have but little in common with the Gospel.

If we could think or talk of God and the world without becoming personally involved and being personally engaged in action and suffering, in fear and hope, then we might discuss in abstract and general terms whether or not God can, will, or might save all. But we are never invited or condemned to be only onlookers or observers of God and of "all" men. Both are too inscrutable to be quietly discussed in armchairs; neither will allow us to sit back in that fashion. According to Ephesians, what knowledge of God we are given, makes us at once, from the beginning, without cessation, to "stand up," "walk," "withstand," "speak the truth," and "be subject." Thus, knowledge of God makes us move among men in a certain "worthy," "fitting," and "right" way. What knowledge we are given of men makes us recognize God's mercy for them, and our solidarity with even the most renegade and obstinate sinners forbids us from presuming to be God's appointed state's attorneys against them. "What have I to do with judging outsiders? . . . God judges those outside" (1 Cor. 5:12-13). We will be faithful to God and act according to our salvation when we plead for them before God as if we were *their* attorneys. Prayer, intercession, and thanksgiving are to be done, if not with them, yet for them. There is a light given to us that will shine even where there is darkness. By words and deeds, a patient, manifold, and hopeful witness can be borne. Consequently, instead of wasting time with pseudo-concern for, and speculations about, some Himalayan monks' possible or impossible salvation, we are to act in prayer and work, in the service of God, and to the benefit of man, as those who know the only Savior and the desperate need of man. As God's children, we cannot speak against men; we can only speak for them. The Gospel is for all. And the Spirit made us ambassadors prepared (only!) "for the Gospel of peace" (6:15, 19; 2:17; 3:6-9).

What, then, shall we say concerning hell? In Ephesians there are only three passages in which something equivalent to our concept of "hell" is mentioned.

In Eph. 4:9 we read that Christ "descended to the deepest places of the earth." This statement refers to the cross as the lowest point of Christ's humiliation (2:16; cf. Phil. 2:8). Hell, therefore, is what Christ has suffered "for us" when he gave himself as an offering and sacrifice to God (2:13-15; 5:2). In whatever lofty or miserable place a man may make his bed, "Thou art there"; so Psalm 139:8 encourages us to conclude. Those living in darkness and doing the works of impurity are already "delivered" by God to bear the consequence of their ignorance and idolatry (Rom. 1:24, 26, 28). But Christ has reached and met them in hell, just where they are. This means, in the language of Ephesians, "that he filled all" (Eph. 4:10), even the lowest places of hell! In 1 Pet. 3:19 the unbelievers are called "spirits in prison"; and it is stated, in a way which resembles Eph. 2:17, that Christ himself "came" into their abode and "preached" to them. Ephesians adds triumphantly that what imprisoned men, Christ made a (i.e., "his") prisoner through the resurrection (4:8). It is reasonable to conclude, therefore, that the first meaning of "hell" in Ephesians gives us reason for a song of gratitude. Hell is what Christ has visited and overcome by his death and resurrection!

A second reference to "hell" may be found in Eph. 2:2. Mention is made of the "aeon of this world . . . the prince of the authority of the air." The devil is also mentioned in 4:27 and 6:11. Little doubt is left concerning his past authority over the Ephesians, and his present "energetic" work in the sons of disobedience. Nothing is said, however, about a future or eternal power given to him for seducing, accusing, and punishing anybody. Much more, this "prince" and his hosts who still cause darkness to enclose and threaten the "children of light" (6:11 f.; 5:8), belong to "all" the powers, principalities, and names, that already are under Christ's feet (1:10, 21-22). Although they bark and bite like chained dogs, their realm is fundamentally a realm of the past. What damage they still can do, cannot prevail against the power of the Spirit, with which God is "energetically at work" (3:20). So the second meaning of hell in Ephesians, although less bright than the first, may be summed up thus: It is the passing-away empire of a forlorn cause. Its defenders may still shoot and kill, but their power is waning and their chances of victory have been lost.

The last hint in the direction of hell is given in 5:5: "Know this: No immoral, impure, or greedy man (that is an idolator), has an inheritance in the Kingdom of Christ and God." We have shown before (on p. 163 ff.) that Paul is speaking here of Christians. How severely the Church is "to judge those inside" is made plain in 1 Cor. 5:1-13: "The man who has done such a thing" has to be "delivered" by the solemn assembly of the saints, in the name of, and with the power of the Lord Jesus Christ, "to Satan for destruction of the flesh." We observe that such delivery of a man to "hell" is executed during his lifetime, and, further, that it is a member of the Church who is treated in this way. In this passage, as in others, hell is not preached to, or predicted for, Gentiles who never heard of Christ, or who only heard of him in such a way that they could not believe. Rather, hell is to be experienced by a man who had stood upon the "foundation of repentance from dead works and faith into God, . . . of resurrection from the dead and eternal judgment" and "who had been enlightened; had tasted of the heavenly gift and become partaker of the Holy Spirit; had the good word of God and the power of the age to come" (Heb. 6:1-5). It is the unworthily-walking Christian who becomes a victim of hell (cf. 1 Cor. 11:27-30). The same is true of all the Gospel passages that mention "outer darkness" (Matt. 8:12, etc.). Not unbelievers who have never heard of God are cast out, but "sons of the kingdom," guests who had been "called," and "servants," who have been appointed by their Lord; even these are threatened with gnawing of teeth and darkness. In none of his missionary sermons did Paul threaten the Gentiles with hell, for they were already deep enough and far enough in darkness. However, he knew that he himself, the "instrument of election," was the first possible victim of hell. "Wretched man who I am! Who will deliver me . . . ?" (Rom. 7:24). "I am the least . . . unworthy . . . I persecuted the Church of God" (1 Cor. 15:9). "Woe to me, if I did not evangelize" (1 Cor. 9:16). The third meaning of hell, as it is presented in Eph. 5:5, is that it is a place only for Christians, only for those "brothers" who abuse the name with which they are called. Still, Paul would not be Paul, unless he added after the so-called excommunication decree concerning the immoral man, the words, "that his Spirit may be saved in the day of the Lord Jesus" (1 Cor. 5:5).

Now there is many a "brother" who, with more or less fitting Bible quotations, and with stories about how the godless perish, illustrates the hell into which his listeners may eventually go. Let him be careful! Speaking of hell to an unbeliever is akin to throwing a boomerang; whenever it is well done, it

returns to hit the head of him who threw it. Of the unbelievers, however, we are compelled to say: "How shall they
believe in him, of whom they have never heard? How shall
they hear without a preacher?" (Rom. 10:14). Since unbelievers already live in death, darkness, and alienation from
God, they need and deserve to be preached nothing else but
the Gospel. They need "good news," i.e., "a good spell," as
the beautiful word "Gospel" implies. In his mercy, God desires that a great sabbatical rest from toiling under sin and
vanity should be announced (Luke 4:18). Who knows whether
those condemned by zealous orators, do in their own way,
often hear and obey much better than their thundering prose-
cutors? At any rate, Ephesians gives good reason to believe
that hell will be populated by Christians who withheld and
betrayed the good news by making of it a legalistic, terrifying,
loveless or saltless judgment and separatist movement, rather
than by those whom fake saints have wished to send into the
abyss, or forever to leave in it.

As to the salvation of non-Christians, we can know, therefore, only this: that we are sent to them to announce in word
and deed their reconciliation by God and with God. We know,
furthermore, that all knees in heaven, on earth, and under
the earth shall bow before Christ, to the Father's glory (Phil.
2:10-11). We make the best of the time which we are granted
(Eph. 5:16), when we invite and encourage all men immediately and joyfully to participate in the glorification of God.
So we cannot give up hope for all. We cannot be particularists, unless we would foolishly choose to have an "evil eye" for
the Lord's goodness; i.e., to "begrudge his generosity" (cf.
Matt. 20:15).

Neither can we be universalists. What Christ said about the
unforgivable sin committed by those belonging to the elect
people (Matt. 12:30-32, etc.) warns us strictly. Also we should
acknowledge that our minds and hands are incapable of removing "hell on earth" by humanitarian actions alone. A

mystic pantheism rejects the specific work of God and despises the proclaimed word of truth. Activistic or sentimental universalism contradicts Ephesians as much as traditional particularism does.

Without God's work, without the Servant-Messiah, without the Spirit who leads in "the truth which is in Jesus" (Eph. 4:21; 1:13) we do not know of any salvation and new life that can last. But because of God's revelation, we know on what ground to stand, we know how to walk worthily, and we know whom to ask for strength, so that in every place, on every occasion, in every occupation, and even in suffering, we may be ambassadors for the Gospel of peace.

This peace which was first preached by Christ himself (2:17) is a political and social event of unlimited dimensions. Such peace, when we consider its breadth, length, height, and depth, surpasses all understanding (3:18 f.), not by its being limited to another world or to man's inner life only, but because it was "made" (2:14 f.) in this world and for this world. Therefore it reaches into the divided soul of both ancient and modern man. It concerns and forbids the crime of preparation for an atomic war. It unmasks and fights the creeping threat of anti-Semitism. It throws burning light into the entangled problems of ecumenical unity and mission work. In short, it is inexhaustible; and yet we are made to know of it and make it known! Christians who are desirous of learning more about it will gain understanding, inasmuch as they actually live in faith and serve God in their daily lives; i.e., when they dare to show that they boldly trust in the validity of God's work and message. They need not be afraid of being too confident, too hopeful, or too daring, for God himself and the Gospel itself are *for* all men everywhere, and at every time. According to this Gospel, through Jesus Christ and the Spirit, God himself does away with all the dividing walls and enmities. In this faith, Christians can stand firm and can grow together.

They have beneath them a solid ground, and they have shoes that bear them securely. Therefore (Eph. 5:14),

> "Stand up, O sleeper,
> And arise from the dead,
> And Christ will give you light!"

BIBLE INDEX

Passages in the Epistle to the Ephesians

TOPICAL INDEX